THE A.A.
SERVICE MANUAL

combined with

TWELVE CONCEPTS
FOR WORLD SERVICE

by Bill W.

ALCOHOLICS ANONYMOUS® is a fellowship of men and women who share their experience, strength and hope with each other that they may solve their common problem and help others to recover from alcoholism.

• *The only requirement for membership is a desire to stop drinking. There are no dues or fees for A.A. membership; we are self-supporting through our own contributions.*

• *A.A. is not allied with any sect, denomination, politics, organization, or institution; does not wish to engage in any controversy; neither endorses nor opposes any causes.*

• *Our primary purpose is to stay sober and help other alcoholics to achieve sobriety.*

Copyright© by A.A. Grapevine Inc.; reprinted with permission

A Declaration of Unity

This we owe to A.A.'s future; to place our common welfare first; to keep our Fellowship united. For on A.A. unity depend our lives, and the lives of those to come.

I Am Responsible...

When anyone, anywhere, reaches out for help, I want the hand of A.A. always to be there. And for that: I am responsible.

THE
A.A. SERVICE MANUAL

Table of Contents

| Note: Vertical lines in outer margins (like that at left) indicate changes made in the 2016-2018 edition.

Chapter Eleven: The General Service Office

Chapter Twelve: The A.A. Grapevine

This is A.A.'s service manual—an outgrowth of the "Third Legacy Manual" which served the movement so well beginning with Bill W.'s first draft in 1951. All of the basic service principles and procedures outlined in that document have been retained. In the interests of convenience and completeness, the material has been edited and rearranged. An overall revision was approved by the 1999 General Service Conference.

The Conference Report and Charter Committee is responsible for reviewing and approving annual updates and revisions of *The A.A. Service Manual/Twelve Concepts for World Service.*

A.A.'s Legacy of Service
by Bill W.[1]

Our Twelfth Step—carrying the message—is the basic service that the A.A. Fellowship gives; this is our principal aim and the main reason for our existence. Therefore, A.A. is more than a set of principles; it is a society of alcoholics in action. We must carry the message, else we ourselves can wither and those who haven't been given the truth may die.

Hence, an A.A. service is anything whatever that helps us to reach a fellow sufferer—ranging all the way from the Twelfth Step itself to a ten-cent phone call and a cup of coffee, and to A.A.'s General Service Office for national and international action. The sum total of all these services is our Third Legacy of Service.

Services include meeting places, hospital cooperation, and intergroup offices; they mean pamphlets, books, and good publicity of almost every description. They call for committees, delegates, trustees, and conferences. And, not to be forgotten, they need voluntary money contributions from within the Fellowship.

Vital to A.A.'s Growth

These services, whether performed by individuals, groups, areas, or A.A. as a whole, are utterly vital to our existence and growth. Nor can we make A.A. more simple by abolishing such services. We would only be asking for complication and confusion.

Concerning any given service, we therefore pose but one question: "Is this service really needed?" If it is, then maintain it we must, or fail in our mission to those who need and seek A.A.

---

1 Bill wrote these words in 1951, therefore, his words reflect that time period in their details.

The most vital, yet least understood, group of services that A.A. has are those that enable us to function as a whole, namely: the General Service Office, A.A. World Services, Inc., The A.A. Grapevine, Inc., and our board of trustees, known legally as the General Service Board of Alcoholics Anonymous. Our worldwide unity and much of our growth since early times are directly traceable to this cluster of life-giving activities.

Until 1950, these overall services were the sole function of a few oldtime A.A.'s, several nonalcoholic friends, Doctor Bob, and me. For all the years of A.A.'s infancy, we oldtimers had been the selfappointed trustees for Alcoholics Anonymous.

Fellowship Ready for Responsibility

At this time, we realized that A.A. had grown up, that our Fellowship was ready and able to take these responsibilities from us. There was also another urgent reason for change. Since we oldtimers couldn't live on forever, newer trustees would be virtually unknown to the A.A. groups, now spread over the whole earth. Without direct linkage to A.A., future trustees couldn't possibly function alone.

This meant that we had to form a conference representing our membership which could meet yearly with our board of trustees in New York, and thus assume direct responsibility for the guardianship of A.A. tradition and the direction of our principal service affairs. Otherwise, a virtually unknown board of trustees and our too little understood service headquarters operations would someday be bound to face collapse.

Suppose that future trustees, acting quite on their own, were to make a serious blunder. Suppose that with no linkage to A.A., they tried to act for us in time of great trouble or crisis. With no direct guidance from A.A. as a whole, how could they do this? Collapse of our top services would then be inevitable. And if, under such conditions, our world services did fall apart, how could they ever be reconstructed?

These, briefly, were the conclusions that led to the formation of the General Service Conference of Alcoholics Anonymous. Later, I will outline in more detail the events that have now become A.A. history.

The deliberative body known as the Conference is made up of elected area delegates from the United States and Canada—now numbering ninety-three—together with the trustees, the directors of A.A.W.S., Inc., and The A.A. Grapevine, Inc., and G.S.O. and Grapevine staff members numbering forty or more. The Conference held its first annual meeting in 1951. Since then it has met annually in April or May in New York.[2] It has proved itself an immense success — establishing a record of advisory actions that have served the Fellowship well during the intervening years of growth and development.

Highlights of A.A. Service History

To go back to the beginning: One day in 1937, at Dr. Bob's Akron home, he and I added up the score of over two years' work. For the first time we saw that wholesale recovery of alcoholics was possible. We then had two small but solid groups in Akron and New York,

---

2 Except for 1955 Conference held in St. Louis, Missouri.

plus a sprinkling of members elsewhere. How could these few recovered ones tell millions of alcoholics throughout the world the great news? That was the question.

Forthwith, Doctor Bob and I met with 18 of the Akron Group at the home of T. Henry Williams, a steadfast nonalcoholic friend. Some of the Akron Group still thought we ought to stick to the word-of-mouth process; but the majority felt that we now needed our own hospitals with paid workers and, above all, a book for other alcoholics that could explain to them our methods and results. This would require considerable money — millions perhaps. (We didn't know that millions would have ruined us even more than no money at all.) So the Akron meeting commissioned me to get to New York and raise funds. Arrived home, I found the New York Group in full agreement with this idea. Several of us went to work at once.

A.A.'s Early Money Problems

Through my brother-in-law, Dr. L. V. Strong, Jr., my only remaining friend and the confidant of the worst of my drinking time, we made a contact with Willard S. Richardson, a friend and longtime associate of the Rockefeller family. Mr. Richardson promptly took fire and interested a group of his own friends. In the winter of 1937, a meeting was called at the office of John D. Rockefeller, Jr. Present were Mr. Richardson and his group, Dr. William D. Silkworth, alcoholics from Akron and New York, Doctor Bob and I. After a long discussion, we convinced our new friends that we urgently needed money—a lot of it, too.

One of them, Frank Amos, soon made a trip to Akron early in 1938 to investigate the group there. He returned with a very optimistic report, of which Mr. Richardson quickly laid before John D. Rockefeller, Jr. Though much impressed, Mr. Rockefeller declined to give any large sum for fear of professionalizing A.A. He did, however, donate $5,000. This was used to keep Doctor Bob and me going during 1938. We were still a long way from hospitals, missionaries, books, and big money. This looked mighty tough at the time, but it was probably one of the best breaks that A.A. ever had.

In spite of Mr. Rockefeller's views, we renewed our efforts to persuade his friends of our crying need for money. At length, they agreed that we did need more money, certainly enough to prepare a textbook on our methods and experience.

In the late spring of 1938, I had drafted what are now the first two chapters of the book "Alcoholics Anonymous." Mimeographed copies of these were used as part of the prospectus for our futile fund-raising operation. At board meetings, then held nearly every month, our nonalcoholic friends commiserated on our lack of success. About half of the $5,000 Mr. Rockefeller advanced had been used to pay the mortgage on Doctor Bob's home. The rest of it, divided between us, would, of course, soon be exhausted. The outlook was certainly bleak.

A.A. Its Own Publisher

Then Frank Amos remembered his oldtime friend Eugene Exman, religious editor at Harper's, the book publishers. He sent me to Harper's, and I showed Mr. Exman two chapters of our proposed book. To my delight, Mr. Exman was impressed. He suggested that Harper's might advance me $1,500 in royalties to finish the job. Broke as we were, that $1,500 looked like a pile of money.

Nevertheless, our enthusiasm for this proposal quickly waned. With the book finished, we would be $1,500 in debt to Harper's. And if, as we hoped, A.A. then got a lot of publicity, how could we possibly hire the help to answer the inquiries—maybe thousands—that would flood in?

There was another problem, too, a serious one. If our A.A. book became the basic text for Alcoholics Anonymous, its ownership would then be in other hands. It was evident that our Society ought to own and publish its own literature. No publisher, however good, ought to own our best asset.

So two of us bought a pad of blank stock certificates and wrote on them "Works Publishing, par value $25." My friend Hank P. and I then offered shares in the new book company to alcoholics and their friends in New York. They just laughed at us. Who would buy stock, they said, in a book not yet written!

Somehow, these timid buyers had to be persuaded, so we went to the *Reader's Digest* and told the managing editor the story of our budding Society and its proposed book. He liked the notion very much and promised that in the spring of 1939 when we thought the book would be ready, the *Reader's Digest* would print a piece about A.A.—mentioning the new book, of course.

This was the sales argument we needed. With a plug like that, the proposed volume would sell by carloads. How could we miss? The New York alcoholics and their friends promptly changed their minds about Works Publishing stock. They began to buy it, mostly on installments.

Ruth Hock, our nonalcoholic secretary, typed away as I slowly dictated the chapters of the text for the new book. Fierce argument over these drafts and what ought to go into them was a main feature of the New York and Akron Groups' meetings for months on end. I became much more of an umpire than I ever was an author. Meanwhile, the alcoholics at Akron and New York and a couple in Cleveland began writing their stories 28—in all.

When the book project neared completion, we visited the managing editor of the *Reader's Digest* and asked for the promised article. He gave us a blank look, scarcely remembering who we were. Then the blow fell. He told how months before he had put our proposition to his editorial board and how it had been turned down flat. With profuse apologies, he admitted he'd plumb forgot to let us know anything about it. This was a crusher.

Meanwhile, we had optimistically ordered 5,000 copies of the new book, largely on a shoestring. The printer, too, had relied on the *Reader's Digest*. Soon there would be 5,000 books in his warehouse, and no customers for them.

The book finally appeared in April 1939. We got the *New York Times* to do a review and Dr. Harry Emerson Fosdick supplied us with another really good one, but nothing happened. The book simply didn't sell. We were in debt up to our ears. The sheriff had appeared at the Newark office where we had been working, and the landlord sold the Brooklyn house, where Lois and I lived. She and I were dumped into the street and then onto the charity of A.A. friends.

How we got through the summer of 1939, I'll never quite know. Hank P. had to get a job. The faithful Ruth accepted shares in the defunct book company as pay. One A.A. friend supplied us with his summer camp; another, with a car.

A.A. Makes News

The first break came in September 1939. *Liberty Magazine*, then headed by our great friend-to-be Fulton Oursler, carried an article, "Alcoholics and God," written by Morris Markey. There was an instant response. About eight hundred letters from alcoholics and their families poured in. Ruth answered every one of them, enclosing a leaflet about the new book, "Alcoholics Anonymous." Slowly, the book began to sell. Then the *Cleveland Plain Dealer* ran a series of pieces about Alcoholics Anonymous. At once, the Cleveland groups mushroomed from a score into many hundreds of members. More books sold. Thus we inched and squeezed our way through that perilous year.

We hadn't heard a thing from Mr. Rockefeller since early in 1938. But in 1940, he put in a dramatic reappearance. His friend Mr. Richardson came to a trustees' meeting, smiling broadly. Mr. Rockefeller, he said, wanted to give Alcoholics Anonymous a dinner. The invitation list showed an imposing collection of notables. We figured them to be collectively worth at least a billion dollars.

The dinner came off early in February at New York's Union League Club. Dr. Harry Emerson Fosdick spoke in praise of us, and so did Dr. Foster Kennedy, the eminent neurologist. Then Doctor Bob and I briefed the audience on A.A. Some of the Akron and New York alcoholics scattered among the notables at the tables responded to questions. The gathering showed a rising warmth and interest. This was it, we thought; our money problems were solved!

Nelson Rockefeller then rose to his feet to speak for his father, who was ill. His father was very glad, he said, that those at the dinner had seen the promising beginning of the new Society of Alcoholics Anonymous. Seldom, Nelson continued, had his father shown more interest in anything. But obviously, since A.A. was a work of pure goodwill, one man carrying the news to the next, little or no money would be required. At this sally, our spirits fell. When Mr. Rockefeller had finished, the whole billion dollars' worth of capitalists got up and walked out, leaving not a nickel behind them.

Next day, John D. Rockefeller, Jr. wrote to all those who had attended the dinner and even to those who had not. Again he reiterated his complete confidence and high interest. Then, at the very end of his letter, he casually remarked that he was giving Alcoholics Anonymous $1,000!

Only much later did we realize what Mr. Rockefeller had really done for us. At risk of personal ridicule, he had stood up before the whole world to put in a plug for a tiny society of struggling alcoholics. For these unknowns, he'd gone 'way out on a limb. Wisely sparing of his money, he had given freely of himself. Then and there John D. Rockefeller, Jr. saved us from the perils of property management and professionalism. He couldn't have done more.

A.A. Grows to Two Thousand Members

As a result, A.A.'s 1940 membership jumped sharply to about two thousand at the year's end. Doctor Bob and I each began to receive $30 a week out of the dinner contributions. This eased us greatly. Lois and I went to live in a tiny room at A.A.'s number one clubhouse, on West 24th Street in Manhattan.

Best of all, increased book sales had made a national headquarters possible. We moved from Newark, N.J., where the A.A. book had been written, to Vesey Street, just north of the Wall Street district of New York. We took a modest two-room office right opposite the Church Street Annex Post Office. There the famous Box 658 was ready and waiting to receive the thousands of frantic inquiries that would presently come into it. At this point, Ruth (though nonalcoholic) became A.A.'s first national secretary, and I turned into a sort of headquarters handyman.

Through the whole of 1940, book sales were the sole support of the struggling office. Every cent of these earnings went to pay for A.A. work done there. All requests for help were answered with warm personal letters. When alcoholics or their families showed continued interest, we kept on writing. Aided by such letters and the book "Alcoholics Anonymous," new A.A. groups had begun to take form.

Beginning of Group Services

More importantly, we had lists of prospects in many cities and towns in the United States and Canada. We turned these lists over to the A.A. traveling businessmen, members of already established groups. With these couriers, we corresponded constantly, and they started still more groups. For the further benefit of our travelers, we put out a group directory.

Then came an unexpected activity. Because the newborn groups saw only a little of their traveling sponsors, they turned to the New York office for help with their innumerable troubles. By mail we relayed the experience of the older centers on to them. A little later, as we shall see, this became a major service.

Meanwhile, some of the stockholders in the book company, Works Publishing, began to get restive. All the book profits, they complained, were going for A.A. work in the office. When, if ever, were they going to get their money back? We also saw that the book "Alcoholics Anonymous" should now become the property of A.A. as a whole. At the moment, it was owned one-third by the 49 subscribers, one-third by my friend Hank P., and the remainder by me.

As a first step, we had the book company, Works Publishing, audited and legally incorporated. Hank P. and I donated our shares in it to the Alcoholic Foundation (as our board of trustees was then called). This was the stock that we had taken for services rendered. But the 49 other subscribers had put in real money. They would have to be paid in cash. Where on earth could we get it?

The help we needed turned up in the person of A. LeRoy Chipman. Also a friend and associate of John D. Rockefeller, Jr., he had recently been made a trustee of the Foundation.

He persuaded Mr. Rockefeller, two of his sons, and some of the dinner guests to lend the Foundation $8,000. This promptly paid off a $2,500 indebtedness to Charles B. Towns,[3] settled some incidental debts, and permitted the reacquisition of the outstanding stock. Two years later, the book "Alcoholics Anonymous" had done so well that we were able to pay off this whole Rockefeller loan.

Jack Alexander Looks at A.A.

The spring of 1941 brought us a ten-strike. *The Saturday Evening Post* decided to do a piece about Alcoholics Anonymous. It assigned one of its star writers, Jack Alexander, to the job. Having just done an article on the New Jersey rackets, Jack approached us somewhat tongue-in-cheek. But he soon became an A.A. "convert," even though he wasn't an alcoholic. Working early and late, he spent a whole month with us. Doctor Bob and I and elders of the early groups at Akron, New York, Cleveland, Philadelphia, and Chicago spent uncounted hours with him. When he could feel A.A. in the very marrow of his bones, he proceeded to write the piece that rocked drunks and their families all over the nation. It was the lead story in *The Saturday Evening Post* of March 1, 1941.

Came then the deluge. Frantic appeals from alcoholics and their families—six thousand of them—hit the New York office. At first, we pawed at random through the mass of letters, laughing and crying by turns. How could this heartbreaking mail be answered? It was a cinch that Ruth and I could never do it alone. Form letters wouldn't be enough. Every single one must have an understanding personal reply. Maybe the A.A. groups themselves would help. Though we'd never asked anything of them before, this was surely their business, if it was anybody's. An enormous Twelfth Step job had to be done and done quickly.

So we told the groups the story, and they responded. The measuring stick for voluntary contribution was at that time set at $1.00 per member per year. The trustees of the Foundation agreed to look after these funds, placing them in a special bank account, earmarking them for A.A. office work only.

We had started the year 1941 with two thousand members, but we finished with eight thousand. This was the measure of the great impact of *The Saturday Evening Post* piece. But this was only the beginning of uncounted thousands of pleas for help from individuals and from growing groups all over the world, which have continued to flow into the General Service Office to this day.

This phenomenal expansion brought another problem, a very important one. The national spotlight now being on us, we had to begin dealing with the public on a large scale. Public ill will could stunt our growth, even bring it to a stand still. But enthusiastic public confidence could swell our ranks to numbers we had only dreamed of before. The *Post* piece had proved this.

Finding the right answers to all our public relations puzzlers has been a long process. After much trial and error, sometimes punctuated by painful mistakes, the attitudes and practices that would work best for us emerged. The important ones can today be seen in

---

3 Owner of Towns Hospital in New York; his loan helped to make the Big Book project possible.

our A.A. Traditions. One hundred percent anonymity at the public level, no use of the A.A. name for the benefit of other causes, however worthy, no endorsements or alliances, one single purpose for Alcoholics Anonymous, no professionalism, public relations by the principle of attraction rather than promotion — these were some of the hard-learned lessons.

Service to the Whole of A.A.

Thus far in our Society story, we have seen the Foundation, the A.A. book, the development of pamphlet literature, the answered mass of pleas for help, the satisfied need of groups for counsel on their problems, the beginning of our wonderful relations with the public, all becoming a part of a growing service to the whole world of A.A. At last our Society really began to function as a whole.

But the 1941–1945 period brought still more developments of significance. The Vesey Street office was moved to Lexington Avenue, New York City, just opposite Grand Central Terminal. The moment we located there, we were besieged with visitors who, for the first time, began to see Alcoholics Anonymous as a vision for the whole globe.

Since A.A. was growing so fast, G.S.O. had to grow too. More alcoholic staff members were engaged. As they divided the work between them, departments began to be created. Today's office has a good many—group, foreign and public relations, A.A. Conference, office management, packing and mailing, accounting, stenographic, and special services to Loners, prisons, and hospitals.[4]

It was chiefly from correspondence and from our mounting public relations activity that the basic ideas for our Traditions came. In late 1945, a good A.A. friend suggested that all this mass of experience might be codified into a set of general principles, simply stated principles that could offer tested solutions to all of A.A.'s problems of living and working together and of relating our Society to the world outside.

If we had become sure enough of where we stood on such matters as membership, group autonomy, singleness of purpose, nonendorsement of other enterprises, professionalism, public controversy, and anonymity in its several aspects, then such a code of principles could be written. Such a traditional code could not, of course, ever become rule or law. But it could act as a sure guide for our trustees, for headquarters people and, most especially, for A.A. groups with bad growing pains.

Being at the center of things, we of the headquarters would have to do the job. Aided by my helpers there, I set to work. The Traditions of Alcoholics Anonymous that resulted were first published in the so called long form in the Grapevine of May 1946.[5] Then I wrote some more pieces explaining the Traditions in detail. These came out in later issues of the Grapevine.

---

4 Other services have been added since 1955.

5 Actually, it was the April 1946 issue of the Grapevine.

Traditions Took Persuasion

The first reception of the Twelve Traditions was interesting and amusing. The reaction was mixed, to say the least. Only groups in dire trouble took them seriously. From some quarters there was a violent reaction, especially from groups that had long lists of "protective" rules and regulations. There was much indifference. Several of our "intellectual" members cried loudly that the Traditions reflected nothing more than the sum of my own hopes and fears for Alcoholics Anonymous.

Therefore I began to travel and talk a lot about the new Traditions. People were at first politely attentive, though it must be confessed that some did go to sleep during my early harangues. But after a while I got letters containing sentiments like this: "Bill, we'd love to have you come and speak. Do tell us where you used to hide your bottles and all about that big, hot-flash spiritual experience of yours. But for heaven's sake, please don't talk any more about those blasted Traditions!"

Time presently changed all that. Only five years later, several thousand A.A. members, meeting at the 1950 Cleveland Convention, declared that A.A.'s Twelve Traditions constituted the platform upon which our Fellowship could best function and hold together in unity for all time to come.

Medicine Takes an Interest

By this time, A.A. had found still more favor in the world of medicine. Two of the great medical associations of America did an unprecedented thing. In the year 1944, the Medical Society of New York invited me to read a paper at its annual meeting. Following the reading, three of the many physicians present stood up and gave A.A. their highest endorsement. These were Dr. Harry Tiebout, A.A.'s first friend in the psychiatric profession, Dr. Kirby Collier, also a psychiatrist friend and an early advocate of A.A., and Dr. Foster Kennedy, world-renowned neurologist. The Medical Society itself then went still further. They permitted us to print my paper and the recommendations of these three doctors in pamphlet form. In 1949 the American Psychiatric Association did exactly the same thing. I read a paper at its annual meeting in Montreal. The paper was carried in the *American Journal of Psychiatry*, and we were permitted to reprint it.[6]

During the 1940's, two hospitals met all these urgent needs and afforded shining examples of how medicine and A.A. could cooperate. At St. Thomas Hospital in Akron, Doctor Bob, the wonderful Sister Ignatia, and the hospital's staff presided over an alcoholic ward that had ministered to five thousand alcoholics by the time Doctor Bob passed away in 1950. In New York, Knickerbocker Hospital provided a ward under the care of our first friend in medicine, Dr. William Duncan Silkworth, where he was assisted by a redheaded A.A. nurse known as Teddy. It was in these two hospitals and by these pioneering people that the best techniques of combined medicine and A.A. were worked out.

Since proper hospitalization was, and still is, one of A.A.'s greatest problems, the General Service Office has retailed this early hospital experience, along with the many

---

6 Now in the pamphlet "Three Talks to Medical Societies by Bill W."

subsequent developments and ramifications, to groups all over the world — still another very vital service.

A Rash of Anonymity Breaks

About this time a serious threat to our longtime welfare made its appearance. Usually meaning well, members began breaking their anonymity all over the place. Sometimes they wanted to use the A.A. name to advertise and help other causes. Others just wanted their names and pictures in the papers. Being photographed with the governor would really help A.A., they thought. (I'd earlier been guilty of this, too.) But at last we saw the appalling risk to A.A. if all our power-drivers got loose at the public level. Already scores of them were doing it.

So our General Service Office got to work. We wrote remonstrances, kind ones, of course, to every breaker. We even sent letters to nearly all press and radio outlets, explaining why A.A.'s shouldn't break their anonymity before the public. Nor, we added, did A.A. solicit money—we paid our own bills.

In a few years the public anonymity-breakers were squeezed down to a handful—thus another valuable G.S.O. service had gone into action.

G.S.O. Services Expand

To maintain all these ever-lengthening service lifelines, the office had to go on expanding. G.S.O. moved to 44th Street.[7]

Our present array of services may look like big business to some. But when we think of the size and reach of A.A. today, that isn't true at all. In 1945, for example, we had one paid worker to every 98 groups; in 1955, one paid worker to every 230 groups.[8] It therefore seems sure that we shall never be burdened with a bureaucratic and expensive service setup.

No description of our world services would be complete without full acknowledgment of all that has been contributed by our nonalcoholic trustees. Over the years they have given an incredible amount of time and effort; theirs has been a true labor of love. Some of them, like Jack Alexander, Fulton Oursler, Leonard Harrison, and Bernard Smith, have given much in their fields of literature, social service, finance, and law. Their example is being followed by more recent nonalcoholic trustees.

As I pointed out earlier, in the 1940's our headquarters was constantly overhung by one great threat to its future existence: Doctor Bob and I and our board of trustees had the entire responsibility for the conduct of A.A.'s services.

In the years leading up to 1950 and 1951, we began to debate the desirability of some sort of advisory board of A.A.'s. Or maybe we needed a conference of larger numbers, elected by A.A. itself; people who would inspect the headquarters yearly, a body to whom

---

7 Later, it moved to 305 East 45th St., and then 468 Park Ave. South. In 1992 it moved to 475 Riverside Dr.

8 In 2016, with services still further expanded, one G.S.O. worker serves approximately 800 groups in the U.S. and Canada.

the trustees could become responsible, a guiding conscience of our whole world effort.

But the objections to this were persistent and nothing happened for several years. Such a venture, it was said, would be expensive. Worse still, it might plunge A.A. into disruptive political activity when conference delegates were elected. Then Doctor Bob fell ill, mortally ill. Finally, in 1950, spurred on by the relentless logic of the situation, the trustees authorized Doctor Bob and me to devise the plan with which this booklet deals. It was a plan for a General Service Conference of A.A., a plan by which our Society could assume full and permanent responsibility for the conduct of its most vital affairs.

Birth of the Conference

It was one thing to say that we ought to have a General Service Conference, but it was quite another to devise a plan which would bring it into successful existence. The cost of holding one was easily dismissed, but how on earth were we going to cut down destructive politics, with all its usual struggles for prestige and vainglory? How many delegates would be required and from where should they come? Arrived at New York, how could they be related to the board of trustees? What would be their actual powers and duties?

With these several weighty considerations in mind, and with some misgivings, I commenced work on a draft of a plan, much assisted by Helen B., an A.A. staff member.

Though the Conference might be later enlarged to include the whole world, we felt that the first delegates should come from the U.S. and Canada only. Each state and province might be allowed one delegate. Those containing heavy A.A. populations could have additional delegates. To give the Conference continuity, delegates could be divided into panels. An odd-numbered panel (Panel One), elected for two years, would be invited for 1951, the first year. An even-numbered panel (Panel Two), elected for two years, would be seated in 1952. Thereafter, one panel would be elected and one would be retired yearly. This would cause the Conference to rotate, while maintaining some continuity.

But how could we pull the inevitable election pressure down? To accomplish this, it was provided that a delegate must receive a two-thirds vote for election. If a delegate got a majority of this size, nobody could kick much. But if he or she didn't, and the election was close, what then? Well, perhaps the names of the two highest in the running, or the three officers of the committee, or even the whole committee, could be put in a hat. One name would be drawn. The winner of this painless lottery would become the delegate.

But when these delegates met in conference, what would they do? We thought they would want to have real authority. So, in the charter drawn for the Conference itself, it was provided that the delegates could issue flat directions to the trustees on a two-thirds vote. And even a simple majority vote would constitute a mighty strong suggestion.

Delegates Encouraged to Question

The first Conference was set for April 1951. In came the delegates. They looked over our offices, cellar to garret, got acquainted with the whole staff, shook hands with the trustees. That evening, we gave them a briefing session, under the name of "What's on your mind?"

We answered scores of questions of all kinds. The delegates began to feel at home and reassured. They inspected our finances with a microscope. After they had listened to reports from the board of trustees and from all the services, there was warm but cordial debate on many a question of policy. Trustees submitted several of their own serious problems for the opinion of the Conference.

So went session after session, morning, afternoon, and evening. The delegates handled several tough puzzles about which we at G.S.O. were in doubt, sometimes giving advice contrary to our own conclusions. In nearly every instance, we saw that they were right. Then and there they proved, as never before, that A.A.'s Tradition Two was correct. The group conscience could safely act as the sole authority and sure guide for Alcoholics Anonymous.

Nobody present will ever forget that final session of the first Conference. We knew that the impossible had happened, that A.A. could never break down in the middle, that Alcoholics Anonymous was at last safe from any storm the future might bring. And, as delegates returned home, they carried this same conviction with them.

Realizing our need for funds and better literature circulation, some did place a little too much emphasis on this necessity; others were a little discouraged, wondering why fellow members in their areas did not take fire as they had. They forgot that they themselves had been eyewitnesses to the Conference and that their brother alcoholics had not. But, both here and at home, they made an impression much greater than they knew.

In the midst of this exciting turn of affairs, the Conference agreed that the Alcoholic Foundation ought to be renamed the General Service Board of Alcoholics Anonymous, and this was done. The word "Foundation" stood for charity, paternalism and maybe big money. A.A. would have none of these; from here out we could assume full responsibility and pay our expenses ourselves.

As I watched all this grow, I became entirely sure that Alcoholics Anonymous was at last safe — even from me.

The Twelve Traditions (Long Form)

Our A.A. experience has taught us that:

1. Each member of Alcoholics Anonymous is but a small part of a great whole. A.A. must continue to live or most of us will surely die. Hence our common welfare comes first. But individual welfare follows close afterward.

2. For our group purpose there is but one ultimate authority — a loving God as He may express Himself in our group conscience.

3. Our membership ought to include all who suffer from alcoholism. Hence we may refuse none who wish to recover. Nor ought A.A. membership ever depend upon money or conformity. Any two or three alcoholics gathered together for sobriety may call themselves an A.A. group, provided that, as a group, they have no other affiliation.

4. With respect to its own affairs, each A.A. group should be responsible to no other authority than its own conscience. But when its plans concern the welfare of neighboring groups also, those groups ought to be consulted. And no group, regional committee, or individual should ever take any action that might greatly affect A.A. as a whole without conferring with the trustees of the General Service Board. On such issues our common welfare is paramount.

5. Each Alcoholics Anonymous group ought to be a spiritual entity *having but one primary purpose* — that of carrying its message to the alcoholic who still suffers.

6. Problems of money, property, and authority may easily divert us from our primary spiritual aim. We think, therefore, that any considerable property of genuine use to A.A. should be separately incorporated and managed, thus dividing the material from the spiritual. An A.A. group, as such, should never go into business. Secondary aids to A.A., such as clubs or hospitals which require much property or administration, ought to be incorporated and so set apart that, if necessary, they can be freely discarded by the groups. Hence such facilities ought not to use the A.A. name. Their management should be the sole responsibility of those people who financially support them. For clubs, A.A. managers are usually preferred. But hospitals, as well as other places of recuperation, ought to be well outside A.A.—and medically supervised. While an A.A. group may cooperate with anyone, such cooperation ought never to go so far as affiliation or endorsement, actual or implied. An A.A. group can bind itself to no one.

7. The A.A. groups themselves ought to be fully supported by the voluntary contributions of their own members. We think that each group should soon achieve this ideal; that any

public solicitation of funds using the name of Alcoholics Anonymous is highly dangerous, whether by groups, clubs, hospitals, or other outside agencies; that acceptance of large gifts from any source, or of contributions carrying any obligation whatever, is unwise. Then, too, we view with much concern those A.A. treasuries which continue, beyond prudent reserves, to accumulate funds for no stated A.A. purpose. Experience has often warned us that nothing can so surely destroy our spiritual heritage as futile disputes over property, money, and authority.

8. Alcoholics Anonymous should remain forever nonprofessional. We define professionalism as the occupation of counseling alcoholics for fees or hire. But we may employ alcoholics where they are going to perform those services for which we might otherwise have to engage nonalcoholics. Such special services may be well recompensed. But our usual A.A. Twelfth Step work is never to be paid for.

9. Each A.A. group needs the least possible organization. Rotating leadership is the best. The small group may elect its secretary, the large group its rotating committee, and the groups of a large metropolitan area their central or intergroup committee, which often employs a full-time secretary. The trustees of the General Service Board are, in effect, our A.A. General Service Committee. They are the custodians of our A.A. Tradition and the receivers of voluntary A.A. contributions by which we maintain our A.A. General Service Office at New York. They are authorized by the groups to handle our overall public relations and they guarantee the integrity of our principal newspaper, the A.A. Grapevine. All such representatives are to be guided in the spirit of service, for true leaders in A.A. are but trusted and experienced servants of the whole. They derive no real authority from their titles; they do not govern. Universal respect is the key to their usefulness.

10. No A.A. group or member should ever, in such a way as to implicate A.A., express any opinion on outside controversial issues — particularly those of politics, alcohol reform, or sectarian religion. The Alcoholics Anonymous groups oppose no one. Concerning such matters they can express no views whatever.

11. Our relations with the general public should be characterized by personal anonymity. We think A.A. ought to avoid sensational advertising. Our names and pictures as A.A. members ought not to be broadcast, filmed, or publicly printed. Our public relations should be guided by the principle of attraction rather than promotion. There is never need to praise ourselves. We feel it better to let our friends recommend us.

12. And finally, we of Alcoholics Anonymous believe that the principle of anonymity has an immense spiritual significance. It reminds us that we are to place principles before personalities; that we are actually to practice a genuine humility. This to the end that our great blessings may never spoil us; that we shall forever live in thankful contemplation of Him who presides over us all.

❖ Chapter One

Introduction to General Service

The Twelve Traditions make clear the principle that A.A., as such, should never be organized, that there are no bosses and no government in A.A. Yet at the same time, the Traditions recognize the need for some kind of organization to carry the message in ways that are impossible for the local groups—such as publication of a uniform literature and public information resources, helping new groups get started, publishing an international magazine, and carrying the message in other languages into other countries.

THE CONFERENCE STRUCTURE—AN OVERVIEW

The U.S./Canada* Conference structure is the framework in which these "general services" are carried out. It is a method by which A.A.'s collective group conscience can speak forcefully and put its desires for Conference-wide services into effect. It is the structure that takes the place of government in A.A., ensuring that the full voice of A.A. will be heard and guaranteeing that the desired services will continue to function under all conditions.

The story of the development of general services and the Conference structure is told in the historical material that appears at the beginning of this manual. Today, general services include all kinds of activities within the Conference structure, carried on by groups, districts, area committees, delegates, trustees, the General Service Office and the Grapevine. Usually, these services affect A.A. as a whole.

An Upside-Down Organization

Alcoholics Anonymous has been called an upside-down organization because, as the structure chart shows, the groups are on top and the trustees at the bottom. Bill W. wrote in Concept I: "The A.A. groups today hold ultimate responsibility and final authority for our world services...." Then, in Concept II, Bill made it clear that the groups "delegated to the Conference complete authority for the active maintenance of our world services and thereby made the Conference... the actual voice and effective conscience for our whole Society."

---

* Bill's early vision was of a worldwide structure. However, the conference structures in countries outside of U.S./Canada evolved as autonomous entities.

STRUCTURE OF THE CONFERENCE
(U.S. and Canada)

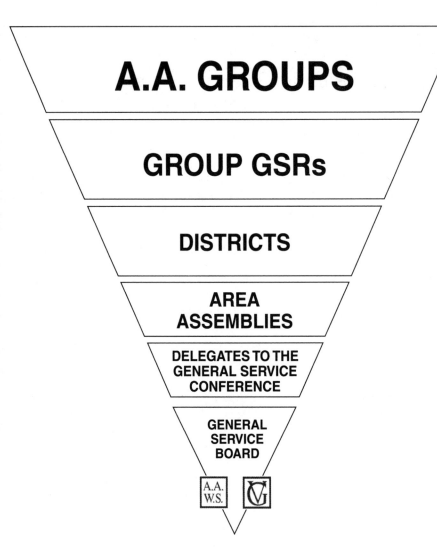

A.A. GROUPS

GROUP GSRs

DISTRICTS

AREA ASSEMBLIES

DELEGATES TO THE GENERAL SERVICE CONFERENCE

GENERAL SERVICE BOARD

A.A. W.S.

Communication Through the Structure

Keeping a balance between ultimate authority and responsibility and the active, day-to-day functioning of world services means there must be constant communication among all elements of the structure.

THE GROUP: The communication process starts with the group, which lets its group conscience—for or against change, approval or disapproval of a proposed action—be known to its elected general service representative (G.S.R.). The G.S.R. (see Chapter Two) makes sure the group's wishes are heard and fully considered at the district and area levels, and that they are part of the delegate's thinking at the Conference. After each annual Conference, the G.S.R. is responsible for making sure that group members are informed about what went on at the Conference and made aware of the full range of Advisory Actions (see Chapter Seven).

THE DISTRICT: Groups are organized into districts, collections of groups located near one another. The G.S.R.s of these groups select district committee members (D.C.M.s), who become part of the area committee (see Chapter Three for more on the district).

THE AREA: The U.S./Canada Conference is divided into 93 areas, made up of a state or province, part of a state or province, or in some cases parts of more than one state or province. At the area assembly, a delegate is elected to represent the area at the annual Conference meeting (see Chapters Four and Five for more on the area and its activities).

THE CONFERENCE AND THE DELEGATE: At the annual Conference meeting, matters of importance to the Fellowship as a whole are first considered and discussed by one of the standing Conference committees, then brought to the full Conference in the form of committee recommendations. All Conference members then have the opportunity to ask questions and discuss the recommendations before they are voted on. Committee recommendations that are approved become Conference Advisory Actions (see Chapters Seven and Eight for more information on the Conference).

After the Conference, the delegate reports back to the area, working through D.C.M.s and group G.S.R.s. At the same time, any Conference Advisory Actions that were referred to the trustees are sent to either the appropriate trustees' committee, G.S.O., or the A.A. Grapevine for implementation.

Membership in the Conference consists of area delegates, trustees, directors of A.A. World Services and the Grapevine, and A.A. staff members of the General Service Office and the Grapevine. Traditionally, area delegates make up at least two-thirds of the Conference body.

THE TRUSTEES: The General Service Board (see Chapter Nine) is made up of 21 trustees. It meets quarterly, and its actions are reported to the Fellowship through quarterly reports and also in the *Final Conference Report*. The board's two operating corporations, A.A. World Services, Inc. and A.A. Grapevine, Inc., report in the same way (see Chapter Ten). A.A.W.S. is the corporation that employs G.S.O. personnel, directs G.S.O. services, and is responsible for book and pamphlet publishing. The Grapevine corporate board employs the magazine's editorial and business staffs and publishes A.A.'s monthly magazine and related materials.

The General Service Conference Structure
(U.S. and Canada)

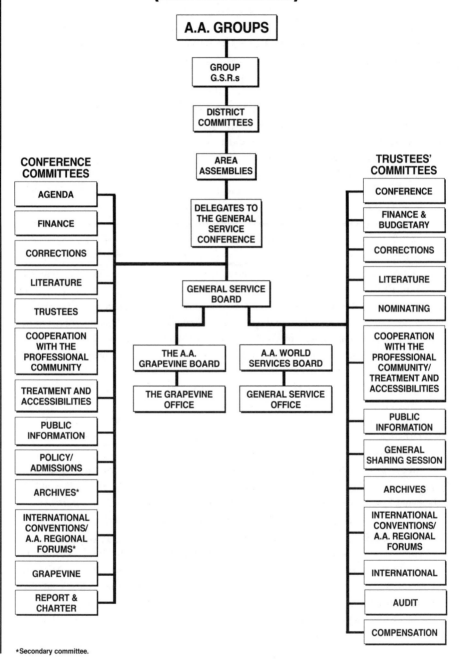

A.A. GROUPS

GROUP G.S.R.s

DISTRICT COMMITTEES

AREA ASSEMBLIES

DELEGATES TO THE GENERAL SERVICE CONFERENCE

GENERAL SERVICE BOARD

CONFERENCE COMMITTEES

- AGENDA
- FINANCE
- CORRECTIONS
- LITERATURE
- TRUSTEES
- COOPERATION WITH THE PROFESSIONAL COMMUNITY
- TREATMENT AND ACCESSIBILITIES
- PUBLIC INFORMATION
- POLICY/ ADMISSIONS
- ARCHIVES*
- INTERNATIONAL CONVENTIONS/ A.A. REGIONAL FORUMS*
- GRAPEVINE
- REPORT & CHARTER

TRUSTEES' COMMITTEES

- CONFERENCE
- FINANCE & BUDGETARY
- CORRECTIONS
- LITERATURE
- NOMINATING
- COOPERATION WITH THE PROFESSIONAL COMMUNITY/ TREATMENT AND ACCESSIBILITIES
- PUBLIC INFORMATION
- GENERAL SHARING SESSION
- ARCHIVES
- INTERNATIONAL CONVENTIONS/ A.A. REGIONAL FORUMS
- INTERNATIONAL
- AUDIT
- COMPENSATION

THE A.A. GRAPEVINE BOARD

THE GRAPEVINE OFFICE

A.A. WORLD SERVICES BOARD

GENERAL SERVICE OFFICE

*Secondary committee.

S18

The Conference Charter

Appendices A and C contain the full text of both the original Conference Charter and the current version. The Charter, adopted in 1955, describes in detail the body of principles and relationships through which A.A. services function as a whole. The Conference itself is not incorporated, and its charter is not a legal document—it is truly an informal agreement between the Fellowship as a whole and its trustees, setting forth the means by which A.A. can give worldwide service.

GLOSSARY OF GENERAL SERVICE TERMS

A.A.W.S.—Alcoholics Anonymous World Services, Inc., one of the two operating corporations of the General Service Board; oversees the operations of the General Service Office and serves as the publishing company for Conference-approved and service literature.

Additional Committee Consideration—An item that was discussed by a Conference committee, but with no action taken or made by the Conference as a whole.

Advisory Action—Represents the informed group conscience of the Fellowship, as the result of the recommendation made by a Conference committee or a floor action, which has been approved by the Conference body as a whole.

Alternate—A service worker who, at group, district, or area level, assists, supports, and participates in service responsibilities, and stands ready to step into the service position if the person occupying it is no longer able to serve.

Appointed committee member—An A.A. member who serves on a specific trustees' committee (for example, public information or correctional facilities) because of his or her knowledge and experience in the field.

Area—A geographical division within a state or province. A Conference delegate comes from an area. Normally there is one area to a state or province, except in heavily A.A.-populated places, where there may be two, three, or more areas in a state or province. Some areas include portions of more than one state or province.

Area assembly—A meeting of G.S.R.s and committee members to discuss area affairs and, every other year, to elect a delegate and committee officers.

Area committee—A committee made up of district committee members (elected by the G.S.R.s in each district) and area committee officers. The area committee generally serves as a "steering committee" for the area.

Conference—The General Service Conference; this can mean either the structure involving committee members, G.S.R.s and delegates in an area, or the annual meeting of Conference delegates each April in New York.

Conference-approved literature, videos, and films—Pamphlets, books, videos, and films, produced under the auspices of various Conference and trustees' committees, which the appropriate Conference committees have reviewed and recommended to the Conference for its approval, and which have been approved by the Conference.

C.P.C.—Cooperation with the professional community. C.P.C. committees at the district, area, trustee, and Conference level help carry the message to professionals who work with alcoholics.

Why Do We Need a Conference?

The late Bernard B. Smith, nonalcoholic, then chairperson of the board of trustees, and one of the architects of the Conference structure, answered that question superbly in his opening talk at the 1954 meeting: "We may not need a General Service Conference to ensure our own recovery. We do need it to ensure the recovery of the alcoholic who still stumbles in the darkness one short block from this room. We need it to ensure the recovery of a child being born tonight, destined for alcoholism. We need it to provide, in keeping with our Twelfth Step, a permanent haven for all alcoholics who, in the ages ahead, can find in A.A. that rebirth that brought us back to life.

"We need it because we, more than all others, are conscious of the devastating effect of the human urge for power and prestige which we must ensure can never invade A.A. We need it to ensure A.A. against government, while insulating it against anarchy; we need it to protect A.A. against disintegration while preventing overintegration. We need it so that Alcoholics Anonymous, and Alcoholics Anonymous alone, is the ultimate repository of its Twelve Steps, its Twelve Traditions, and all of its services.

"We need it to ensure that changes within A.A. come only as a response to the needs and the wants of all A.A., and not of any few. We need it to ensure that the doors of the halls of A.A. never have locks on them, so that all people for all time who have an alcoholic problem may enter these halls unasked and feel welcome. We need it to ensure that Alcoholics Anonymous never asks of anyone who needs us what his or her race is, what his or her creed is, what his or her social position is."

The A.A. Service Manual/Twelve Concepts for World Service—Both titles in a single booklet. The manual opens with a history of A.A. services; explains the Conference structure and its year-round importance; includes the Conference Charter and General Service Board Bylaws. The Concepts—principles of service that have emerged from A.A.'s service accomplishments and mistakes since its beginning—are set forth by Bill W.

Delegate—The man or woman elected every other year to represent the area at the annual Conference meeting in New York and to bring back to the area the results of that meeting.

Director—A person who serves on the corporate board of directors of either A.A.W.S. or Grapevine. Nontrustee directors are A.A. members selected for business or professional experience that relates to the activities of the corporation. The directorate of both corporate boards also includes trustees and A.A. staff.

District—A division within an area, represented by committee member(s).

D.C.M.—District committee member. An experienced G.S.R. elected by other G.S.R.s to represent the groups of their district in area committee meetings and to coordinate service activities in the district.

District meetings—Meetings of the D.C.M.s and G.S.R.s of groups in a district.

General services—Movement-wide services, performed by anyone in the general service structure (G.S.R., D.C.M., delegate, etc.).

G.S.O.—The General Service Office, which provides services to groups in the U.S. and Canada and publishes A.A. literature.

G.S.R.—General service representative. The group contact with the General Service Office; voting member of the area assembly.

Grapevine (G.V.)—The international journal of Alcoholics Anonymous is available online and in print. A.A. Grapevine, Inc. is one of the two operating corporations of the General Service Board and is responsible for Grapevine operations and finances.

GvR—Grapevine representative: the group or district contact with the Grapevine office.

La Viña—Bimonthly Spanish-language magazine published by the A.A. Grapevine.

P.I.—Public information. P.I. committees at the district, area, trustee, and Conference level help carry the message by working with the media.

Region—A grouping of several areas from which a regional trustee comes to the board of trustees. There are six regions in the U.S., two in Canada.

RLV—La Viña representative; the group or district contact with the Grapevine office.

Rotation—The spiritual principle of sharing the responsibility for A.A. through changing leadership.

Sharing session—A group, district, area, or Conference meeting in which everyone is invited to contribute ideas and comments on A.A. matters, and during which no actions are taken.

Third Legacy—A.A.'s Third Legacy is Service, the sum total of all A.A. services, from a Twelfth Step call to coast-to-coast and worldwide service activities. The first two Legacies are Recovery and Unity.

Trustee—A member of A.A.'s General Service Board. Fourteen trustees are A.A. members (Class B); seven are nonalcoholic (Class A).

THIRD LEGACY PROCEDURE

A.A.'s Third Legacy Procedure is a special type of electoral procedure, used primarily for the election of delegates and regional and at-large trustees. It is considered to be unique to A.A., and at first glance, appears to introduce a strong element of chance into a matter that should depend solely on the judgment of the majority. In practice, however, it has proved highly successful in eliminating the influence of factions or parties that seem to thrive on most political scenes. The railroading of a candidate for election is made difficult, if not impossible, since voters have a wide selection of candidates to choose from. More importantly, a second-place candidate who may be extremely well qualified but without early popular support is encouraged to stay in the balloting rather than withdraw.

Third Legacy Procedure is as follows:

- The names of eligible candidates are posted on a board. All voting members (of the area or Conference body) cast written ballots, one choice to a ballot. The tally for each candidate is posted on the board.
- The first candidate to receive two-thirds of the total vote is elected.
- Withdrawals start after the second ballot. If any candidate has less than one-fifth of

The Third Legacy Procedure

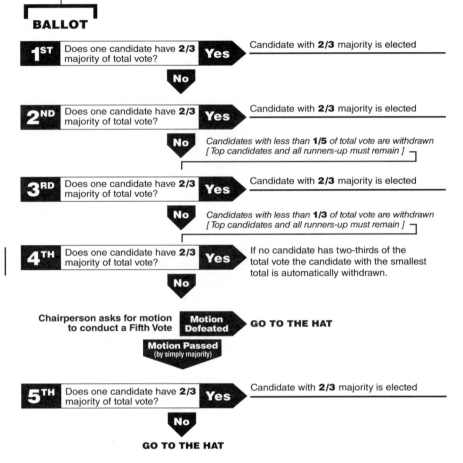

BALLOT

1ST Does one candidate have **2/3** majority of total vote? **Yes** → Candidate with **2/3** majority is elected

No

2ND Does one candidate have **2/3** majority of total vote? **Yes** → Candidate with **2/3** majority is elected

No → *Candidates with less than **1/5** of total vote are withdrawn [Top candidates and all runners-up must remain]*

3RD Does one candidate have **2/3** majority of total vote? **Yes** → Candidate with **2/3** majority is elected

No → *Candidates with less than **1/3** of total vote are withdrawn [Top candidates and all runners-up must remain]*

4TH Does one candidate have **2/3** majority of total vote? **Yes** → If no candidate has two-thirds of the total vote the candidate with the smallest total is automatically withdrawn.

No

Chairperson asks for motion to conduct a Fifth Vote **Motion Defeated** → **GO TO THE HAT**

Motion Passed (by simply majority)

5TH Does one candidate have **2/3** majority of total vote? **Yes** → Candidate with **2/3** majority is elected

No

GO TO THE HAT

the total vote, his or her name is automatically withdrawn[1]—except that the top two candidates must remain. (In case of ties for second place, the top candidate and all tied runners-up remain as candidates.)

- After the third ballot, candidates with less than one-third of the total vote will be withdrawn automatically, except the two top candidates remain. (In case there are ties for second place, the top candidate and all tied runners-up remain as candidates.)
- After the fourth ballot, if no candidate has two-thirds of the total vote, the candidate with the smallest total is automatically withdrawn, except that the top two candidates remain. In case there are ties for second place, the top candidate and all tied second-

---

1 The 1969 General Service Conference approved the change from optional to automatic withdrawal of candidates.

place candidates remain. At this point, the chairperson asks for a motion, second, and a simple majority of hands on conducting a fifth and final ballot. If this motion is defeated, balloting is over and the choice is made by lot—"going to the hat"—immediately. If the motion carries, a fifth and final ballot is conducted.

- If after the fifth ballot no election occurs, the chairperson announces that the choice will be made by lot (from the hat). At this point, the top two candidates remain. In case there are ties for first place, all tied first place candidates remain. In case there are no ties for first place, the top candidate and any tied second-place candidates remain.
- Lots are then drawn by the teller, and the first one "out of the hat" is the delegate (or trustee or other officer).

STIMULATING INTEREST IN GENERAL SERVICE

Most A.A. members are primarily interested in their groups, in their own sobriety, and in helping other drunks one-on-one. And that is as it should be. While the work of general service has precisely the same objective—carrying the message to the alcoholic who still suffers—the connection is not always direct or obvious. Some stimulators are usually needed to get the attention of A.A. members—to show them that service can add a rich dimension to their sober lives and Twelfth Step work, and that their participation is vital to the future of A.A.

Good communication is of vital importance. In personal Twelfth Step work, there is no end to communication. The sponsor talks with the drunk; speakers share their experience; we share with each other. But when it comes to general service work, communication has a tendency to break down. It can take hard work to get the attention of alcoholics, but with a creative approach, they can be encouraged to take time out from the nuts and bolts of recovery to think about another phase of their new lives. Once A.A. members are well informed about service, they often want to become involved and to take on their own service responsibilities.

In many areas, the delegate and area committee members make themselves available to visit groups or district meetings and talk about general service. Workshops on the Traditions, Concepts, or other aspects of service are often an effective way of spreading the word of service. Sometimes two or more districts will work together to sponsor a service event.

Here is the experience of two areas: "We let committee members be responsible for running sharing sessions in their districts, then reporting on them at the monthly assembly. We created as many jobs as possible for G.S.R.s and committee members and encouraged visitors to our assemblies, so they could see what was being done."

Video meetings: "Altogether, we showed service and informational videos 239 times at group meetings. We have no records of the hundreds of questions about general services that were answered during that period."

Reactivating districts: Frequently, there is a need within an area to attempt to reactivate districts or groups that have become inactive or are unrepresented. Areas encourage participation in general service in many ways, especially by direct contact with groups by district/area officers to provide information about service events and opportunities to carry the message beyond the group level. Sometimes there is district-to-district sponsorship in which an active district shares its experience and suggestions to "jump start" activity among groups within the inactive neighboring district.

THE PRINCIPLE OF ROTATION

Traditionally, rotation ensures that service positions, like nearly everything else in A.A., are passed around for all to share. Many positions have alternates who can step into the service positions if needed.

To step out of an A.A. office we love can be hard. If we have been doing a good job, if we honestly don't see anyone else around willing, qualified, or with the time to do it, and if our friends agree, it's especially tough. But it can be a real step forward in growth—a step into the humility that is, for some people, the spiritual essence of anonymity.

Among other things, anonymity in the Fellowship means that we forgo personal prestige for any A.A. work we do to help alcoholics. And, in the spirit of Tradition Twelve, it ever reminds us "to place principles before personalities."

Many outgoing service position holders find it rewarding to take time to share their experience with the incoming person. Rotation helps to bring us spiritual rewards far more enduring than any fame. With no A.A. "status" at stake, we needn't compete for titles or praise—we have complete freedom to serve as we are needed.

Tools Available from G.S.O.

These communication tools are available from the General Service Office (Box 459, Grand Central Station, New York, NY 10163). They are designed to show groups the kind of help that is offered to groups everywhere by G.S.O., and thus to get more people interested in service activity (See Chapter Eleven).

G.S.O's A.A. WEBSITE (www.aa.org): Provides immediate access to information about A.A. for anyone with a drinking problem; A.A. members will find literature, service material and other useful information.

VIDEOCASSETTEs and DVDs: These include "Your A.A. General Service Office, the Grapevine, and the General Service Structure" (and its accompanying service piece), "Markings on the Journey" (made up of rare materials from the A.A. archives; pictures 45 years of A.A. history), and "Carrying the Message Behind These Walls" (correctional facilities work).

AUDIO TAPEs and CDs: These include "Voices of Our Co-Founders," "Bill Discusses the Twelve Traditions," "Three Legacies, by Bill W.," *Alcoholics Anonymous, Twelve Steps and Twelve Traditions, A.A. Comes of Age, Living Sober,* and "Pioneers of A.A." (stories from the Big Book).

CD ROM: *Alcoholics Anonymous.*

LITERATURE DISPLAY: Poster and format for setting up a display of Conference-approved pamphlets and books. Also, the Literature Order Form (lists all pamphlets, books, and films). Other order forms list literature in languages other than English.

GUIDELINES DISPLAY: Samples of all available guidelines, covering service areas common to most A.A.s.

SHARING SESSIONS: A service piece on sharing sessions is available.

❖ Chapter Two

The Group and Its G.S.R.

For most A.A.s, membership in a home group is one of the keys to continuing sobriety. In a home group, they accept service responsibilities and learn to sustain friendships. The home group affords individual A.A.s the privilege of voting on issues that affect the Fellowship as a whole; it is the very basis of the service structure. While most A.A. members attend other groups regularly, the home group is where they participate in business meetings and cast their vote as part of the group conscience of the Fellowship as a whole. As with all group conscience matters, each member has one vote.

The Long Form of Tradition Three and a section of Warranty Six, Concept 12, aptly describe what an A.A. group is:

Tradition Three: "Our membership ought to include all who suffer from alcoholism. Hence we may refuse none who wish to recover. Nor ought A.A. membership ever depend upon money or conformity. Any two or three alcoholics gathered together for sobriety may call themselves an A.A. group, provided that, as a group, they have no other affiliation."

Warranty Six: "…much attention has been drawn to the extraordinary liberties which the A.A. Traditions accord to the individual member and to his group: no penalties to be inflicted for nonconformity to A.A. principles; no fees or dues to be levied—voluntary contributions only; no member to be expelled from A.A.— membership always to be the choice of the individual; each A.A. group to conduct its internal affairs as it wishes—it being merely requested to abstain from acts that might injure A.A. as a whole; and finally that any group of alcoholics gathered together for sobriety may call themselves an A.A. group provided that, *as a group,* they have no other purpose or affiliation."

Group service—from coffee maker to secretary, treasurer, or chairperson—is usually the way members first experience the joy and the growth that can be derived from A.A. service. (The pamphlet "The A.A. Group" provides extensive information on group organization and opportunities for service.)

The General Service Representative (G.S.R.)

The general service representative has the job of linking his or her group with A.A. as a whole. The G.S.R. represents the voice of the group conscience, reporting the group's thoughts to the district committee member and to the delegate, who passes them on to the Conference. This communication is a two-way street, making the G.S.R. responsible for bringing back to the group Conference Actions that affect A.A. unity, health, and growth. Only when a G.S.R. keeps the group informed, and communicates the group conscience, can the Conference truly act for A.A. as a whole.

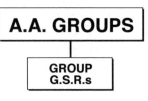

FINANCIAL SUPPORT: Current experience indicates that many groups provide financial support for their general service representatives to attend service functions.

Qualifications

- Experience shows that the most effective G.S.R.s have been active in group, intergroup, or other service, where they have developed a desire to serve, and encountered situations in which the Twelve Traditions have been called upon to solve problems.
- Usually, prospective G.S.R.s have at least two years of continuous sobriety.
- They have time available for district meetings and area assemblies.
- They have the confidence of the group, and an ability to listen to all points of view.

Duties

- G.S.R.s attend district meetings.
- They also attend area assemblies.
- G.S.R.s serve as the mail contact with the General Service Office, and they are listed in the A.A. directories as contacts for their groups. They receive the G.S.O. bulletin *Box 4-5-9*, and keep their groups abreast of A.A. activities all over the world.
- They serve as mail contact with their district committee member and with the area committee.
- G.S.R.s supply their D.C.M.s with up-to-date group information, which is relayed to G.S.O., either directly to the Records department or through the area registrar updating G.S.O.'s database, for inclusion in the directories and for G.S.O. mailings.
- They are knowledgeable about material available from G.S.O.—new literature, guidelines, bulletins, videos, tapes, kits, etc.,—and they are responsible for passing such information on to the groups.
- They learn everything they can about the Twelve Traditions and Twelve Concepts and are familiar with this manual, the books *Twelve Steps and Twelve Traditions* and *A.A. Comes of Age, Twelve Concepts for World Service,* and the pamphlets "The A.A. Group," "A.A. Tradition – How It Developed," "The Twelve Traditions Illustrated," and "The Twelve Concepts Illustrated."
- They usually serve on group steering committees.
- They work with group treasurers to develop practical plans for group support of G.S.O., such as the Regular Contribution Plan and the Birthday Plan. They encour-

age the group to support the area and district committees and local central offices or intergroups, and they are familiar with the leaflet "Self-Support: Where Money and Spirituality Mix."

- They participate in district and area service meetings, and often help with planning for area get-togethers and conventions. Following these events, they make reports to their groups for the benefit of those who could not attend.

Term and Method of Election

G.S.R.s serve for two years and the term frequently runs concurrently with those of committee members and the delegate. They represent their home group and are nominated and elected by group members.

Service Structure Inside the A.A. Group

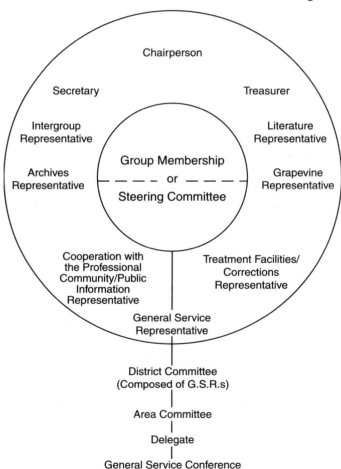

Chairperson

Secretary

Treasurer

Intergroup
Representative

Literature
Representative

Group Membership

Archives
Representative

or

Grapevine
Representative

Steering Committee

Cooperation with
the Professional
Community/Public
Information
Representative

Treatment Facilities/
Corrections
Representative

General Service
Representative

District Committee
(Composed of G.S.R.s)

Area Committee

Delegate

General Service Conference

Some groups hold a special election for the G.S.R. To emphasize the need for selecting strong G.S.R.s, such a meeting can provide information on the role of G.S.R.s and their work in the district and area. (A basic resource is the pamphlet "G.S.R.: May be the Most Important Job in A.A.") Nominations can be made by a steering committee or during a group business meeting. A plurality is generally sufficient for election.

NOTIFICATION: As soon as a G.S.R. is elected, the group should provide the district and area committees, the local intergroup/central office, and G.S.O. with the following information: 1) group name and service number, 2) the new G.S.R.'s name, address, and telephone number, and 3) the previous G.S.R.'s name (so it can be removed from the mailing list).

G.S.R. KIT: When G.S.O. has been notified, the new G.S.R. receives a kit containing a covering memo, *The A.A. Service Manual/Twelve Concepts for World Service*, useful pamphlets and leaflets, and a literature order form.

ALTERNATE G.S.R.: An alternate should be elected at the same time, in case the G.S.R. is unable to attend all district and area meetings. Alternates should be encouraged to assist, participate, and share in the responsibilities of the G.S.R., attending district and area meetings when feasible, depending on local needs.

Inactive General Service Representative

A.A. relies on the autonomy of each group regarding the period of time and involvement that constitutes inactivity. While the group needs to establish its own practices or guidelines, it is generally suggested that a service worker be asked to resign if he or she is unable to carry out the responsibilities of the position.

Group Information

It is important for the group to send information to each of the following entities: G.S.O., and the district, the area *and* to the local intergroup/central office. While local, area and national offices communicate regularly, they have different purposes and different mailing lists.

Two simplified forms (see following pages) have been developed to facilitate transmittal of information to G.S.O.: 1) *Alcoholics Anonymous New Group Form* is for one-time use only, when a new group is started; 2) the *Group Information Change Form* is to be filled in whenever a group changes its name or meeting address, elects a new G.S.R., reports a change of address and/or phone number, reports the designation of a new second contact, or reports a change of address or phone number for the second contact. The group information provided on these two forms is stored in G.S.O.'s database, which is accessible to the area registrar.

G.S.O. also uses this database to generate mailing lists for A.A. newsletters. Group information included in G.S.O.'s database may be used by areas and districts for various purposes: the delegate may use it to communicate with groups; some areas use it for their meeting locators or to generate mailing lists. To assure direct and regular communication between the group and G.S.O., each group is assigned a service number. It is helpful to refer to this number when writing to G.S.O. and when sending contributions.

If a group wishes to be listed in the appropriate U.S. or Canadian A.A. directory, this can be indicated in filling out the New Group Information Form.

ALCOHOLICS ANONYMOUS NEW GROUP FORM

"Our membership ought to include all who suffer from alcoholism. Hence we may refuse none who wish to recover. Nor ought A.A. Membership ever depend upon money or conformity. Any two or three alcoholics gathered together for sobriety may call themselves an A.A. group, provided that, as a group they have no other affiliation." — Tradition Three (the long form)

"Each Alcoholics Anonymous group ought to be a spiritual entity having but one primary purpose — that of carrying its message to the alcoholic who still suffers." — Tradition Five (the long form)

"Unless there is approximate conformity to A.A.'s Twelve Traditions, the group... can deteriorate and die." — Twelve Steps and Twelve Traditions, page 174.

A.A.'s Traditions suggest that a group not be named after a facility or member (living or deceased), and that the name of a group not imply affiliation with any sect, religion, organization or institution.

GROUP NAME: Tangelo Group   GROUP START DATE: 4|1|11

GROUP MEETING LOCATION: United Methodist Church   NUMBER OF MEMBERS: 25

ADDRESS: Peekskill Hollow Road

CITY/TOWN: Putnam Valley   STATE/PROVINCE: N.Y.   ZIP CODE: 10579

MEETING DAY	MON ☑	TUES ☐	WED ☐	THURS ☑	FRI ☐	SAT ☐	SUN ☐
MEETING TIMES	8.00 P			8.00 P			

LANGUAGE (Please check one ✓)   ENGLISH ☑   SPANISH ☐   FRENCH ☐   OTHER _____ (Specify)

GENERAL SERVICE REPRESENTATIVE

NAME: Andrea Soprano   E-MAIL: xxxx@yahoo.com

ADDRESS: 1 Lake Drive   CITY/TOWN: Lake Peekskill

STATE/PROVINCE: N.Y.   ZIP CODE: 10537   TELEPHONE: (xxx)xxx-xxxx

ALTERNATE G.S.R. ☐   OR MAIL CONTACT ☐   (Please check one ✓)

NAME: _____   E-MAIL: _____

ADDRESS: _____   CITY/TOWN: _____

STATE/PROVINCE: _____   ZIP CODE: _____   TELEPHONE: _____

Does your Group meet in a hospital, treatment center or detox center?   ☐ Yes   ☑ No
If yes, is it open to A.A. members in the community as well as to patients in the center?   ☐ Yes   ☐ No

If the Group is to be listed in the Directory, please provide a telephone number and mailing address for the G.S.R., Alternate G.S.R., or Group contact. Listing in the Directory is for Twelfth Step referral and/or for meeting information. The G.S.R.'s (or other contact) name and telephone number will be included in the Directory with the group's name and service number.

OK TO LIST IN THE DIRECTORY? ☑ Yes ☐ No

SIGNATURE: Andrea Soprano   DATE: 5|1|11

THREE WAYS TO RETURN THIS FORM:

☐ Postal Mail to: A.A. World Services, Inc.   ☐ By Fax: 212-870-3003 (Attn: Records)   ☐ E-mail: records@aa.org
Grand Central Station
P.O. Box 459
New York, NY 10163

FOR G.S.O. RECORDS DEPT. USE ONLY

DELEGATE AREA NUMBER:	DISTRICT NUMBER:	GROUP SERVICE NUMBER (ASSIGN BY G.S.O.)

GROUP SERVICE No. 000701122   **DATE:** 5|1|11

DELEGATE AREA No. 7   **DISTRICT No.** 40   **No. OF MEMBERS:** 27

OLD INFORMATION	NEW INFORMATION

GROUP NAME: By the Book Group

Group Meeting Location: 1st Pres. Church

Street: Rte. 47

City/Town: _____

State/Province: _____

Zip Code: _____ Telephone: _____

GROUP NAME: Same

Group Meeting Location: United Methodist Church

Street: Clarkston Street

City/Town: _____

State/Province: _____

Zip Code: _____ Telephone: _____

MEETING DAY

MON ☐ | TUES ☐ | WED ☐ | THUR ☐ | FRI ☐ | SAT ☑ | SUN ☐

MEETING DAY

MON ☐ | TUES ☐ | WED ☐ | THUR ☐ | FRI ☐ | SAT ☑ | SUN ☐

MEETING TIMES
___ | ___ | ___ | ___ | ___ | 8 AM| ___

MEETING TIMES
___ | ___ | ___ | ___ | ___ | 8 AM| ___

GENERAL SERVICE REPRESENTATIVE (G.S.R.)

Name: Laura Reynolds

Street: 789 First Ave So.

City/Town: Englewood

State/Province: Colo

Zip Code: 80110 Telephone: 720-123-4567

E-mail: _____

GENERAL SERVICE REPRESENTATIVE (G.S.R.)

Name: Same

Street: _____

City/Town: _____

State/Province: _____

Zip Code: _____ Telephone: _____

E-mail: _____

ALTERNATE G.S.R. ☐ **or MAIL CONTACT** ☐ (Please check one ✓)

Name: None

Street: _____

City/Town: _____

State/Province: _____

Zip Code: _____ Telephone: _____

E-mail: _____

ALTERNATE G.S.R. ☐ **or MAIL CONTACT** ☐ (Please check one ✓)

Name: _____

Street: _____

City/Town: _____

State/Province: _____

Zip Code: _____ Telephone: _____

E-mail: _____

If the Group is to be listed in the Directory, please provide a telephone number and mailing address for the G.S.R., Alternate G.S.R., or Group contact. Listing in the Directory is for Twelfth Step referral and/or for meeting information. The G.S.R.'s (or other contact) name and telephone number will be included in the Directory with the group's name and service number.

OK TO LIST IN THE DIRECTORY? ☑ Yes ☐ No

SIGNATURE: Laura Reynolds   DATE: 5|1|11

"Our membership ought to include all who suffer from alcoholism. Hence we may refuse none who wish to recover. Nor ought A.A. Membership ever depend upon money or conformity. Any two or three alcoholics gathered together for sobriety may call themselves an A.A. group, provided that, as a group they have no other affiliation." — Tradition Three (the long form)

"Each Alcoholics Anonymous group ought to be a spiritual entity having but one primary purpose — that of carrying its message to the alcoholic who still suffers." — Tradition Five (the long form)

"Unless there is approximate conformity to A.A.'s Twelve Traditions, the group... can deteriorate and die." — Twelve Steps and Twelve Traditions, page 174.

THREE WAYS TO RETURN THIS FORM:

☐ **Postal Mail to:** A.A. World Services, Inc.
Grand Central Station
P.O. Box 459
New York, NY 10163

☐ **By Fax:** 212-870-3003 (Attn: Records)

☐ **E-mail:** records@aa.org

❖ Chapter Three

The District and the D.C.M.

THE DISTRICT

A district is a geographical unit containing the right number of groups—right in terms of the committee member's ability to keep in frequent touch with them, to learn their problems, and to find ways to contribute to their growth and well-being.

The number of groups per district varies widely, from as few as five in a rural district to 90 or more in a metropolitan district. Population density and the geographic size of the district, which will affect the ability of the D.C.M. to communicate with the groups, would be key factors determining the number of groups a district will have.

LINGUISTIC DISTRICTS: To encourage participation of the maximum number of groups, some areas have incorporated linguistic districts within their structure. These districts are made up of groups that conduct meetings in a non-English language. They usually have a bilingual D.C.M. or liaison. Their boundaries may be independent of the conventional geographic district boundaries.

THE DISTRICT COMMITTEE MEMBER

The district committee member (D.C.M.) is an essential link between the group G.S.R. and the area delegate to the General Service Conference. As leader of the district committee, made up of all G.S.R.s in the district, the D.C.M. is exposed to the group conscience of that district. As a member of the area committee, he or she is able to pass on the district's thinking to the delegate and the committee. (The pamphlet "Your D.C.M.," available from the General Service Office, provides basic information on this service job.)

FINANCIAL SUPPORT: Current experience indicates that many districts provide financial support for their D.C.M.s to attend service functions. Invariably, this pays off in increased activity, interest, and group participation.

Qualifications

- The district committee member has usually served as a G.S.R. and is elected by other G.S.R.s to take responsibility for district activities. If the person chosen is a current G.S.R., a new G.S.R. should be elected to fill his or her position.
- A D.C.M. should have enough sobriety (generally four or five years) to be eligible for election as delegate.
- He or she also needs to have the time and energy to serve the district well.

Duties

The D.C.M.'s job is primarily that of two-way communication. The D.C.M.:

- Regularly attends all district meetings and area assemblies.
- Receives reports from the groups through G.S.R.s and through frequent personal contacts with groups in the district.
- Holds regular meetings of all G.S.R.s in the district.
- Helps the Conference delegate cover the area, which would be impossible for the delegate to do on a group-by-group basis.
- Assists the delegate in obtaining group information in time to meet the deadline for A.A. directories.
- Keeps G.S.R.s informed about Conference activities; this

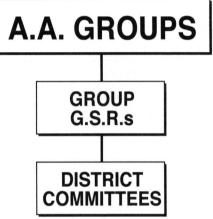

A.A. GROUPS

GROUP G.S.R.s

DISTRICT COMMITTEES

includes setting up opportunities for the delegate's Conference report, occasionally making the Conference report if the delegate cannot be present, and inviting the delegate to regular district meetings.

- Makes sure that G.S.R.s are acquainted with *The A.A. Service Manual,* the *Twelve Concepts for World Service,* the G.S.O. bulletin *Box 4-5-9,* workbooks and guidelines from G.S.O., and any other service material.
- Helps G.S.R.s make interesting reports to groups, and encourages them to bring new A.A. members to service events.
- Keeps groups informed about Conference-approved books and pamphlets.
- Organizes workshops and/or sharing sessions on service activities.
- Regularly keeps in touch with the alternate D.C.M. and the delegate; sends district minutes to the delegate and alternate, and exchanges them with other districts.
- Brings Traditions problems to the attention of the delegate.
- Makes a regular practice of *talking to groups* (new and old) on the responsibilities of general service work.

Term, Eligibility, and Election Procedures

The D.C.M.'s term of office is two years, coinciding in most areas with the terms of the delegate, committee officers, and G.S.R.s. Some areas, however, rotate half their committee members each year. D.C.M.s are generally elected in the fall of the year. The election should take place *after* the G.S.R. election and *before* that of the area delegate, because the D.C.M. is chosen either from among currently serving G.S.R.s or from a combination of past and present G.S.R.s. In most areas, a candidate for an area committee officer or Conference delegate must be a committee member before being eligible for election.

While district meetings to elect committee members are most often held in advance of area assemblies, and separate from them, occasionally travel distances make this impractical and/or a hardship. (This usually means more districts should be set up.) If necessary, therefore, meetings to elect committee members can be held immediately before area assemblies at the place where the assembly meets.

The committee member who is finishing a term sets up the election meeting and, in most districts, notifies the G.S.R.s who have just been elected and those who are going out of office.

The method of election should be decided by the area assembly or by the district committee. Some options are:

- Most district committees allow all current voting members of the district committee to vote in district elections.
- Some committees also allow newly elected G.S.R.s a vote, even though they might not take office until some time after the election.

Many district committees include alternate D.C.M.s, a secretary and/or treasurer, and other officers or service committee chairpersons in addition to the D.C.M and G.S.R.s. Sometimes, these jobs are held by the G.S.R.s already on the committee; sometimes, they call for additional voting members, who are eligible to stand for D.C.M.

Election is either by written ballot or show of hands, with a majority needed to elect. A district may also choose to follow Third Legacy Procedure (see page S21), which requires a two-thirds majority.

Inactive District Committee Member

A.A. relies on the autonomy of each district regarding the period of time and involvement that constitutes inactivity. While the district needs to establish its own practices or guidelines, it is generally suggested that a service worker be asked to resign if he or she is unable to carry out the responsibilities of the position.

The Alternate D.C.M.

The alternate is a backup for the D.C.M. If the D.C.M. resigns or is unable to serve for any reason, the alternate steps in. Usually, the alternate is elected at the same time as the D.C.M., by the same procedure. Alternate committee members should be encouraged to assist, participate, and share in the D.C.M.'s responsibilities at district and area meetings.

Redistricting

If it were not for adding committee members to take care of new groups as A.A. grows, the General Service Conference might well become unwieldy. As the number of groups increases and it becomes too difficult for the D.C.M. to communicate with them all, several courses can be followed:

- *New districts:* Divide the district into two or more districts, each with its own D.C.M.
- *Local Committee Member* (L.C.M.): A large district could divide itself into smaller districts (often called subdistricts or local districts), each electing a local committee member. Depending on area practice, these L.C.M.s may or may not be voting members of the area committee and may or may not hold regular meetings with the G.S.R.s they serve.
- *District Committee Member Chairperson* (D.C.M.C.): A large district in a city or county may hold regular meetings led by a D.C.M.C., who serves as the link between the district and the area. Within this large district, there are as many district subdivisions as needed to adequately serve the groups. Each of these may be called a subdistrict, local district, or zone. Each is served by a D.C.M., who may hold regular meetings of G.S.R.s. In some areas, these D.C.M.s are voting members of the area committee and assembly; in some, they are not.

Good communication and cooperation among groups, districts, and areas is important when redistricting or other changes in district structure are undertaken. There are many variations, but the goal is the same: to take care of expansion at the district level.

When additional committee members are elected to respond to expansion, qualifications and election methods listed for a D.C.M. can serve as guidelines.

District Information

It is important that the district send information to the area, G.S.O. and to the local intergroup/central office, if applicable. While local, area and national offices communicate regularly, they have different purposes and different mailing lists.

There may be one person in the area, frequently the area secretary or the area registrar, who is responsible for transmitting district contact information changes to G.S.O. One simple form has been developed to facilitate this, the District Information Change Form (F-43) shown on the following page. The form is used whenever a district elects a new D.C.M. or D.C.M.C., or when any contact information for the D.C.M. or D.C.M.C. changes. When filling out the form, it is important to fill the sections in for the old information and for the new information, and to note at the top of the form the area and the date when the new information will become effective.

The information provided on this form is stored in G.S.O.'s database, which is accessible to the area registrar. G.S.O.'s database also provides the capability for the area registrar to identify district officers and service chairs with local or specific information that then can be used to facilitate communication.

A.A. District Committee Member & District Committee Member Chair Change Form

Area#:_____   Effective Date: _____

Outgoing DCM (District Committee Member)	Incoming DCM (District Committee Member)
District:_____	District:_____
(Please indicate District #)	(Please indicate District #)
District Language: ☐ English ☐ Spanish ☐ French	District Language: ☐ English ☐ Spanish ☐ French
Name:_____	Name:_____
Address:_____	Address:_____
City:_____	City:_____
State/Province:_____	State/Province:_____
Zip/Postal Code:_____	Zip/Postal Code:_____
Email:_____	Email:_____
Phone:_____	Phone:_____
☐ Home ☐ Business	☐ Home ☐ Business

Outgoing DCMC (District Committee Meeting Chair)	Incoming DCMC (District Committee Meeting Chair)
District:_____	District:_____
(Please indicate District #)	(Please indicate District #)
District Language: ☐ English ☐ Spanish ☐ French	District Language: ☐ English ☐ Spanish ☐ French
Name:_____	Name:_____
Address:_____	Address:_____
City:_____	City:_____
State/Province:_____	State/Province:_____
Zip/Postal Code:_____	Zip/Postal Code:_____
Email:_____	Email:_____
Phone:_____	Phone:_____
☐ Home ☐ Business	☐ Home ☐ Business

Please return to: A.A. World Services, Inc.
Records Department
P.O. Box 459, Grand Central Station
New York, NY 10163

Or fax to: (212) 870-3003
Attn: Records

❖ Chapter Four

The Area Assembly and Activities

An area may be part of a state or province, or all of it, or may include parts of more than one state or province, depending on the size and needs of the A.A. population. In any case, the area holds an important middle position in the Conference structure—through the elected delegate, it participates in A.A. worldwide, while through the D.C.M.s and G.S.R.s, it is close to the local scene.

THE AREA ASSEMBLY

Any meeting of area G.S.R.s and the area committee (see Chapter Five) is an assembly. The area assembly is the mainspring of the Conference structure—the democratic voice of the movement expressing itself. Assemblies are the responsibility of the area committee, and are conducted by its chairperson.

In the beginning, general service assemblies were held only to elect committee officers and the delegate to the Conference meeting, and without such meetings, there might be no area service structure today. Now, assembly meetings consider a variety of issues, from General Service Conference business to area problems and solutions and financial affairs, while sharing sessions, public information programs, workshops, and video programs keep A.A. strong and participation in service growing.

An election assembly is held at least once every two years to choose a delegate and committee officers. It is usually scheduled in the fall of the year, prior to November 1. (Generally, the newly elected delegate and officers take office as of January 1.)

Nonelection assemblies or meetings may be held at any interval the area wishes. In some areas they may be called "workshops" or "general sharing sessions." However, most areas call them assemblies and include workshops and other activities; and the election meeting is always called an "assembly."

Composition

G.S.R.s, D.C.M.s, and area officers make up the assembly. Any A.A. member may attend, and in many areas members are encouraged to attend assemblies as a way of encouraging them to become active in general service.

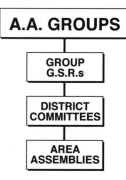

Eligibility to Vote

Generally speaking, all area committee members and officers and all G.S.R.s have one vote each in an assembly. Experience indicates that even though committee members and area officers are members of a group in the area that is represented by a G.S.R., they are entitled to a vote at the assembly. Alternates normally vote only if the regular D.C.M. or G.S.R. is not present.

AREA PROCEDURES: Uniform practices throughout the Fellowship are in no way obligatory, or even practical in many cases. It is important for the area to agree upon a set of procedures, and each individual assembly is the best judge of whom it will seat. Several areas have developed written procedures for all aspects of area operations.

Procedures should answer such commonly asked questions as: Do both incoming and out-going D.C.M.s and G.S.R.s vote? Do the chairpersons of special committees have a vote? How long must a group have been in existence before it is entitled to a vote? (Usually, if an A.A. group has submitted the name of a G.S.R., the G.S.R. is permitted to vote.) Can one G.S.R. represent two groups? (Each group should have its own G.S.R., who votes for one group only.) When the G.S.R. cannot be present, can he or she vote by proxy? (Normally the alternate votes; proxies may be used in some areas, but this is not a common practice.)

The assembly also needs to decide whether or not G.S.R.s of prison and hospital groups are to have a vote (some do, and find it helpful).

Inactive Service Workers

How does the area deal with area officers and committee chairs who have been absent from two or more assemblies? While the area assembly needs to establish its own practices or guidelines, it is generally suggested that a service worker be asked to resign if he or she is unable to carry out the responsibilities of the position.

Timing and Location of Assemblies

The majority of areas hold assembly meetings quarterly or every other month—a few meet monthly. When travel distances are great, assemblies may be held semiannually or even annually, with more emphasis being placed on district meetings, which are more accessible to G.S.R.s.

Some areas hold all their assemblies at a convenient central spot, while others rotate the meeting from one district to another. Assemblies may run from half a day to a full weekend.

A Typical Election Assembly

Election assemblies are held every two years, and the delegate and other area officers are elected for two-year terms. The order of business is generally something like this:

1. Chairperson opens meeting with a moment of silence followed by the Serenity Prayer.
2. Secretary, delegate, other officers, and D.C.M.s report on activities since the last meeting.
3. Chairperson announces procedure for the election of committee members and acceptance of members already elected by G.S.R.s in their districts.
4. When a district committee member has not been elected in advance of the assembly, G.S.R.s from each district caucus to elect one. Chair announces a recess for this purpose and G.S.R.s gather in groups by district.
5. Chairperson reviews the election procedure and the area's guidelines for who votes in the assembly and asks approval of it, and of the order of election—whether chairperson and other officers are to be elected before or after the delegate. Early in the growth of the Conference structure, the delegate was elected last; more recently, the delegate has usually been chosen first, followed by the alternate delegate, chairperson, secretary, treasurer, etc.
6. The delegate is usually elected by Third Legacy Procedure (see page S21).
   - Before balloting starts, eligible committee members' names (suggest full names be used) and districts are read to the assembly or written on the board. Those eligible may be present or past committee members. (In some areas, the chair asks who among those eligible wish to stand for delegate, and those names go on the board.)
   - The chairperson asks whether anyone is unable to serve, and if so, that person's name is removed. Some areas allow nominations from the floor.
   - Paper and pencils are distributed for written ballots. (Some areas use color-coded ballots to speed up the process.)
   - The secretary calls the roll of voting members.
   - Two nonvoting members are selected as tellers, two as collectors of ballots, and one to record and tally votes.
   - Written ballots are cast, collected, and given to tellers to count, and votes are written on the board as the election proceeds.
7. The alternate delegate is elected next, by the same procedure, followed by other area officers.
8. The chairperson directs the secretary to send a report of the assembly, together with names and addresses, of delegate, officers, committee members, and G.S.R.s attending, to the Conference secretary at G.S.O. by December 1. All those elected usually take office January 1.
9. The chairperson then adjourns the meeting.

A Typical Non-Election Assembly

When no election is scheduled, assembly meetings deal with a variety of area concerns. To keep agendas lively and meaningful, some areas appoint agenda committees, which typically include the officers and three, four, or more G.S.R.s. Some areas choose to keep business to a minimum and use most of the time for sharing sessions or workshops. Special speakers who have experience with A.A. worldwide can shed light on worldwide services. The agenda for a regular assembly might be something like the following:

1. A moment of silence followed by the Serenity Prayer.
2. Chairperson's report on committee activities since the last meeting.
3. Delegate's Conference report, or recent communications from G.S.O.
4. Secretary's report.
5. Treasurer's report (usually a good time to remind everyone of the leaflet "Self-Support: Where Money and Spirituality Mix," a useful guide for helping each group decide how to plan its regular contributions to A.A. services).
6. Reports from chairs of special committees—correctional facilities, treatment facilities, public information, cooperation with the professional community, Grapevine, literature, convention, etc.
7. District reports from committee members—on district meetings, district problems, growth, etc.
8. G.S.R. time—ideas, opinions, and suggestions from G.S.R.s.
9. Sharing session.
10. Videos from G.S.O.
11. Newsletter editor's report.
12. Brief "information session" on G.S.O. services—conducted by delegate.
13. Reports from central offices or intergroups.
14. Local problems, ideas, and suggestions.

SENDING MINUTES TO G.S.O.: The General Service Office appreciates receiving copies of area minutes, notes on sharing sessions and workshops, and letters about the meetings. This enables the office to keep up with what is happening in the areas, and to share the experience of areas that have found solutions with others that need help with a problem.

AREA ACTIVITIES

Help on the Annual Conference Program

Every A.A. member has something to say about the Fellowship's present and future—and A.A.'s welfare is central to the agenda of every General Service Conference. Thus, one of the most important program items for an assembly (or a district meeting) is a good look at what might help A.A. on a broad basis. A certain problem may appear to be peculiar to one area, but it is surprising how many are found to be common to every corner of A.A., once they are widely discussed. Assemblies and district meetings provide an ideal time to find out what problems and solutions are shared by A.A. groups everywhere.

The area assembly is a vital part of the communication process from the group to the Conference. Many Conference agenda items follow a path from the A.A. group through the G.S.R and on through district and area. And after the Conference, assemblies and district meetings are occasions for hearing full reports on what took place at the Conference, for asking questions of the delegate, and for deciding what may need attention at future Conferences.

Sharing Sessions

In a sharing session, everyone has a chance to use their experience, strength and hope to contribute ideas and opinions about the welfare of A.A. It can be set up anywhere for any group of people, and is especially useful for assemblies and district meetings. Its format is aimed at drawing out the ideas of even the shyest participant, and keeps the more articulate from dominating the meeting. Each person offers an opinion, and never needs to defend it. The chairperson or leader functions more as a timekeeper than as a participant. Here is how it works:

Let's say that the topic is "How can we get more A.A.s interested in general service?" The leader, armed with a loud bell and a watch or stopwatch, reads the question and explains the rules. Each person present may talk for a specified time (a minute and a half or two minutes is typical—whatever the group agrees upon). Usually no one is permitted to speak twice on the same subject until all who wish to have spoken. The leader continues until the topic has been fully explored.

A member takes down the essence of the meeting; these notes will provide good ideas for use by committee officers and members and by G.S.R.s.

GOOD TOPICS FOR SHARING SESSIONS: Local situations will always provide fodder for a productive session.

- When a group's meeting attendance has fallen, what steps can be taken to rebuild it? How can other groups help?
- Sponsorship… the hand of A.A.
- Group conscience… the voice of A.A.
- G.S.O. services: What kind of help do groups need and want? How useful are the bulletin *Box 4-5-9* and other services? How can they be made more useful?
- How can an area committee work productively with central offices/intergroups in the area?
- What methods are there for getting a group to provide its share of the area and G.S.O. budget?
- Are groups supporting local, district, area and G.S.O. services? If not, why not?

Area Archives

In a growing number of areas, archives committees are engaged in the work of setting up an area archives to collect and preserve area history. Written materials (books, pamphlets, newsletters, written histories), photographs, and audiotapes are the foundations of a collection. Local A.A. historical material is sought out from oldtimers, past delegates, committee members, and others with experience to share. Guidelines on archives are available from the General Service Office.

Area Newsletters or Bulletins

Newsletters and bulletins published by area committees or intergroups/central offices may include local A.A. news, information about groups and committees, and reprinted material from A.A. literature. As in most A.A. service activities, it has been found prudent to make a committee (rather than one or two individuals) responsible for the format, planning, and content.

Here are some ideas taken from local experience with A.A. newsletters and bulletins: scheduling "theme issues" on some aspect of the A.A. program and using excerpts from A.A. literature relating to the theme; asking for and publishing letters from A.A. readers (with the writer's permission, and provided anonymity is protected); carrying minutes of various committee meetings; running a Calendar of Events feature; conducting a subscription campaign (perhaps making announcements at group meetings) to build paid readership.

Local A.A. publications are permitted to reprint the Steps, Traditions, and/or the Concepts, and to quote a phrase, sentence or brief paragraph excerpted from A.A. literature such as the Big Book, *Alcoholics Anonymous,* the *Twelve Steps and Twelve Traditions, The A.A. Service Manual* and Conference-approved pamphlets without a prior, written request to do so. When this occurs, the proper credit line should be included to ensure that the copyrights of A.A. literature are protected. After a quotation from a book or pamphlet, the credit line should read: *Reprinted from (name of publication, page number), with permission of A.A. World Services, Inc.*

The A.A. Preamble is copyrighted by A.A. Grapevine. Beneath it, and beneath any article reprinted from Grapevine and La Viña, these words should appear: *Copyright © (Month, Year) A.A. Grapevine, Inc. Reprinted with permission.* For more information on reprinting other material from A.A. Grapevine, Inc., see Chapter 12.

Any group or district of the Fellowship is free to use the symbol of a circle and triangle on newsletters, meeting schedules, or other A.A. material.

Working with Local Intergroups and Central Offices

Traditionally, general service committees and intergroup/central offices have performed different functions. Central offices provide local services; general service committees maintain the link between the A.A. groups and the A.A. General Service Board by means of the Conference. So these two separate but vital service structures coexist in many areas in mutual cooperation and harmony.

At the time the Conference was started, there were already well-established central offices in several large cities, providing services for local A.A. groups and members. Today, there are many more central offices throughout the U.S. and Canada, supported by the A.A. groups in the communities they serve. Each group elects a representative to attend central office meetings.

These offices provide such services as:

1. Receiving, arranging, and following up Twelfth Step calls.
2. Answering inquiries about A.A.
3. Establishing local public information committees
4. Maintaining information about local hospitals and recovery facilities for alcoholics.
5. Publishing local A.A. meeting lists.
6. Providing a newsletter.
7. Ordering, selling, and distributing A.A. Conference-approved literature.

In contrast, the Conference structure is the method through which all A.A. groups in an area can provide the most effective communication within the area and between the groups and the General Service Board and G.S.O. on matters of policy that affect A.A. as a whole. These include policy on: Conference-approved literature, A.A. public information, A.A. cooperation with the professional community, A.A. activity in treatment and correctional facilities, A.A. finances, the A.A. Grapevine, and the election of trustees to the General Service Board.

Many areas find that a liaison between the intergroup/central office and the area committee is very helpful in maintaining good relations and communication. In some areas the liaison has a vote at the assembly; in others, a voice but no vote.

More information on working together is available through G.S.O. and in the pamphlets "The A.A. Group" and "Self-Support: Where Money and Spirituality Mix," as well as in the Guidelines on Central or Intergroup Offices.

Area, State, Provincial and Regional Conventions

Conventions are a special type of A.A. meeting—usually weekend affairs, but sometimes extending several days. They are frequently set up and guided by area committees or by special committees appointed by area chairpersons. Usually, assembly meetings are not held during conventions, but occasionally they can take place just before or after. A.A. Guidelines on Conferences and Conventions are available from the General Service Office.

Forming a New Delegate Area

If the A.A. population seems to have grown to the point where the current delegate and other trusted servants can no longer provide adequate service and communication, there may be local interest in forming a new area. In such a case, the area committee or committees involved may write to G.S.O. and request an application for an Additional Delegate Area.

This four-page form, first worked out in 1968 and revised in 1992 and 2002, requests detailed information about the current area structure, such as: How often assemblies are held; whether there is an alternate delegate; how often district meetings are held; the number of active D.C.M.s and whether they assist the delegate and alternate; the number of active G.S.R.s in the area; geographical and A.A. population information about the area and its pattern of growth over the past five years, broken down to yearly figures.

The application form is designed to determine problems regarding geography and A.A. population, as well as whether or not the current area service structure is as well developed as it might be to provide support for the delegate.

When such a request came up at the 1961 Conference, a memo from co-founder Bill W. provided background on the subject. Bill wrote (in part):

"The Conference Committee on Admissions [now Policy/Admissions] should weigh each new application for a new delegate on its own merit, taking into consideration the primary factors of population, geography—and also expense. But this process of adding delegates ought to be gradual, aiming at the remedying of obvious and marked flaws in local communications. We should, our budget allowing, continue to remedy obvious flaws in local communication, and that is all.

"It should be reemphasized that the Conference is not a political body, demanding a completely rigid formula of representation. What we shall need will always be enough delegates at the Conference to afford a reliable cross section of A.A. plus enough more to make sure of good local communication."

Requesting a Change of Region

An area may decide that it should be part of a different region. In that case:

1. The G.S.R.s in the area will be informed in advance by the area committee of the necessary facts—both advantages and disadvantages—in order to make a sound decision in requesting a change of region. A simple majority (one-half plus one) of G.S.R.s should be present (or respond to a mail poll). Two-thirds of the majority present or responding should agree before an area petitions for a change of region.

2. Upon notification by the delegate of the plan to change regions, the General Service Office will provide a form to be filled in by the delegate, indicating that the conditions outlined have been fulfilled.

3. The delegate from the requesting area will write, on behalf of the assembly, to the secretary of the trustees' Nominating Committee, stating the request and enclosing the completed form. The delegate will also send copies of the letter and form to the trustees in the two regions involved.

4. The delegate will ask G.S.O. to send a letter to all of the area delegates in the two regions involved, requesting that they obtain the group conscience of their respective areas on the proposed change of region, and that they indicate approval/disapproval on an enclosed card, as soon as possible.

5. Approval by two-thirds of the delegates from each region involved is required before the proposal is presented to the General Service Conference for action.

6. A change of region will become effective *at the end* of the Conference at which it was approved.

Guidelines for Changing Regional Boundaries

The 1996 General Service Conference accepted suggested procedural guidelines for changing regional boundaries, and they are available from G.S.O.

❖ Chapter Five

The Area Committee

Perhaps more than any other group of people in A.A., the area committee is responsible for the health of the Conference structure and thus for growth and harmony in the A.A. Fellowship. If G.S.R.s are lax, if there is lack of harmony in a district, if there are difficulties in public information or some other service area, the committee member knows it and can turn to the full committee for help.

An active committee deals with all kinds of service problems: Is experience being shared among groups? Is the A.A. message getting into hospitals, prisons, jails, and rehabilitation centers? Are news media and professionals who deal with suffering alcoholics well informed about A.A.? Are new groups and Loners being visited and helped?

Composition

Basically, the committee is composed of all district committee members, area officers, and chairs of area service committees. There should be enough districts and committee members to ensure good communication between the committee and the groups. In the absence of a D.C.M., the alternate D.C.M. is a voting member.

In some areas, past delegates serve on the committee, with or without a vote; in others, only the outgoing delegate is a committee member, with or without a vote. The decision on the status of past delegates is up to the group conscience of the area assembly.

Chairperson

DUTIES: The chairperson is responsible for the smooth running of area assemblies, consulting with the committee before setting the date and time, making sure that all groups are notified, consulting with officers and committee members on the program, and chairing the assembly meetings. The chairperson, more than any other officer, keeps the delegate informed about what is going on in the area, and makes sure that committee members are aware of what goes on in world services.

QUALIFICATIONS: The chairperson should have a solid period of sobriety (minimum three to five years), and experience in group, central office, institutional, and/or area affairs. Area chairpersons need a sound understanding and appreciation of the Steps, the Traditions, and the Concepts, along with a good fund of experience gained through applying these guiding principles successfully to local problems. Communication skills, leadership qualities, and sensitivity to the wishes of the local area are also important.

SUGGESTIONS ON CHAIRING ASSEMBLY MEETINGS: Much depends on the chairperson's ability to conduct a smoothly functioning meeting. These suggestions should be helpful:

```
┌─────────────────┐
│  A.A. GROUPS    │
└─────────────────┘
        │
┌─────────────────┐
│     GROUP       │
│   G.S.R.s       │
└─────────────────┘
        │
┌─────────────────┐
│   DISTRICT      │
│  COMMITTEES     │
└─────────────────┘
        │
┌─────────────────┐
│     AREA        │
│  ASSEMBLIES     │
└─────────────────┘
        │
┌─────────────────┐
│     AREA        │
│  COMMITTEES     │
└─────────────────┘
```

- Keep the issues clear. If a motion is offered, be sure it is stated clearly and distinctly so that all know what they are voting for or against.

- Stick close to Third Legacy Procedure for elections; discourage departures from it.

- On simple matters, a majority vote is enough—even a "sense of the meeting" can take the place of a vote at times. In such a case, the chair asks: "Is it the sense of the meeting that…?" If there are no "nays," it is apparent there is accord.

- Meetings may be fairly informal, but the attention of the entire meeting should be on one subject at a time, without the disruptive influence of private conversations.

- An assembly makes its own rules, and the chairperson should be sure that all members are aware of current suggested procedures in the manual. If members want to make a change in the rules, it should be done *before* a vote is taken, or *before* an election is conducted.

Secretary

DUTIES: The secretary records and distributes minutes of area meetings; keeps mailing lists up to date and sends out area mailings; sometimes the secretary is responsible for preparing lively bulletins that will encourage attendance at committee meetings and assemblies. The secretary is in a good position to act as liaison between officers and committee members.

QUALIFICATIONS: The secretary should have a "reasonable period of sobriety," which might mean two years in an area where A.A. is still young, four or five years in an older area. Some service in group or central office or general service is useful. So is some background in general office work — more and more, computer knowledge is helpful. An effective secretary needs to have a sense of order, and the ability to capture the essentials of what is happening at a meeting. The job is time-consuming and needs to be carried out on schedule, and the secretary needs to be sure that ample time is available.

Registrar

DUTIES: In many areas, *registrars* now develop and maintain records of all groups in the area, including group name, meeting location, time, and G.S.R. or group contact. Registrars may also be responsible for names, addresses, email addresses and phone numbers of the G.S.R.s, D.C.M.s, district and area officers and area committee members. They may provide mailing labels for area publications such as a monthly newsletter or a mailing of minutes.

Area registrars also assist the G.S.O. Records Department to keep their records up-to-date.

QUALIFICATIONS: Registrars should be familiar with the area and district structure. For this job, an organized approach is important as there are many details that need to be recorded. Ideally, it would be very helpful if the area registrar possessed some practical, working computer knowledge, and were comfortable relaying information via email to G.S.O. and within the local area.

Treasurer

DUTIES: The treasurer keeps financial records for the area and reports regularly to the assembly. In most cases, the treasurer is responsible for encouraging contribution support for area and G.S.O. services.

QUALIFICATIONS: The treasurer should be a responsible person with a solid period of sobriety. He or she should be organized enough to keep good records, and some accounting or bookkeeping experience is useful. Otherwise, the person elected may need help in setting up a system, and possibly some clerical assistance. Persuasiveness, firmness, and diplomacy will help the treasurer do the job. If the committee includes a finance chairperson, the treasurer is free for record keeping and financial controls.

Other Officers

An area committee usually has other officers who are responsible to the committee for special activities. Examples are public information and cooperation with the professional community chairs to head up the area P.I. and C.P.C. committees; correctional and treatment facilities chairs to coordinate this vital Twelfth Step work; a literature chairperson to act as a liaison between various service entities; a Grapevine and La Viña chairperson to disseminate information on the magazines and other Grapevine materials (see p. S90); an archives chairperson to gather area history and maintain the area archives; a convention chairperson to facilitate this event; a finance chairperson to encourage self-support for both area needs and those of G.S.O.; a liaison chairperson to foster communication between the area and the central office/intergroup; and other committee assignments and responsibilities as suggested by area needs.

Alternate Committee Officers

Some areas find it helpful to select alternates for all committee officers, especially for the chairperson. The alternates can provide continuity at the area level; they may or may not be seated as voting members, depending on local decision and area needs. In this as in all other levels of service, alternates should be encouraged to participate in committee activities as fully as possible. Qualifications of alternates are generally the same as the qualifications for the positions they may be called upon to assume.

Past Delegates

A.A. has in past delegates a wealth of experience, which is sometimes used and sometimes not. The A.A. practice of rotation prevents delegates from succeeding themselves or from returning later as delegates, but a role for past delegates is gradually emerging that involves them in area activities and gives the area the benefit of their experience with worldwide A.A., but leaves area committees and new delegates free to run their own show.

It is suggested that past delegates not hold office as G.S.R.s or D.C.M.s, but find other ways to become involved in area service. As stated above, in some areas they serve on the area committee. They are called in for consultation or for special assignments, such as chairing area sharing sessions, speaking at special meetings designed to inform members about A.A. worldwide, or conducting workshops or orientation meetings for new G.S.R.s. Frequently, they are in line for committee chairperson or chairperson of a state or provincial convention. Or they may be appointed by the area chairperson to be responsible for area public information, or to urge more widespread distribution of Conference-approved literature and the A.A. Grapevine.

In addition, several regions hold annual meetings of past delegates, with newly elected delegates and alternates invited as well. Started as a breakfast meeting for past delegates at a regional convention, this event has proved to be a valuable way of passing on experience to new delegates. In some regions, the meeting now spans a full weekend. Its purpose is first and foremost communication, strengthening the lines of communication among the General Service Conference, G.S.O., the General Service Board, Grapevine Board and A.A. as a whole. There is no attempt to discuss or recommend actions that would interfere with or supersede the functions of the area or the Conference.

Financial Support

Typical of most financial undertakings in A.A., the cost of supporting an area committee is small in relation to comparable activities in business firms and other organizations. Nonetheless, sufficient funds are needed, or the work of the committee will be hampered. Most areas today maintain solvent treasuries and report regularly to their G.S.R.s on the financial picture.

AREA EXPENSES: There are, of course, the routine expenses of postage, phone calls, and bulletin printing. The delegate needs money for the trip to the Conference meeting in New York in April. Delegates and committee members incur further travel expenses when they report to groups following the Conference meeting. Many active area committees support public information programs and buy literature for groups in institutions. Each area sends at least $1,600.00 U.S. (sixteen hundred dollars) to G.S.O. to help defray the cost of the annual meeting of the Conference, and a number of areas send additional funds. (The $1,600.00 is sent no later than March 1 of each year—a reminder from G.S.O. is sent in January.)

METHODS OF SUPPORT: Here are some of the ways areas remain solvent and effective:
- They take collections at assembly and district meetings.
- They share in the Regular Contribution Plan whereby groups contribute monthly or quarterly to the intergroup/central office, G.S.O., district, and area. (See also the leaflet "Self-Support: Where Money and Spirituality Mix.")
- They receive contributions from area and state convention treasuries.

Area Information

The outgoing delegate provides G.S.O. with contact information for all incoming area officers and committee chairs. This information is stored in G.S.O.'s database, which is also accessible to the area registrar, and is used to communicate with these officers and committee chairs throughout their rotation.

❖ Chapter Six

The Delegate

The delegate has a demanding job, not only because a large amount of time and work are involved, but because it is the delegate's responsibility to serve the US/Canada Conference as a whole. As voting members of the Conference, delegates bring to its deliberations the experiences and viewpoints of their own areas. Yet they are not representatives of their areas in the usual political sense; after hearing all points of view and becoming fully informed during Conference discussion, they vote in the best interests of A.A. as a whole.

Duties

Though the high point is the Conference meeting, the delegate's job goes on year-round and involves all aspects of the Conference structure. The delegate should:

- Attend the annual Conference meeting fully prepared. Immediately upon election, every delegate is put on the G.S.O. mailing list to receive Conference materials.
- Communicate the actions of the Conference to area committee members and encourage them to pass on this information, and the delegate's enthusiasm, to groups and to intergroups/central offices. If an area is too large for the delegate to cover in person, he or she will ask area officers and committee members to share the load.
- Be prepared to attend all area and regional service meetings and assemblies applicable to his/her respective area. From these meetings, delegates come to better understand their own areas and can make suggestions for the Conference agenda. Here, too, they come in contact with A.A. members who might not be reached otherwise.
- Help area committees obtain financial support for the area and G.S.O.
- Provide leadership in solving local problems involving the A.A. Traditions.
- Remind G.S.R.s to inform groups and individuals about the A.A. Grapevine and Conference-approved literature.
- Cooperate with G.S.O. in obtaining information—for example, making sure that up-to-date information reaches G.S.O. in time to meet the deadline for each issue of the A.A. directory and helping carry out the triennial membership surveys.
- Visit groups and districts in the area whenever possible.

- Work closely with committee members and officers, sharing experience throughout the year. After G.S.R.s and committee members have reported on the Conference, learn from these A.A.s how groups and members have reacted.
- Assume added responsibility if the area chair and alternate chair are unable to serve. Or, if an area committee is not functioning effectively, the delegate may take an active role in remedying the situation.
- Keep the alternate delegate fully informed and active, so that the alternate can replace the delegate in an emergency.
- Late in the second year of the term, work with newly elected delegates to pass along a basic knowledge of Conference proceedings and problems.

A.A. GROUPS
GROUP G.S.R.s
DISTRICT COMMITTEES
AREA ASSEMBLIES
AREA COMMITTEES
DELEGATES TO THE GENERAL SERVICE CONFERENCE

Term of Office

A delegate serves one term of two years, and the Conference strongly recommends that a delegate serve only one term—with the exception of an alternate delegate who, after attending one Conference in place of the delegate, may be elected to serve a full term. Half the delegates are elected in one year, the other half the next (see Appendix D for a list of Conference Panels). This ensures that at any Conference, there is a core of experienced delegates along with first-year delegates.

Expenses

A delegate's expenses to the Conference are covered in this way: The area contributes at least $1,600.00 (U.S.) toward Conference expenses (and many areas are able to send additional funds). The General Fund of the General Service Board pays the balance, but this does not take care of the many incidental expenses the delegate will have during Conference week. Upon arrival in New York, each delegate receives cash to cover basic expenses during Conference week. In addition, the areas generally provide some money to cover extra expenses. The amount differs, depending on the area's financial circumstances.

Many areas also provide funds to cover travel and incidental expenses the delegate incurs in reporting back to groups and districts within the area.

Qualifications

Like other A.A. members, delegates come in all shapes and sizes. But some characteristics seem to make for well-qualified delegates. For example:

- Several years of active participation in local and area affairs, as a G.S.R. and as a committee member.
- Time available, not only for the week-long Conference meeting in April but for all the efforts needed before and after the Conference.

- Five or six years of continuous sobriety. The sobriety requirement varies from area to area; in any case, a delegate should have been sober long enough to be responsible and informed.
- The ability to make and take suggestions—and criticisms, too.
- Experience in chairing meetings.
- Knowledge of A.A. affairs, and of where to find the correct information when they do not know the answers.
- Thorough familiarity with the Twelve Traditions and the Twelve Concepts and how they apply to local problems.
- The ability to be open-minded, to sit down with A.A.s in the area and with other delegates to discuss and act on matters vital to A.A.

If you are thinking about standing for a term as delegate, ask yourself these questions:
- How well did you do as a G.S.R.? As a committee member? Did you enjoy the responsibilities? Were you active?
- Have you discussed the possibility with your family and your employer? Will the time be available for the amount of work required?
- Are you familiar with this manual? With *A.A. Comes of Age?* And of course, with the Twelve Steps, Twelve Traditions, and Twelve Concepts?
- Have you talked with past delegates to get an idea of the time and effort required and the sort of work you will need to do?

Geographical Rotation Within the Area

Some areas have adopted their own policy of "rotation" from rural to urban sections or from one part of an area to another, to avoid domination by one or more heavily populated locations. However, no well-qualified A.A. should be passed over in the interest of geographical rotation.

The Alternate

The Conference recommends that all areas elect alternate delegates. The alternate serves as a valuable assistant, often traveling with the delegate or giving reports for him or her. In some areas, the alternate serves some special function of the committee. Many area committee treasuries recognize the need to support the alternate's expenses separately from the delegate's.

An alternate who replaces the delegate at the annual Conference meeting will remain on the G.S.O. mailing list as the delegate until G.S.O. is informed otherwise by the area committee.

PERSONAL EXPERIENCE
(past delegates offer practical suggestions)

Preparing for the Conference

"Although you may have been involved in A.A. service for some time, don't take your knowledge for granted. Do some reviewing as quickly as possible. Read and reread this manual, *A.A. Comes of Age*, and *Twelve Concepts for World Service.* Get copies of the full Conference Reports for the past two or three years for further study. Seek out some past delegates to share their experience.

"Start a Conference file, because you'll get lots of letters from the Conference coordinator at G.S.O., containing background information and requests. Read them thoroughly;

Leadership in A.A.: Ever a Vital Need

(Excerpts from Bill W.'s article in the April 1959 Grapevine.

See Concept IX, page 36 of "Twelve Concepts for World Service" for the full article)

Somewhere in our literature there is a statement to this effect: "Our leaders do not drive by mandate: they lead by example." In effect, we are saying to them, "Act for us, but don't boss us."...

Therefore, a leader in A.A. service is a man (or woman) who can personally put principles, plans, and policies into such dedicated and effective action that the rest of us want to back him up and help him with his job. When a leader power-drives us badly, we rebel; but when he too meekly becomes an order-taker and he exercises no judgment of his own—well, he really isn't a leader at all....

Good leadership originates plans, policies, and ideas for the improvement of our Fellowship and its service. But in new and important matters, it will nevertheless consult widely before taking decisions and actions. Good leadership will also remember that a fine plan or idea can come from anybody, anywhere. Consequently, good leadership will often discard its own cherished plans for others that are better, and it will give credit to the source....

Good leadership never passes the buck. Once assured that it has, or can obtain, sufficient general backing, it freely takes decisions and puts them into action forthwith, provided, of course, that such action be within the framework of its defined authority and responsibility....

Another qualification for leadership is give-and-take, the ability to compromise cheerfully whenever a proper compromise can cause a situation to progress in what appears to be the right direction. Compromise comes hard to us all-or-nothing drunks. Nevertheless, we must never lose sight of the fact that progress is nearly always characterized by a series of improving compromises. We cannot, however, compromise always. Now and then, it is truly necessary to stick flat-footed to one's conviction about an issue until it is settled. These are situations for keen timing and careful discrimination as to which course to take....

Leadership is often called upon to face heavy and sometimes long-continued criticism. This is an acid test. There are always the constructive critics, our friends indeed. We ought never fail to give them a careful hearing. We should be willing to let them modify our opinions or change them completely. Often, too, we shall have to disagree and then stand fast without losing their friendship.

Copyright © by The A.A. Grapevine, Inc.; excerpted with permission make notes on what you're asked to do; do it. You'll receive questionnaires; expedite replies. G.S.O. may request material from you; expedite this, too. Promptness is necessary so that, by the time the Conference opens, your material will have been compiled for use in a report, a panel discussion, a workshop, a floor discussion, or a committee agenda item.

"Early on, you'll receive two important communications. One will ask your area treasurer to send in a check for your area's share of expenses. Be sure this deadline is met. Another will seek information on your arrival time, transportation costs, and housing details. Be sure this is supplied at once. G.S.O. will send a check to cover your travel expenses. When you arrive in New York you will receive cash to cover most of your local expenses, such as meals. Generally, areas supply extra allowances also.

"Before you leave New York, make sure your committee members are arranging the times and places of the Conference reports you'll give on your return.

"Finally, don't plan any big social events in New York or figure you'll make a few business calls there. The Conference schedule runs from 9:00 a.m. to 9:00 p.m., or even later at times.

"And remember, even if you're the new kid on the block, you're just as important to the Conference proceedings as anyone else. Your voice expresses your informed area conscience. Your thoughts and your questions must be shared—loud and clear—for the benefit of all."

Reporting on the Conference

Reporting to groups, districts, and the area back home is a big part of the delegate's job, and one that can prove challenging. One past delegate says: "On my return from the Conference, I traveled some 4,000 miles in the first six weeks visiting groups. If I was not asked to speak at group meetings, I asked them to let me speak. I made a point of never talking too long, but I gave literally hundreds of these talks. I talked of service and unity and G.S.O. and area assembly." That same delegate reports the results: more new groups than ever before, a stronger service structure, and the first state convention. "We have grown, and if I were asked to pick out the one part of our activities that contributed most, it would be improved communications."

"What I Saw and Heard and Felt"

"My report on the Conference consisted of a description of what I saw and heard and felt at the Conference meeting in New York. (I also made copies of my report and made them available.)

"The distances between towns in my state are great, and it seemed best to make my reports to district or intergroup meetings when possible, with an A.A. talk after the report. In addition, I frequently reported to members, G.S.R.s and groups by mail. I try to do a bulletin a month, each on one or more subjects. My Conference report gives me all the material I need."

If You Attract—You Can't Miss

"Make an announcement a month before you give your report; set up dates with district committee members. Where districts are small, have two or three combined. (Refreshments help.) Ask to be invited—or invite yourself. Get in somehow! It costs groups and G.S.O. money to bring in delegates; groups should see and hear the reports on the Conference.

"Give as much of your time to the small group as to the large one. Don't pass up the opportunity to share with them all. Let them know about the staff at G.S.O. and the service work that they encourage all over the world.

"Invite groups to attend special area meetings with programs of questions and answers about world services and G.S.O. Include one or more past delegates. Hold meetings often—and in different districts. Remember our key word: attraction. If you attract, you can't miss."

Taped Talk: Effective, Inexpensive

"In addition to detailed reporting of the material *and* spirit of the Conference sessions at our state convention, copies of my notes were made available to the area committee members upon their request. Fortunately, we were able to make arrangements for my talk to be taped and made available throughout our area—an inexpensive and effective way of carrying the Conference message in some detail."

❖ Chapter Seven

The Annual Conference Meeting

In all its proceedings, the General Service Conference shall observe the spirit of the
A.A. Tradition, taking great care that the Conference never becomes the seat of
perilous wealth or power; that sufficient operating funds, plus an ample reserve, be
its prudent financial principle; that none of the Conference Members shall ever
be placed in a position of unqualified authority over any of the others; that all
important decisions be reached by discussion, vote, and whenever possible,
by substantial unanimity; that no Conference action ever be personally punitive
or an incitement to public controversy; that though the Conference may act for the
service of Alcoholics Anonymous, it shall never perform any acts of government;
and that, like the Society of Alcoholics Anonymous which it serves, the Conference
itself will always remain democratic in thought and action.

— General Warranties of the Conference
Concept XII, *Twelve Concepts for World Service*

While the General Service Conference operates all year round, the annual meeting, held in New York City, usually in April, is the culmination of the year's activities, the time when the collective group conscience of U.S./Canada A.A. comes together to take actions that will guide the groups in the years to come.

The Conference comes closer to "government" than anything else in A.A., but as Bill W. put it in the first edition of this manual: *"Of course it cannot be too often said that while the Conference can issue orders to the General Service Office, it can never mandate or govern the Society of Alcoholics Anonymous which it serves. The Conference represents us, but cannot rule us."*

The Conference itself is not incorporated, but the General Service Board (board of trustees) is, as are A.A. World Services, Inc. and A.A. Grapevine, Inc. Incorporation of these entities is necessary to carry out policies established by the Conference, handle funds, and conduct A.A.'s business.

Note: See Appendix D for Conference Panels.

What Goes On at the Conference

A typical Conference lasts a full week, with sessions running from morning to evening. The opening day features roll call, keynote address, an opening dinner and a five-speaker A.A. meeting. Business sessions from Sunday to Friday include committee meetings, presentations, workshops, and new trustee elections. Each delegate serves on one of the standing Conference committees, which meet early in the week and do the principal work of the Conference. (Some delegates also have a secondary committee assignment.) The committees bring recommendations to the full Conference for consideration as possible Advisory Actions (see Chapter Eight for more on the committee system), and generally the last two days (or more) are devoted to discussion and voting on committee recommendations. Although outside of the Conference, a delegates-only meeting is often held prior to the opening day of the Conference. On Saturday, following the last day of Conference business, a closing breakfast provides an opportunity for goodbyes, and for rotating trustees to say their farewells. In alternate years, a visit to G.S.O./Grapevine offices or the home of Bill W. and Lois in Westchester County is scheduled.

Sources of Agenda Items

The final agenda for any Conference consists of items suggested by individual A.A. members, groups, delegates, trustees, area assemblies, area committee members, and directors and staff members of A.A.W.S. and the Grapevine. The Conference considers matters of policy for A.A. as a whole, and there are tried-and-true procedures for placing an item on the agenda in the most effective way—or, when the suggestion does *not* concern overall policy, for routing it to the most appropriate part of the service structure.

If a G.S.R. has an idea for an agenda item, chances are that he or she will want to discuss it first with the group, then at a district or area meeting, which can then forward it to the staff member at G.S.O. currently serving as Conference coordinator. An A.A. who is not part of the general service structure can give the idea to the group's G.S.R. or write directly to the Conference coordinator.

Whatever its origin, any agenda item follows the same path to the Conference agenda: The A.A. staff studies it in the light of previous Conference actions, then passes it on to the trustees' Conference Committee or the appropriate Conference committee. Usually, the trustees' committee determines the most appropriate way of programming it—as a workshop or presentation subject, a proposal, or a committee concern.

S56

Conference Membership

Voting membership of the Conference includes area delegates (who make up at least two-thirds of the Conference body), the directors and A.A. staff of A.A. World Services, Inc. and A.A. Grapevine, Inc., and the trustees. The Conference may wish to invite visitors from other countries to attend as nonvoting observers.

Each Conference member has one vote, even if he or she attends in more than one capacity (for example, a trustee who serves as a director of A.A.W.S. or the Grapevine as well as on the General Service Board).

Historically, the voting ratio has never been important, since no issue has ever divided Conference opinion along the lines of delegates opposed to other Conference members. But it could conceivably be important at some time. To take care of that situation, the Conference Charter provides "as a matter of tradition, that a two-thirds vote of Conference members voting shall be considered binding upon the General Service Board and its related corporate services, provided the total vote constitutes at least a Conference quorum. But no such vote ought to impair the legal rights of the General Service Board and the service corporations to conduct routine business and make ordinary contracts relating thereto."

The Voting Process

Each Conference committee (see Chapter Eight) brings to the Conference floor a report of its deliberations, which usually includes recommendations for consideration and voting. In addition, recommendations may come from the floor in the course of discussion. Even if a committee reports decisively on its solution to a problem, the Conference is not obligated to accept the report. It can refuse a committee decision, and if it does, the matter is discussed and decided upon in general session. While in the majority of cases the Conference *does* accept a committee recommendation, in typical A.A. fashion, a Conference committee does not represent "authority."

The Conference, through ample discussion, always strives for substantial unanimity. Before a vote is taken, plenty of time is allotted for full discussion, including questions about the background of a recommendation and the committee's reasons for coming to its conclusions. In order to become an Advisory Action, a recommendation must be approved by "substantial unanimity"—defined as a two-thirds majority. A simple majority vote of the Conference shall be considered a suggestion to the General Service Board and to G.S.O. or the Grapevine.

Discussion, both in general sessions and during committee meetings, can at times be hot and heavy, but Conference members always strive to reach a group conscience and to make decisions in the best interests of the Fellowship. After the vote, the Conference chairperson calls for minority opinions—and occasionally, a well-reasoned minority opinion can result in another vote, reversing the first decision. Ideally, of course, that is the rare exception; any matter should be so thoroughly considered *before* a vote is taken that the Conference's original conclusion will stand.

Conference Advisory Actions

Conference Advisory Actions represent recommendations of the Conference committees, or floor actions, that have been approved by the Conference body as a whole with substantial unanimity.

Can the Conference Act for A.A. as a Whole?

Here is what co-founder Bill W. has to say about that in Concept III of *Twelve Concepts for World Service:*

"Excepting for its Charter provisions to the contrary, the Conference should always be able to decide which matters it will fully dispose of on its own responsibility, and which questions it will refer to the A.A. groups (or more usually, to their Committee Members or G.S.R.s) for opinion or for definite guidance.

"Therefore it ought to be clearly understood and agreed that our Conference Delegates are primarily the world servants of A.A. as a whole, that only in a secondary sense do they represent their respective areas. Consequently they should, on final decisions, be entitled to cast their votes in the General Service Conference according to the best dictates of their own judgment and conscience at that time.

"Similarly, the Trustees of the General Service Board (operating of course within the provisions of their own Charter and Bylaws) should be able at all times to decide when they will act fully on their own responsibility and when they will ask the Conference for its guidance, its approval of a recommendation, or for its actual decision and direction.

"Within the scope of their defined or implied responsibilities, all Headquarters service corporations, committees, staff or executives should also be possessed of the right to decide when they will act wholly on their own and when they will refer their problems to the next higher authority."

What kind of business is transacted at the Conference? A quick tour through the Advisory Actions over the years reveals a wide-ranging collection of issues:

- affirmations of the importance of anonymity and actions delineating how anonymity may be applied in relations with the general public;
- approval of various methods of contributing to G.S.O. and/or the areas; recommendations for increasing area contributions for the support of the annual Conference meeting;
- approval of new Conference-approved literature and changes to literature already published, including new editions of the Big Book;
- solutions to group issues such as that of "family groups," special-purpose groups, and groups meeting in treatment facilities;
- recommendations concerning the composition and functioning of the General Service Board;

- suggestions for displaying and selling A.A. literature in groups;
- recognition of the A.A. Grapevine as the international journal of Alcoholics Anonymous;
- various recommendations concerning the content of *The A.A. Service Manual* and suggested practices in the service structure;
- recommendations against the production or sale of chips and medallions by G.S.O. or the Grapevine;
- recommendations for the development of new literature, as well as films, videos, and audiocassettes to carry the A.A. message;
- guidelines for forming new delegate areas, changing regional boundaries, as well as the acceptance of new delegate areas;
- recommendations regarding carrying the A.A. message to the general public, to members of the professional community, and to A.A.s in prisons or treatment centers.

A compilation of Conference Advisory Actions is available from G.S.O.

Reporting to the Membership

The most productive Conference sessions are of little value unless area committees and groups back home hear about them. So the delegate's reporting job is as important as the program for the Conference itself. No delegate could possibly report everything that took place, and over the years G.S.O. and delegates, working together, have developed a system of reporting that has proved tremendously helpful in communicating information throughout the Fellowship.

It begins, in a sense, with the advance information mailed to delegates, which includes significant questions to take to the areas for input before the Conference. During the Conference, delegates take reams of notes, and much of the information is provided in writing in the Conference Handbook. (Chapter Six contains suggestions for reporting techniques that have worked well.)

The *Final Conference Report* comes off press during the summer and provides a complete record of reports, discussions, workshops, and actions. It is not a verbatim account, but no significant aspect of the Conference is omitted.

Throughout the year, delegates are kept informed of G.S.O. and Grapevine activities, results of meetings of the General Service Board, and the work being done by the various committees of the board.

❖ Chapter Eight
Conference Committees

Without committees, it is doubtful that any Conference would be able to function effectively. Most questions suggested for the Conference agenda are assigned to a committee, where items can be discussed in a small group before they are forwarded for discussion to the full Conference body.

Extensive background material is mailed to committee members well in advance of the actual Conference meeting. Most Conference committees work closely with a corresponding committee of the General Service Board, and the two maintain communication throughout the year and meet at the beginning of Conference week for a joint session. The joint meeting is designed to share information; no actions are taken.

Committee Meetings

Each delegate committee then meets twice early in Conference week (and occasionally more often, if necessary), reviews and discusses everything on its agenda, and prepares a report, which is presented to the full Conference, discussed, and voted on (see the section on "The Voting Process" in Chapter Seven). Generally, the committee reaches a conclusion as a result of its deliberations, and presents a recommendation to the full Conference. On some items, the committee may choose to make no recommendation, or simply to report a suggestion or observation. The committee may also defer an item to the next year's Conference, or seek further information from the Fellowship or the trustees before making a decision at a subsequent Conference.

Selection of Committee Members

Each delegate serves on one Conference committee, the same one for both years of the term. Normally, a committee is made up of four or five first-year delegates and four or five second-year delegates. Committee members are selected by lot in December by one or two trustees or members of the trustees' Conference Committee and the Conference coordinator. The names of new delegates are drawn from the hat to replace outgoing delegates on each committee.

Committee chairs and alternate chairs are elected by plurality at the committee's last meeting during Conference week. The new chair takes office as soon as the Conference ends, and serves through the end of the next year's Conference.

An A.A. staff member serves as the nonvoting secretary of the committee corresponding to his or her assignment; the controller of A.A.W.S. is secretary of the Finance

Committee. Staff members help prepare the committee report and serve as resources, sharing knowledge gained from their day-to-day work on the assignment.

The Conference Committees

At its first meeting in 1951, the Conference established committees, and new ones have been added when necessary. Currently, these committees are:

AGENDA *(trustees' committee: General Service Conference)*: Reviews and approves the overall format and content of the agenda for the annual Conference meeting; considers proposed Conference themes, presentation/discussion topics and Conference Evaluation Questionnaire.

COOPERATION WITH THE PROFESSIONAL COMMUNITY *(trustees' committee on C.P.C./Treatment and Accessibilities)*: Responsible for suggesting policies and recommending activities that will help carry the message to the still-suffering alcoholic through sharing information about the A.A. program with professional groups and individuals who have contact with alcoholics, furthering mutual understanding and cooperation between A.A. and professionals, and increasing awareness of members and outside groups and organizations on ways of cooperating with others without affiliating.

CORRECTIONS *(trustees' Corrections Committee)*: Encourages A.A. members to assume responsibility for carrying the message to alcoholics behind the walls, reviews all aspects of service to A.A. groups in correctional facilities, and makes recommendations for changes and/or improvements. It is also concerned with clarifying what A.A. can and cannot do, within the Traditions, to help inmate alcoholics both inside and upon release.

FINANCE *(trustees' Finance and Budgetary Committee)*: Reviews the budget and financial reports of A.A. World Services and the Grapevine, and reviews or initiates Conference recommendations that involve finances. The Finance Committee, since it first convened in 1951, has kept abreast of the movement's needs: it has looked into annual budgets, been concerned with the income needed to carry out service work, and has almost invariably recommended the expansion of services to groups and to the public.

GRAPEVINE *(meets jointly with members of the Grapevine Corporate Board)*: Responsible for reviewing the development and circulation of the Grapevine and La Viña for the past year at the group level; its members also seek suggestions and recommendations in any area of the Grapevine and La Viña, including material and format. The Grapevine Committee has been helpful in clarifying matters of policy for A.A.'s international journal, in helping develop material related to the magazine and, most recently, enabling the Grapevine to reach Spanish-speaking alcoholics through La Viña, a bimonthly magazine in Spanish.

LITERATURE *(trustees' Literature Committee)*: This Committee is primarily concerned with recovery literature; material related to specific areas of service e.g., Corrections material is developed by the relevant committee. Reviews new literature and audiovisual needs, reviews existing pamphlets and new pamphlet drafts as they are prepared, and recommends special action to the trustees' Literature Committee. The Literature Committee has played a vital part in the development of A.A. pamphlets and books. It has never hesitated to put on the brakes if it feels that A.A.'s literature is expanding too rapidly—or to urge A.A.'s publishing operation into action when there is a real need for a new pamphlet or book. In recent years it has been instrumental in the development of audiovisual materials.

POLICY/ADMISSIONS *(no corresponding trustees' committee)*: Responsible for matters of policy pertaining to the Conference itself and for reviewing all requests for admissions to the annual meeting of the General Service Conference. All changes in the Conference plan, all steps in the expansion of the Conference, and all procedures affecting the cost of the Conference are taken to the Committee on Conference Policy and Admissions. This committee has the job of approving or disapproving requests for additional delegate areas.

PUBLIC INFORMATION *(trustees' Public Information Committee)*: Responsible for creating greater understanding of—and preventing misunderstandings of—the A.A. program through the public media, electronic media, P.I. meetings, and speaking to community groups.

REPORT AND CHARTER *(no corresponding trustees' committee)*: Responsible for *The A.A. Service Manual*, the *Final Conference Report*, and the A.A. directories. The Report and Charter Committee reads drafts of the Conference Report and checks them for accuracy. This committee receives any suggestions for changes in the Conference Charter and makes recommendations on them.

TREATMENT AND ACCESSIBILITIES *(trustees' Committee on C.P.C./Treatment and Accessibilities)*: Coordinates the work of individual A.A. members and groups who carry the A.A. message of recovery to alcoholics in treatment facilities, and sets up means of bridging the gap from treatment to A.A. In addition, the committee supports the work of individual A.A. members and groups endeavoring to insure that those with special needs have access to the A.A. message. The committee will review all aspects of service to A.A. groups/meetings in treatment facilities and other noncorrectional institutional environments as well as to A.A.s with accessibilities issues and make recommendations for changes and/or improvements.

TRUSTEES *(trustees' Nominating Committee)*: Reviews all resumes of nominees for the General Service Board and corporate board directors and presents the slates to the Conference for disapproval, if any. Members of this committee are part of the voting body that nominates regional and at-large trustees during the week of the Conference.

Secondary Committees

Two committees have been formed to consider matters of importance that do not require the length of time devoted to standing committee agenda items. Some delegates serve on one of these secondary committees in addition to their primary assignment.

INTERNATIONAL CONVENTIONS/REGIONAL FORUMS: This committee, composed of eight delegates chosen by lot, one from each region, works on plans for forthcoming International Conventions, Regional Forums, and Local Forums. It meets once during the Conference in a dinner meeting with the trustees' Committee on International Conventions/ Regional Forums. Direct action may be taken by the Conference committee at this meeting.

ARCHIVES: The 1998 General Service Conference approved the formation of this committee as a secondary committee assignment to consider matters of practice and policy related to A.A. archives. Members, chosen by lot, meet once during the Conference at a dinner meeting with the trustees' Archives Committee. Direct action may be taken by the Conference committee at this meeting.

❖ Chapter Nine

The General Service Board

The General Service Board (the trustees) is the chief service arm of the Conference, and is essentially custodial in its character... Excepting for decisions upon matters of policy, finance, or A.A. Tradition liable to seriously affect A.A. as a whole, the General Service Board has entire freedom of action in the routine conduct of the policy and business affairs of the A.A. service corporations....

— excerpt from the Conference Charter*

The trustees of Alcoholics Anonymous are concerned with everything happening inside and outside A.A. that may affect the health and growth of the movement. However, as the Charter points out, their duties are essentially custodial. Whenever a decision on movement-wide policy is needed, they turn to the Conference. And because trustees are members of the Conference body, they participate in these decisions—but as individual Conference members, not as a group.

The trustees do much of their work through two operating corporations, A.A. World Services, Inc. and A.A. Grapevine, Inc. (see Chapter Ten), and through the trustees' committees.

The chart "The General Service Conference Structure" (Chapter One) shows how the General Service Board fits into the whole picture and demonstrates that the trustees derive from the Conference what "authority" they have. This relationship was established when the Conference structure was first set up, and over the years, the only changes considered necessary have been in the composition of the General Service Board, not in its duties or responsibilities.

The Bylaws of the General Service Board (see Appendix E) describe fully all aspects of the workings of the board.

---

* The two service corporations, A.A.W.S., Inc. and A.A. Grapevine, Inc., although affiliates of the General Service Board of Alcoholics Anonymous, Inc., are organized as separate, not-for-profit corporations, and, as such, the routine conduct of policy and business affairs of each resides in the respective boards of the two corporations.

Composition

The Board of Trustees today consists of 21 men and women, 14 alcoholics (Class B) and seven nonalcoholics (Class A), who bring varying talents and backgrounds to their service responsibilities.

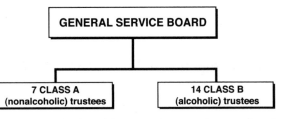

There is always a careful balance on the board between trustees who are elected primarily to bring regional and A.A. service experience to the board and those selected primarily for business or other professional backgrounds.

In 1951, the first year of the General Service Conference, the board consisted of eight Class A trustees and seven Class B trustees. Most lived in the New York City area. Two major changes in board composition have taken place over the years. The first was in 1962, when because of the Fellowship's growth, it was necessary to broaden the base of trusteeship to bring in A.A.s who had service experience in different areas of the U.S. and Canada. At that time, the board was increased in size to make room for several A.A. trustees from states and provinces away from New York City.

There had always been a majority (of one) of nonalcoholics on the board. By the mid-1960s, however, A.A. had solid experience in running its own affairs and had developed a practical method for bringing in trustees from a distance. So the Fellowship took a second major step in 1966 and reorganized its board into the current configuration of seven nonalcoholics and fourteen alcoholic members.

Election of Trustees and Officers

The trustees' Nominating Committee is responsible for recommending to the General Service Board candidates for general service trustee, Class A trustee, and nontrustee director. The candidates approved by the General Service Board are subject to the approval of the General Service Conference. The trustees' Nominating Committee receives advice from and consults with the A.A.W.S. and the A.A. Grapevine Boards with respect to potential general service trustees, nontrustee directors, and regional trustees to serve on the respective boards. The trustees' Nominating Committee also recommends a slate of trustees to serve as officers of the General Service Board. Trustees and officers of the General Service Board for the upcoming year are elected by the trustees (acting as the members of the General Service Board) at the annual meeting of members which is held immediately following the General Service Conference. During the Conference, a proposed slate of trustees is presented to the Conference, and becomes the final slate unless a majority of the Conference members votes to disapprove any one or all proposed trustees listed. The nominating procedures used in developing the slate vary with the different types of trustees, and are described below.

The proposed slate of officers of the board for the upcoming year is determined by the board prior to the Conference and presented to the Conference in the same manner as the slate of trustees. The chair of the board, who may be a Class A or Class B trustee, serves a four-year term in that position, including years after the date when the trustee would otherwise have rotated from the board.

Qualifications of an Effective Trustee

A.A. has been fortunate over the years in having many competent trustees, both A.A. members and nonalcoholics, and the choice of trustees remains one of the most important factors in ensuring A.A.'s future. There are no hard-and-fast rules governing qualifications. In general, though, there are certain things to look for.

NONALCOHOLIC TRUSTEES: In seeking candidates for Class A trustee, the board looks for men and women with a proven track record in their own fields, a demonstrated interest in Alcoholics Anonymous, some experience in working with A.A. and its members, and a willingness to serve. The qualifications listed below for alcoholic trustees have generally proved to be important considerations for nonalcoholic trustees as well.

ALCOHOLIC TRUSTEES: The Conference feels that ten years of continuous sobriety is right for regional trustees and trustees-at-large, though it is not mandatory. For general service trustees, the Conference has approved seven years of continuous sobriety. It is important for trustees to be thoroughly familiar with the A.A. structure and all its elements, from the group through the area to the board and the Conference, as well as A.A. history and the trends that affect its future. In addition, experience has shown that strength in the following areas is helpful:

• *Business or professional background*: While business experience is not necessary for all alcoholic trustees, it has proved essential for general service trustees, who deal with the business affairs of the two corporate boards. Regional trustees and trustees-at-large with sound professional qualifications are always valuable to the board, but may also be stronger in other areas.

• *Leadership*: In A.A. this quality enables a member to deal with A.A. growth and affairs with good feeling and a minimum of friction. Good leaders can bring to the board the quality of resoluteness and the courage of their convictions, along with good judgment, objectivity, and the willingness to stand up and express themselves. Such candidates generally have the love and respect of A.A.s in their community, state, or province, and can represent the board and interpret its actions back home.

TIME COMMITMENT OF TRUSTEES: Prospective trustee candidates should carefully consider how much time they have available for A.A. service as a trustee. Trustees must be available for quarterly board meetings, each of which takes three to five days, plus travel time, and the week-long Conference in April. Throughout the year, trustees communicate with their colleagues on the board and with members of the Fellowship, and participate in projects and other matters which require attention between regularly scheduled meetings. Trustees may be asked from time to time to attend Regional Forums and to appear at local A.A. events; the trustees-at-large also serve as delegates to the World Service Meeting and to the zonal Meeting of the

Americas, described at the end of this chapter. In addition to these commitments, general service trustees must be available for all meetings of their respective boards (eight or more each year) and for consultation with G.S.O. or Grapevine staff members at any time. A Class A trustee may also be asked to serve on a service corporation's board of directors for a two or three year period. Regional trustees and trustees-at-large have especially time-consuming jobs. Regional trustees serve as a member of the board of directors of either A.A.W.S. or the Grapevine for two years, and, along with trustees-at-large, often have demanding travel schedules.

Chairperson of the A.A. General Service Board

The chairperson of the General Service Board of A.A. presides over the trustees' meetings, co-chairs the General Service Conference, and functions on behalf of the General Service Board between board meetings. The chairperson appoints members of the trustees' committees, subject to G.S.B. approval, and is an ex-officio member of all trustees' committees. In addition to board meetings and the Conference, the chairperson participates in all Regional Forums and may participate in a number of other events.

Nonalcoholic (Class A) Trustees

A.A.'s debt to those who do not share our disease but willingly share our problems is immense, going back to the beginning. Bill W. wrote: "In the days when A.A. was unknown, it was the nonalcoholic trustees who held up our hands before the general public. They supplied us with ideas.... They voluntarily spent hours on end, working side by side with us and among the grubbiest of details. They gave freely of their professional and financial wisdom. Now and then they helpfully mediated our difficulties." Written in 1966, those words hold true today. Nonalcoholic trustees remain a rich source of wisdom and perspective, and since they need not maintain anonymity, they are available to appear in public on behalf of A.A.

Class A trustees serve two consecutive three-year terms. The chair of the General Service Board may recommend to the trustees that a Class A member trustee be permitted to serve for a third successive three-year term. In order to provide the board with a sufficient degree of flexibility, the trustees can permit this. (See Appendix E, Bylaws of the General Service Board, Inc., page S110).

Board members make an effort to choose Class A trustees from a variety of professional backgrounds, and the board has included doctors, lawyers, clergy, sociologists, business people, and financial experts among its members. Whatever their backgrounds, the bylaws make one key provision for nonalcoholic trustees: they "shall be persons who are not and have not been afflicted by the disease of alcoholism and who express a profound faith in the recovery program upon which the Fellowship of Alcoholics Anonymous is founded."

NOMINATION PROCEDURE: The General Service Board nominates Class A trustees after an extensive search and interview process that begins by asking current and past members of the board, directors, delegates, and G.S.O. and Grapevine staff to submit names and background information for "friends of A.A." to fill a vacancy. The list is narrowed down by the trustees' Nominating Committee, and the remaining prospects are invited to a quarterly trustees' meeting to meet all members of the board. The Nominating Committee then recommends the election of one person for each vacancy to the General Service Board, and, after approval by the board, the candidate is included on the slate, which is presented to the Conference as described above.

Regional Trustees

There are eight regional trustees, six from the United States and two from Canada (see regional map), who serve four successive annual terms. While no trustee can be said to "represent" a geographical section—all trustees represent only the Fellowship as a whole—regional trustees bring to the board's discussions a regional A.A. point of view and experience that is invaluable.

Candidates for regional trustee are proposed by the areas, either one candidate from each area or, in some cases, a candidate is put forward by two or more areas acting together. This responsibility should be considered carefully by the A.A.s involved. It is suggested that the bylaws of the General Service Board, along with the qualifications and responsibilities required to fill the trustee position, be carefully reviewed before a selection is made.

Delegates and area officers in a region scheduled to select a regional trustee candidate are informed by G.S.O. in a May mailing. G.S.O. notifies all A.A. groups in the region of the opening in an issue of the newsletter *Box 4-5-9*.

The schedule of elections is as follows:

Region	Election Years	Region	Election Years
Northeast U.S.	2019-2023-2027-2031	Southwest	2019-2023-2027-2031
Western Canada	2020-2024-2028-2032	West Central	2020-2024-2028-2032
Southeast	2017-2021-2025-2029	East Central	2017-2021-2025-2029
Eastern Canada	2018-2022-2026-2030	Pacific	2018-2022-2026-2030

NOMINATION PROCEDURE

1. At the area level, Third Legacy Procedure (see page S21) should be used to select the area's candidate for regional trustee.
2. Prior Conferences have recommended that no area submit the same person as a candidate for both regional trustee and trustee-at-large/U.S. or Canada at the same Conference. Also, a General Service Conference delegate is not eligible as a trustee candidate until one year after his or her last Conference.
3. A candidate's signed resume, covering professional, business, and A.A. service qualifications, with name and address, must be forwarded to G.S.O., by the area delegate only, by registered mail—return receipt requested.
4. Any resumes received after the January 1 deadline will be returned by G.S.O. to the delegate and will not be considered. If an area's candidate withdraws after the deadline, the area may not submit another candidate.

The trustees' Nominating Committee reviews all candidates for eligibility. Then, at the Conference, a nominating session chooses one regional trustee nominee from the

Regional Map of U.S. & Canada

This map represents a general outline of Regi

candidates. The session is co-chaired by the chairs of the trustees' Nominating Committee and the Conference Committee on Trustees. It meets in a roped-off section and can be observed by all Conference members.

Voting members of the nominating session are: 1) delegates from the region, and 2) an equal number of voters—one-half from the Conference Committee on Trustees and one-half from the trustees' Nominating Committee.

The session follows the Third Legacy Procedure.

Trustees-at-Large

There are two trustees-at-large, one from the U.S. and one from Canada. Each serves a four-year term. The trustees-at-large are members of the trustees' International Committee and other trustees' committees, and can be appointed as directors of one of the corporate boards. They may fill in for regional trustees, as needed or requested.

Trustees-at-large serve as the World Service Meeting delegates representing the U.S. and Canada. As such, they participate in two World Service Meetings, which are held every two years. They also serve as delegates to the Meeting of the Americas, a zonal meeting held in alternate years when the World Service Meeting is not being held. Each trustee-at-large is requested to attend Regional Forums in both the U.S. and Canada. If schedules permit, each trustee-at-large could attend one Regional Forum in each of the eight North American regions over the course of their four-year term. They are also available for other A.A. service activities as requested by areas or regions, and additional activities as requested by the board of trustees.

NOMINATION PROCEDURE: All areas in the U.S. or Canada are notified of a vacancy and asked to submit qualified candidates. Prior Conferences have recommended that no area submit the same person as a candidate for both regional trustee and trustee-at-large/U.S. or Canada at the same Conference. Also, a General Service Conference delegate is not eligible as a trustee candidate until one year after his or her last Conference.

The trustees' Nominating Committee reviews all candidates for eligibility, and, before the nominating session during Conference week, area delegates from each region caucus (generally at a regional lunch) and reduce the list of names to one for each U.S. region, and two for each region in Canada. The names are given to the secretary of the trustees' Nominating Committee following the regional lunches. A maximum of six candidates for trustee-at-large U.S. or four for trustee-at-large Canada will be presented to the voting members of the Conference for election. The Third Legacy Procedure as used in the nomination of regional trustees is used at the Conference to select one nominee for each vacancy, with the area delegates from either the U.S. or Canada and the members of the trustees' Nominating Committee participating in the voting.

General Service Trustees

There are four general service trustees, two from the A.A. World Services Board and two from the Grapevine, who serve on these boards and are available at any time for the solution of problems on which G.S.O. or Grapevine staff members need help. Because of this requirement, all general service trustees originally came from New York City or its commuting area and were sometimes known as "in-town trustees." With the advent of faster and more efficient communication, these positions are no longer restricted to residents of New York City and its vicinity.

A.A. has been fortunate to have general service trustees with the kind of business or professional acumen that is particularly applicable to the problems at hand, whether their backgrounds are in publishing, public relations, or administration. General service trustees can share with the General Service Board the operations of A.A.W.S. and the Grapevine, thus increasing the awareness of all trustees on these matters. They serve as trustees for four years.

NOMINATION PROCEDURE: General service trustees are chosen from among current or past nontrustee directors of the two corporate boards, A.A. World Services, Inc. and A.A. Grapevine, Inc. Since nontrustee directors are already serving (or have served) on one of the corporate boards, their qualifications are well known to the members of the respective boards.

The resume of one qualified candidate, who has served for at least one year on the A.A.W.S. or Grapevine board is submitted to the trustees' Nominating Committee in a single recommendation. If the candidate is acceptable to the Nominating Committee, the nominee's name is forwarded to the full board with a recommendation that the candidate be included on the slate of trustees presented to the Conference. If the candidate forwarded by the operating corporation board is not acceptable to the committee, the committee may select another qualified candidate, or request that the affiliate corporate board submit another qualified candidate for consideration.

"Choosing Nontrustee Directors for A.A. World Services and the A.A. Grapevine" in Chapter Ten describes the process for selecting nontrustee directors.

Trustees Emeriti

The General Service Board has designated rotating board chairpersons as trustees emeriti. Trustees emeriti are invited to attend quarterly board meetings of the General Service Board and the annual General Service Conference. They are a resource of corporate memory and are often asked to share their experience with past board decisions, how previous General Service Boards conducted business, and the processes they used to reach a group conscience. Trustees emeriti do not vote on any matter before the General Service Board or the Conference.

General Service Board Committees

There are thirteen committees of the General Service Board that, for the most part, mirror the General Service Conference Committees. Trustees' committees meet quarterly, and often form subcommittees to work on specific projects, which, for several of the committees, may include preparation of written and audiovisual materials for approval by the Conference. Membership averages about eight or nine per committee and consists of trustees and directors of A.A.W.S. and the Grapevine; a few committees also include appointed committee members with particular expertise in the subject area. The chair is a trustee, and the secretary is usually a G.S.O. staff member.

ARCHIVES (*corresponding Conference committee—Archives*): Ensures, with the guidance of the Archivist, that the preservation, organization and use of the Archives is consistent with the highest professional and ethical standards, and in accord with copyright laws and the Tradition of anonymity.

COOPERATION WITH THE PROFESSIONAL COMMUNITY/TREATMENT AND ACCESSIBILITIES (*corresponding Conference committees—Cooperation With the Professional Community,* and *Treatment and Accessibilities*): Seeks to create mutual understanding and cooperation between the Fellowship and those professional groups and individuals concerned with alcoholism and the still-suffering alcoholic, to further the acceptance of A.A. in hospitals, rehabilitation centers, and similar facilities, and to bring additional help to alcoholics under treatment there. Encourages A.A. members to assume responsibility for providing information about A.A. to alcoholics with special needs.

CORRECTIONS *(corresponding Conference committee—Corrections)*: Develops programs and materials that support carrying the message to alcoholics confined in correctional institutions.

FINANCE AND BUDGETARY *(corresponding Conference committee—Finance)*: Oversees all G.S.O. and Grapevine financial matters, the General Fund, the Reserve Fund and the Postretirement Medical Fund. The treasurer of the General Service Board serves as chair, and the chief financial officer of the General Service Office serves as secretary.

GENERAL SERVICE CONFERENCE *(corresponding Conference committee—Agenda)*: Works on procedures, agenda, and theme for the annual Conference meeting.

INTERNATIONAL *(no corresponding Conference committee)*: Suggests ways to carry the message to alcoholics internationally, particularly in countries where there is no established structure.

INTERNATIONAL CONVENTIONS/REGIONAL FORUMS *(corresponding Conference committee—International Conventions/Regional Forums)*: Develops plans for each forthcoming Convention and for all Regional Forums and Local Forums, assesses the effectiveness of these events, and suggests future modifications to better serve the Fellowship.

LITERATURE *(corresponding Conference committee—Literature)*: Develops new and revised Conference-approved literature, evaluates literature needs, and oversees the final editing of *The A.A. Service Manual.*

NOMINATING: *(corresponding Conference committee—Trustees)*: Reviews procedures for selection of candidates. Reviews and passes on all candidates for trustee, for directors of A.A. World Services, Inc. and A.A. Grapevine, Inc. and for general service trustees nominated by the two corporate boards. In addition, some of its members serve as part of the Conference sessions that select regional trustees and trustees-at-large.

PUBLIC INFORMATION *(corresponding Conference committee—Public Information)*: Has responsibility for determining ways to increase public understanding of A.A.—or preventing misunderstanding of the A.A. program. Among its activities are the preparation of public service announcements, letters to the media about A.A.'s anonymity Traditions, and the triennial A.A. Membership Survey.

The following three trustee committees are concerned with oversight of the activities of the board and its affiliate corporations and assuring that appropriate practices are being followed. These committees have no corresponding Conference committees.

AUDIT COMMITTEE: Meets at least once a year with the independent auditor of the General Service Board, Inc., A.A.W.S., Inc. and A.A. Grapevine, Inc. to receive the audit report and discuss the adequacy of internal controls, the independence of the auditor, and any other matter the auditor wishes to bring to the attention of the committee. The committee annually recommends the selection of an independent auditor to the General Service Board.

COMPENSATION COMMITTEE: Meets annually with compensation consultants to assure that the compensation practices of the affiliate corporations are appropriate. Matters covered include overall compensation philosophies and policies, annual salary increase process, best compensation practices, and executive compensation. Actual compensation decisions are made by the boards of the respective affiliates.

LEGAL AFFAIRS COMMITTEE: Meets when needed to oversee the handling of any legal matters which require the attention of the board.

Finally, during each quarterly trustee weekend the board conducts a General Sharing Session to give an opportunity for sharing among trustees, directors, committee members, and A.A. staff on a wide range of topics that concern A.A. as a whole.

Appointed Committee Members

Several trustees' committees seek the participation of A.A. members with strong experience —A.A. service or professional— in such areas as corrections, treatment facilities, cooperation with the professional community, public information, or literature. Suggestions for candidates are sought from trustees, delegates, staff members, directors, and committee members past and present. The committee chair makes sure that all resumes received are carefully evaluated, using the following criteria: special qualifications, service experience, and dedication. (If the candidate is a past Conference delegate, he or she is not eligible until one year after rotation.) Eligible candidates are then interviewed by the chair or someone designated by the chair. The name of the candidate is referred to the trustees' Nominating Committee for approval, and the candidate who is selected is then appointed to the committee by the chair of the General Service Board. Appointed committee members are appointed for one year, but the term may be extended depending on committee projects (maximum four years).

Regional Forums

Regional Forums, which originated in 1975, are weekend-long sharing and informational sessions which provide unique opportunities to share and exchange valuable experience, ask questions and spark new ideas. They are also designed to help the General Service Board, A.A. World Services, and A.A. Grapevine, and G.S.O. and Grapevine staff members stay in touch with A.A. members, trusted servants and newcomers throughout the A.A. service structure. G.S.O.'s staff member on the Regional Forums assignment coordinates details for the Forum and works closely with the volunteer host chair who recruits volunteers to assist staff with hospitality, set-up and registration during the Forum. Forums are held on a rotating basis, at the request of each region. There is no registration fee for Regional Forums. The General Service Board covers the expenses of meeting rooms. As all Forums are intended to be sharing sessions, no formal actions result. Sharing is captured in Forum Final Reports, which are distributed to all attendees, and are available on G.S.O.'s website. Regional Forums carry A.A.'s message of love and service by improving communication at all levels of our Fellowship.

Local Forums

In October 2006, the concept of Local Forums was approved by the General Service Board. The purpose of Local Forums is to bring Forum information to A.A. members in remote, sparsely populated areas, urban neighborhoods or underserved A.A. communities. Any

A.A. community or service entity may request a one-and-a-half or two day Local Forum. Unlike Regional Forums, the responsibility for Forum expenses, such as meeting room rental and miscellaneous expenses, are assumed by the Local Forum Committee. The General Service Board will send two participants, one from the Board and one from the General Service Office or Grapevine office and display literature at Board expense. Like Regional Forums, Board participation in Local Forums requires the approval of the trustees' Committee on International Conventions/Regional Forums. The Regional Forums Coordinator works closely with the Local Forum organizing committee to create an agenda that is responsive to local needs.

World Service Meeting

A World Service Meeting is held every two years, in locations alternating between New York City and another country. The World Service Meeting serves as a forum for sharing the experience, strength, and hope of delegates who come from all parts of the world. It seeks ways and means of carrying the A.A. message to the alcoholic who still suffers, in any nation and any language. It can also represent an expression of the group conscience worldwide. It encourages the planning of sound service structures and exploration of expanding A.A. services to reach the alcoholic through internal communication, literature distribution, sponsorship, public information, community relations, and institutions work.

QUALIFICATIONS OF WORLD SERVICE MEETING DELEGATES: At least one of the delegates from each of the member conference structures should come from its general service board or equivalent overall service committee. Delegates should have leadership qualities, genuine service interest, organizational ability, a knowledge and love of A.A., time to attend the World Service Meetings, and they should be fully informed about A.A. in their countries or zones. Perhaps even more important, the delegates should have the time to present and carry out the decisions reached at the World Service Meetings. The two trustees-at-large of the General Service Board typically serve as delegates to these meetings.

Meeting of the Americas

The Meeting of the Americas (REDELA) is a zonal meeting of the general service structures of North and South America. It is held every other year, in the years when the World Service Meeting is not held. The location rotates among member countries. The two trustees-at-large of the General Service Board typically serve as delegates to these meetings.

❖ Chapter Ten

The Board's Operating Corporations

The General Service Board is responsible for the General Service Office (G.S.O.) and the Grapevine, and it takes care of its administrative duties through two operating corporations. One is A.A. World Services, Inc., which oversees the General Service Office and its service activities in the U.S. and Canada, as well as communications with A.A. service boards and offices around the world. In addition, A.A.W.S. publishes and distributes A.A.'s books, pamphlets and other items. The other is A.A. Grapevine, Inc., which oversees the Grapevine office and publishes and distributes the A.A. Grapevine magazine, the Spanish edition, La Viña, and related items. The two entities handle all aspects of the day-to-day operation of A.A.'s business.

The General Service Board has custodial oversight over both of these corporations, which it exercises by electing the directors of each. While the General Service Board does not interfere with the daily operation of either corporation, it does have the ultimate responsibility for seeing that both operate in the best interest of the movement as a whole. The trustees' Finance and Budgetary Committee is responsible for reviewing the financial results of both corporations and reviews and approves, for recommendation to the General Service Board, the budgets of the General Service Office, inclusive of A.A.W.S. and of A.A. Grapevine, Inc. Shortly after the end of each year, cash held by A.A.W.S. and A.A. Grapevine, Inc. in excess of their respective operating needs is transferred to the General Service Board Reserve Fund.

The makeup of the two boards of directors is a good example of the application of the Concept IV right of participation. "If it wishes, the board could elect none but its own trustees to these corporate directorships. But a powerful tradition has grown up to the effect that this never ought to be done," Bill W. wrote. "The principle of participation has resulted in well-informed and highly unified boards of directors, and ruled out authoritarian and institutional operating styles that would conflict with A.A. principles."

The General Service Board Reserve Fund

In 1954, the Board of Trustees established a Reserve Fund whose principal purpose is to provide the financial resources necessary to continue the essential services of G.S.O. and the

Grapevine in the event of emergency or disaster, to fund costs beyond the means of the G.S.O. and the Grapevine, such as major leasehold improvements or technical upgrades, and to allow the General Service Board and its two operating affiliates time to formulate and implement plans needed to adjust to changed

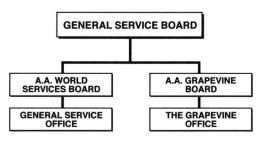

economic or other conditions. Withdrawals from the Reserve Fund may be authorized by the board of trustees (on recommendation of the trustees' Finance and Budgetary Committee).

Currently, the fund is limited to no more than one year's combined operating expenses of A.A. World Services, Inc., A.A. Grapevine, Inc., and the General Fund of the General Service Board. If the Reserve Fund exceeds the 12-month upper limit, a one-year period is allowed to review the Reserve Fund level, followed by a second year to formulate actions to adjust the Reserve Fund below 12-months' operating expenses.

In practice, however, the office, as well as the trustees' Finance Committee, continuously monitors the Reserve Fund balance, as well as the number of months of operating expenses, in an attempt to allow for orderly management of the Fellowship's financial affairs, keeping in mind our primary goal of carrying the message to the alcoholics who still suffer.

A.A. World Services, Inc.

CORPORATE BOARD: Currently, A.A. World Services, Inc. has nine directors: two general service trustees, two regional or at-large trustees, three nontrustee directors, one paid staff member, and the general manager of G.S.O., who is president of the corporation. The board meets eight times a year and considers agenda items such as budget preparation for the service and publishing operations, pricing of new and revised publications, G.S.O. service activities, implementation of Conference and General Service Board recommendations, copyright concerns, and reprint permissions.

Committees of the board: Because of the number and complexity of the issues A.A.W.S. must deal with, the board does much of its work through four committees, which meet separately from the full board meeting and make reports and recommendations to the full board. These committees are:

- Technology/Communication/Services (TCS): Addresses the needs of all service assignments and seeks to improve communication between the A.A.W.S. Board and the Fellowship, including innovative technologies. This committee is responsible for oversight of G.S.O.'s A.A. website.
- Finance: Has responsibility for salary, and budget, and audit reviews; and self-support initiatives.
- Publishing: Addresses reprints, foreign literature, translations, licensing and publishing concerns.
- Nominating: Nominates new A.A.W.S. directors and general service trustees. All members of this committee are trustee-directors.

FINANCIAL SUPPORT: According to the Seventh Tradition, every group should be self-supporting. Fellowship contributions to the General Service Office enable the A.A. message to reach vast numbers of alcoholics in the United States, Canada, and worldwide.

The General Service Office has two sources of revenue: group and member contributions to the General Service Board's General Fund, and income from A.A.W.S. publishing. For operating and reporting purposes, expenses of G.S.O. are divided into two categories: service and publishing. For many years, A.A. groups and members have contributed enough to cover some, but not all, of the service expenses. Net income from publishing activities provides the remaining funds needed to enable G.S.O. to provide its vital services.

In recent years, less than 50% of groups listed with G.S.O. make contributions to G.S.O. Group participation in A.A. is part of our spiritual heritage, and is more important than the dollar amount of the contributions. Making regular contributions to G.S.O. ties a group to A.A. worldwide.

Many groups have found it convenient to set up a *regular contribution plan* whereby they send in a predetermined amount or percentage each month or each quarter. Another method for encouraging regular participation in support of A.A. service is the Birthday Plan. On their A.A. birthdays each year, members make their personal contributions, either directly to G.S.O. or through their groups, in an amount determined by the individual for each year of sobriety. G.S.O. will supply Birthday Plan envelopes on request at no charge. Contributions, including Birthday Plan and recurring contributions, may also be made by groups and individuals by going to www.aa.org and clicking on "Online Contributions."

In keeping with the Seventh Tradition, G.S.O. accepts contributions only from A.A. members, groups or other A.A. entities (for example, delegate areas, districts, A.A. Conventions, A.A. Roundups, Intergroup/Central Offices). Furthermore, the General Service Conference has set a limit on the contributions of an individual member to $3,000 per year, and also limits contributions by the estate of a deceased member to a one-time bequest of $5,000. In memoriam contributions are sometimes made to honor the memory of a deceased member. Of course, in memoriam contributions of this type, like those of any other, can be accepted only from A.A. members and groups, and in the case of individual members are subject to the $3,000 limit. There is no limit on the amount of contributions which may be made to G.S.O. by an A.A. group.

A.A. Grapevine, Inc.

CORPORATE BOARD: A.A. Grapevine, Inc. currently has nine directors: two general service trustees, two regional trustees, one Class A trustee, three nontrustee directors, and the executive editor/publisher, who serves as president of the corporation. The board meets quarterly to consider such matters as circulation, finance, and publishing operations for both Grapevine and La Viña. It also holds four additional meetings a year as a planning committee of the whole.

FINANCIAL SUPPORT: A.A. Grapevine Inc.'s goal is to be supported by revenues from the purchase of print and online subscriptions and other related items. In contrast to

G.S.O., where group contributions are applied to support group services, A.A. Grapevine, Inc., does not accept contributions from individuals or groups. Nor does it accept revenue from ads or membership fees. A.A. Grapevine, Inc. relies on A.A. groups, committees, and individual members who value Grapevine and La Viña in their recovery and in their Twelfth Step work to purchase subscriptions. "After all," as Bill W. once wrote, "the Grapevine is to be their Voice—their newspaper. I am quite sure they will support it."

Over the years, the General Service Conference has continued to encourage the Fellowship to purchase bulk or monthly subscriptions to carry the A.A. message to prisons, hospitals and other institutions, professionals, as well as to newcomers in their groups. In 1996, when the General Service Conference asked A.A. Grapevine, Inc. to publish La Viña, the Spanish-language magazine, it recognized that the Grapevine Board could not be expected to cover the full cost of publishing it alone, so the Conference asked the General Service Board to help. (see page S88)

Choosing Nontrustee Directors
For A.A. World Services and A.A. Grapevine

Vacancies are announced to the Fellowship through the bulletin *Box 4-5-9* and in a mailing to area delegates, past and present trustees and directors, G.S.O. and Grapevine staff, central and intergroup offices, and current appointed committee members.

Working in concert with the trustees' Nominating Committee, the nominating committee of the corporate board reviews all of the resumes received. The committee then reduces the number of candidates by considering business or professional background, length of sobriety, A.A. service experience, and the candidates' availability for commitments, keeping in mind that nontrustee directors are the pool from which general service trustees are selected. The specific skills needed to administer the affairs of a corporation are a consideration.

The remaining candidates are interviewed by the corporate board's nominating committee. A.A.W.S. recommends a nominee to its full board, and A.A. Grapevine recommends its selection(s) to its full board for final interview. The name and resume of the nominee are then forwarded to the trustees' Nominating Committee, for approval by the General Service Board and the General Service Conference. Per the A.A.W.S. and A.A. Grapevine bylaws, a nontrustee director can serve up to four one-year terms.

Trademarks, Logos and Copyrights

A.A. World Services and Grapevine have registered a number of trademarks and logos, and the guidelines for using them are based partly on legal considerations and partly on the nature of A.A.

In 1993, Alcoholics Anonymous World Services, Inc., announced that official use of all of the several circle/triangle trademarks and service marks was being discontinued. The following is a complete list of registered trademarks and service marks that symbolize Alcoholics Anonymous, its work and its purpose: *A.A.; Alcoholics Anonymous;*

The Big Book; The Grapevine; A.A. Grapevine; GV; La Viña; AA Grapevine Digital Archive, Grapevine and Audio Grapevine.

Use of these marks on goods or services that do not emanate from A.A., and have not been approved by A.A., both infringes upon and dilutes A.A. marks, in legal terms. The resulting harm is that the marks and A.A. itself, since A.A. is what the marks symbolize, will come to be associated with a variety of products and services that are not part of A.A., and are not consistent with A.A.'s purpose. This will cause the marks to lose their meaning and significance as symbols of Alcoholics Anonymous.

Substantially all of the publications and other material produced and distributed by A.A.W.S. and the Grapevine, including service material, are protected by copyrights that have been registered by the respective corporations. These materials are valuable Fellowship assets, and are held for the benefit of A.A. as a whole. Therefore, the reprinting and/or copying of these materials is carefully monitored by A.A.W.S. and the Grapevine in order to avoid any erosion or loss of the copyrights. In an earlier section of this manual, entitled "Area Newsletters or Bulletins," guidance is provided regarding use of such materials.

❖ Chapter Eleven

The General Service Office

The General Service Office of A.A. ("G.S.O.") and the Grapevine are located at 475 Riverside Drive in New York City. G.S.O. serves all A.A. groups in the United States and Canada, and also offers services to A.A. overseas, especially in countries where there is no service structure. While many other countries have their own G.S.O.s, the U.S./Canada General Service Office, the earliest to be established, is generally regarded as the "senior" office. It serves as a clearinghouse and exchange point for the wealth of A.A. experience accumulated over the years, coordinates a wide array of activities and services, and oversees the publication, all translations of, and distribution of A.A. Conference-approved literature and service materials.

Visitors to New York are invited to take a guided tour of the G.S.O. and Grapevine offices, and to attend the A.A. meeting that takes place every Friday at 11:00 a.m. in the conference room.

STRUCTURE

The *general manager*, an A.A. member, provides leadership and overall management in the daily operations of the General Service Office through its four main functions: services, archives, publishing, and finance.

SERVICES

A.A. *staff members* help with group problems by sharing G.S.O.'s store of accumulated A.A. experience through extensive correspondence and telephone calls, and by traveling on request to A.A. events. All staff members have subject assignments (such as literature, public information, international, and correctional and treatment facilities), which rotate every two years. Staff serve as support to both Conference and trustees committees in their respective assignments. Most staff members also handle correspondence for a geographic area.

Staff assistants in the *support services department* produce correspondence, minutes, reports, and copy for bulletins.

OTHER SERVICES: In addition to help with group problems, G.S.O. offers an array of services that include:

GENERAL SERVICE OFFICE OF ALCOHOLICS ANONYMOUS AND A.A. WORLD SERVICES, INC.

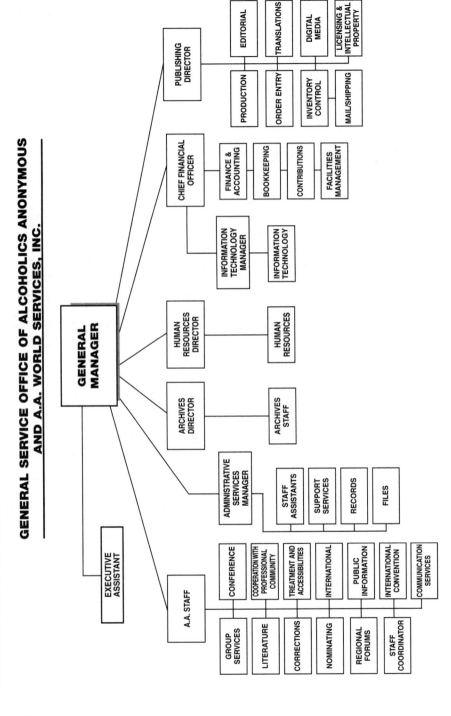

- *Group services:* Provides complimentary literature packages, the Group Handbook, and the A.A. directories. Equal services are provided in Spanish and French, whenever possible.

- *Help for groups in treatment and correctional facilities:* Corresponds with groups; provides bulletins and films; helps in bridging the gap from treatment and prisons into regular A.A. groups.

- *International:* Communicates with members and groups in countries that have no structure, and with overseas service offices; coordinates the World Service Meeting every other year; and helps with translations of A.A. literature.

- *Loners and Internationalists:* Supplies bulletins, letters, and directories for members who cannot attend meetings and for seagoing A.A.s.

- *Public information:* Provides accurate information for the media, answers inquiries from the general public, and coordinates with local P.I. committees.

- *Anonymity breaks:* Upon learning that an A.A. member's anonymity has been broken in the media, G.S.O. communicates with the area delegate, who can either remind the member of the anonymity Tradition or ask G.S.O. to send a reminder.

- *Cooperation with the professional community:* Supplies information to professionals who work with alcoholics, sends the professional exhibit to their conferences on request, and works with local C.P.C. committees.

- *Idea exchange for central offices/intergroups:* A staff member acts as liaison between G.S.O. and local offices, sharing common problems and solutions.

- *Self-support:* Encourages groups and members to support their area committees, local intergroups/central offices, and G.S.O.

- *General Service Conference:* Coordinates the program and arrangements for the annual meeting in April, gathers ideas and solutions from Conference committees, and helps delegates keep their areas informed.

- *Regional Forums:* Works on the agenda and arrangements with the regional trustee and current delegates in each region where a Forum is scheduled.

- *International Conventions:* Arranging programming, finances, and Convention facilities requires considerable advance work each year. Conventions are held every five years.

- *Area, state, and provincial conventions:* G.S.O. helps by exchanging programming ideas; often, A.A. staff and trustees are invited as speakers.

- *Alcoholics Anonymous website:* A website (www.aa.org), in English, Spanish, and French, offers information for anyone interested in A.A., including newcomers, professionals, and students, and provides services for members, lists of U.S./Canada central offices/intergroups and international general service offices.

- *Files:* The File Department has a folder for every A.A. group known to G.S.O., and in addition to information about group origins, many are full of correspondence aimed at solving a variety of critical problems.

- *Group records:* A manager and several assistants handle the job of maintaining and updating records on groups, delegates, committee members, G.S.R.s, Loners and

Internationalists, and so on. This is where the job of producing the A.A. directories is largely done—a job that relies on accurate information provided by the groups.

THE A.A. ARCHIVES

The Archives—a high spot of any tour of G.S.O.—opened in 1975 and serves as a repository for every aspect of A.A. history. Under the direction of a professional archivist, archival projects include digitizing old records, collecting oral histories from early members and re-recording older tapes, gathering material on local histories from members and groups, and being available to researchers, both A.A.s and nonalcoholics.

PUBLISHING

Very early, A.A. made the decision to be its own publisher, a decision that has meant a great deal to the unity, growth, and good health of the movement. By acting as its own publisher, A.A. can be sure that its recovery program is not tampered with by those who may be well-meaning but uninformed.

A.A. publishes all its own books and pamphlets, as well as its own magazine (see Chapter Twelve). The addition of a new book or pamphlet is not approached lightly. Usually, the need is well researched by Conference and trustees' committees, the Publishing Department, and the A.A. staff. If the need does not appear to be urgent or broad enough to justify a new publication, the project is abandoned or deferred; if the need is clear, work is started. The first four books were written by Bill W. Since then, all literature has been written by thoroughly knowledgeable A.A.s. From the first draft to the last, committee and staff members—and occasionally a broadly representative special panel—are free to criticize and to suggest, underlining what they feel will best express the A.A. point of view. This process takes time—months or even years. When all the preparation work is completed, a manuscript is forwarded to the appropriate Conference committee for discussion. When the committee recommends approval and two-thirds of Conference members agree, the new piece of literature is entitled to bear the designation, "This is A.A. General Service Conference-approved literature." The same process is used for developing audiovisual materials.

In addition to Conference-approved materials, G.S.O. publishes service materials such as guidelines, bulletins, reports, and A.A. directories.

The Publishing Department at G.S.O. manages the logistics of this process, hiring writers when a piece of literature needs to be developed, then implementing the printing and distributing of completed and approved manuscripts. A publishing director oversees the department, which includes editors, translators for Spanish materials, production people, and support staff. Processing literature orders is also a responsibility of this department.

In addition to the routine translation of most A.A. literature into French and Spanish, there are translations of A.A. material into many other languages as well. When A.A.W.S. produces a translation, the translation is created by a professional linguist; and when the translation is created overseas, it is checked by professional linguists. All of these translations are copyrighted, and all of the copyrights are assigned to A.A.W.S. Much of the material published by A.A.W.S. is also available in different formats, such as hard and soft cover editions, pocket editions, CD and DVD editions.

Mail Room and Shipping and Receiving: The mail room handles thousands of pieces of correspondence annually, incoming and outgoing, and sends out complimentary materials for new groups, service committees, and Loners. Shipping is responsible for shipping literature orders by the hundreds (large orders are handled by an outside service).

FINANCE

Finance: The Finance Department consists of several units: contributions, cash receipts, bookkeeping, accounts receivable, inventory valuation, payroll, office management, and copy center. The obvious common goal of these units is the processing of information, which allows the office to carry on the day-to-day business; the end result is the preparation of monthly, quarterly, and annual financial statements. In addition, this group is involved with G.S.O. budgeting, meeting planning, assistance with International Convention planning, management, and reporting, as well as providing information necessary for trusted servants to make appropriate decisions about the General Service Board's Reserve Fund and the A.A.W.S. and A.A. Grapevine Employees Retirement Plans (defined benefits and defined contribution).

Office Management: The office management responsibilities include purchasing, copy center operations, and arranging for space and food requirements for in-house meetings, such as A.A.W.S. Board Meetings. The office management group also tends to the space and refreshment needs of the many large groups of visitors that tour the office each year.

Information Technology: Information Technology is responsible for overseeing implementation of requests for new data and information, and for monitoring the work of outside contractors who provide maintenance and support of the "system" needs of the office.

LITERATURE PUBLISHED BY A.A.W.S.*

…we have seen the Foundation (the board of trustees), the A.A. book, the development of pamphlet literature, the answered mass of pleas for help, the satisfied need of groups for counsel on their problems, the beginning of our wonderful relations with the public, all becoming part of a growing service to the whole world of A.A. At last, our Society really began to function as a whole.

— Bill W. in his introduction to this manual

*(Note that A.A.W.S. publishes most of its literature in French and Spanish, as well as English.)

BOOKS

Alcoholics Anonymous	Dr. Bob and the Good Oldtimers
Alcoholics Anonymous Comes of Age	"Pass It On"
Twelve Steps and Twelve Traditions	Daily Reflections
As Bill Sees It	Experience, Strength and Hope

BOOKLETS

Came to Believe...	A.A. in Prison: Inmate to Inmate	Living Sober

PAMPHLETS*

A.A. and the Armed Services

A.A. as a Resource for the Health
 Care Professional

A.A. for the Alcoholic with Special Needs

A.A. for the Black and African
 American Alcoholic

A.A. for the Older Alcoholic
 —Never Too Late

A.A. for the Woman

The A.A. Group

A.A. in Correctional Facilities

A.A. in Treatment Settings

A.A. Membership Survey

The A.A. Member—Medications and
 Other Drugs

A.A. Tradition—How It Developed

Bridging the Gap

A Brief Guide to A.A.

Carrying the Message Into
 Correctional Facilities

Circles of Love and Service

The Co-founders of A.A.

Do You Think You're Different?

Frequently Asked Questions About A.A.

G.S.R.

How A.A. Members Cooperate

If You Are a Professional...

Inside A.A.

Is A.A. for Me?

Is A.A. for You?

Is There an Alcoholic in Your Life?

Is There an Alcoholic in the Workplace?

A.A. at a Glance (flyer)

A.A. and the Gay/Lesbian Alcoholic

A.A. for the Native North American

It Happened to Alice

It Sure Beats Sitting in a Cell

The Jack Alexander Article

Let's Be Friendly With Our Friends

Many Paths to Spirituality

A Member's-Eye View of A.A.

Members of the Clergy Ask about A.A.

Memo to an Inmate Who May Be
 an Alcoholic

A Message to Corrections Professionals

A Newcomer Asks...

Problems Other Than Alcohol

Questions and Answers on Sponsorship

Speaking at Non-A.A. Meetings

Self-Support: Where Money and
 Spirituality Mix

This is A.A.

Three Talks to Medical Societies
 by Bill W.

Too Young?

The Twelve Concepts Illustrated

Twelve Steps Illustrated

The Twelve Traditions Illustrated

Understanding Anonymity

What Happened to Joe

Young People and A.A.

Your A.A. General Service Office

*Also available on G.S.O.'s website (aa.org).

S84

SERVICE LITERATURE

Many groups rely on G.S.O. service literature; others don't know it is available. It deals solely with the experience A.A. has had with problems that affect group unity and growth. One set of the A.A. Guidelines is available free. Also available on G.S.O.'s website (aa.org).

1. *Central or Intergroup Offices*
2. *Relationship Between A.A. and Clubs*
3. *Conferences and Conventions and other area or regional A.A. get-togethers. These Guidelines are sent when news of conferences or conventions is received at G.S.O.*
   a. *Material for assembling a 4'x4' Literature Display*
   b. *It is suggested Responsibility Placards also be displayed (see Literature Order Form).*
4. *Cooperating with Court, D.W.I., and Similar Programs*
5. *For A.A. Members Employed in the Alcoholism Field*
6. *Cooperation With the Professional Community*
7. *Corrections Committees*
8. *Treatment Committees*
9. *Public Information—ways A.A. members work together to carry the message to the public*
10. *Relationship between A.A. and Al-Anon—ways of cooperating but not affiliating*
11. *Carrying the A.A. Message to the Deaf Alcoholic*
12. *Finance*
13. *Literature Committees*
14. *A.A. Answering Services*
15. *Serving Alcoholics With Special Needs*
16. *Archives*
17. *Internet*

SPECIAL LITERATURE AND SERVICE MATERIAL

A trilingual (English, French and Spanish) Literature Catalog and Order Forms, sent on request, lists items that may be ordered from G.S.O. Literature may also be ordered online: https://b2c.aaws.org.

A.A. AUDIOVISUAL MATERIAL

VIDEOs/DVDs

*Bill's Own Story

*Bill Discusses the Twelve Traditions

**A New Freedom

A.A. Videos for Young People

Young People's Animation Video

*Markings on the Journey

Hope: Alcoholics Anonymous

A.A. for the Alcoholic With Special Needs (in American Sign Language)

Alcoholics Anonymous (in American Sign Language)

Twelve Steps and Twelve Traditions (in American Sign Language)

Carrying the Message Behind These Walls

Your A.A. General Service Office, the Grapevine, and the General Service Structure

A.A. in Correctional Facilities

CD
History of Service
A.A. Comes of Age
A.A. in Prison: Inmate to Inmate
A.A. for the Alcoholic with Special Needs

TAPE CASSETTEs/CDs
Three Legacies, by Bill
Voices of Our Co-Founders
Bill Discusses the Twelve Traditions
Alcoholics Anonymous (The Big Book)
Twelve Steps and Twelve Traditions
A Brief Guide to A.A.
Living Sober

DIRECTORIES
*A.A. directories: four-part annual listings of A.A. offices, groups, and contacts; *International A.A. Directory; Eastern U.S.; Western U.S.; Canada*

REPORTS
*Conference Report: annual summary of proceedings at the April meeting of the General Service Conference (U.S. and Canada)
*World Service Meeting Report: biennial summary of proceedings.

BULLETINS FROM G.S.O.
**Box 4-5-9: quarterly; general and notes; special departments cover public information, cooperation with the professional community, and correctional and treatment facilities activities; English, French, and Spanish editions.
**About A.A.: three issues a year; newsletter designed to inform professionals interested in alcoholism (the only bulletin aimed primarily at non-A.A.'s).
*Loners-Internationalist Meeting: confidential bimonthly bulletin of A.A. Loners (Lone Members) Homers (housebound members) and Internationalists (seagoing A.A.s); excerpts of correspondence and lists of names and addresses of LIM members who wish to correspond with each other.
*Quarterly Report: covers activities of the General Service Board, including A.A. World Services Inc., and The A.A. Grapevine, Inc.
**Sharing from Behind the Walls: four issues a year; contains excerpts from inmate letters received at G.S.O., and distributed by local correctional facilities committees to A.A. groups behind the walls.

*For A.A. internal use only.
**Available electronically, free of charge.

❖ Chapter Twelve

Grapevine

Grapevine mirrors the Fellowship by publishing members' stories of recovery from alcoholism in print, audio and online. It was started by a group of six volunteers in June 1944 as a newsletter for A.A.s in the New York City area, but Bill W. and the editors soon saw that it had a broader potential for unifying widespread groups and letting the public know about the new program. "May its rays of hope and experience ever fall upon the current of our A.A. life and one day illumine every dark corner of this alcoholic world," Bill W. wrote in the first issue, which was sent to all known groups in the U.S. and Canada and to A.A.s serving in the armed forces during World War II. A year and a half later, Bill W. wrote to the groups and asked if they would like Grapevine to be their national publication. He called for a magazine that "reflects, as accurately as possible, the Voice of all A.A." as he put it, and "not the views of any one individual, group, or organization—even our Central Office or the Alcoholic Foundation—though it should, of course, be tied loosely to the Alcoholic Foundation to insure its continuity and basic soundness." The groups adopted the magazine immediately and by 1949 it was being called "the international monthly journal of Alcoholic Anonymous" as well as popularly called "our meeting in print."

Between 1944 and 1971, Bill W. published approximately 150 articles and editorials in Grapevine, including two sets of essays introducing the Twelve Traditions. Bill also used Grapevine to try out his proposal to change the ratio of alcoholic to non-alcoholic trustees on the General Service Board and to introduce the General Service Conference to the Fellowship. For him, the magazine was a primary means of communication with the groups; and in later years, his Grapevine articles clarified and developed his thoughts on many of A.A.'s fundamental spiritual principles.

First published in the June 1947 issue, the A.A. Preamble (based on the foreword to the first edition of the Big Book) was written by a Grapevine editor, and a number of Grapevine articles have been reprinted as stories in the second, third and fourth editions of the Big Book and in other Conference-approved books and pamphlets.

In 1986, a Conference Advisory Action stated "since each issue of the Grapevine cannot go through the Conference-approval process, the Conference recognizes the

A.A. Grapevine as the international journal of Alcoholics Anonymous." This recognition extends to La Viña as well.

Nature of the Magazine

When Grapevine was a year old, Bill W. told readers: "We of the Grapevine once more affirm that this is your periodical. It will be the vehicle for your thoughts, your feelings, your experiences, and your aspirations—if you care to make it that. While we can only publish a fraction of the material which will come to hand you may be sure that we shall do our fairest and best in making the selections. Always wishing to reflect A.A. and nothing but A.A., it will be the ideal of the Grapevine to always serve, never to dictate or command."

As a basic editorial statement, those words still hold true. The Steps, Traditions, and Concepts are the magazine's guidelines, and Grapevine articles articulate these unchanging principles through the current experiences and informed opinions of individual members/writers. In addition to personal experiences of gaining sobriety and working the program, articles deal with sensitive issues—often in topical sections grouping different points of view. Wide participation on topics of current importance in A.A. is ensured through "Dear Grapevine" (letters from readers), the "What's On Your Mind?" column and an occasional "Your Move," which collects brief pro and con opinions on a given subject. "A.A. News" contains news and information about the Fellowship as a whole.

Structure and Support

A.A. Grapevine, Inc., is one of two operating entities of the General Service Board. (See Chapter Ten for information on corporate structure and financial support.) Grapevine staff, directors, and trustees are voting members of the Conference, and there is a Conference Committee on Grapevine, which reviews the proposed topics for every Grapevine and La Viña book. The Conference also reviews Grapevine policies and in a 1986 Advisory Action, formally recognized the A.A. Grapevine as the international monthly journal of Alcoholics Anonymous.

EDITORIAL ADVISORY BOARD: In addition to the corporate board, a volunteer Editorial Advisory Board and La Viña Editorial Advisory Board are important to the A.A. Grapevine corporation. Their members, A.A.s with expertise in multi-media publishing, technology, digital communications, and graphic arts, with at least four years of sobriety, serve a maximum of one four-year term on the Editorial Advisory Boards.

The boards meet up to five times a year. They are nonvoting bodies, which make no formal recommendations to staff, the Grapevine Board, or the General Service Board, and have no direct responsibility for the day-to-day operation and production of the magazine. Their members advise the editorial staff by lending their experience, insight, and perspective, both as professionals and as A.A. members, to various aspects of the editorial content, graphics, and readership of the magazine. Members become familiar with current issues and the website, aagrapevine.org; make suggestions for special sections, features, related books or audios; suggest ways to increase reader participation in the magazines or website; and read and review manuscripts upon request.

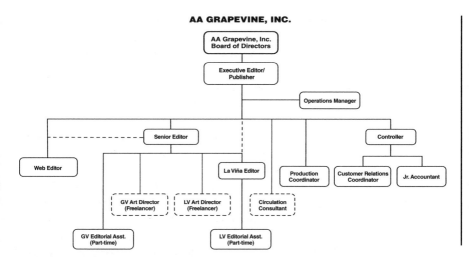

AA GRAPEVINE, INC.

What Gets Done at Grapevine?

The work of the Grapevine office is primarily distributed into four areas: editorial, circulation, office administration and finance, typically accomplished by nine full-time and two part-time employees, as well as several freelancers and outside vendors. The executive editor/publisher has managerial oversight responsibility for the entire organization and reports directly to Grapevine's board of directors. The financial and production operations of the office are supervised by the controller, while the editorial department, which produces Grapevine, La Viña, the website, and all other Grapevine publications, is overseen by the senior editor. The web editor reports to the executive editor/publisher while collaborating with the senior editor. All members of the editorial department making editorial decisions about the content of the magazines and their design are members of the Fellowship. The executive editor/publisher, with assistance from the management team, handles public information and publicity for the magazines, website and all other print and digital items, as well as communication with Conference members, intergroups and central offices, and Grapevine and La Viña representatives. The executive editor/publisher and controller also oversee fulfillment and customer service. The office manager provides administrative support to the executive editor/publisher, Grapevine Board and staff and acts as the primary liaison to the A.A.W.S. staff, GVRs and RLVs. In addition, the operations manager oversees the day-to-day operations of Grapevine.

Articles for the magazines are contributed by A.A. members, with the exception of a few by nonalcoholic friends of A.A. Articles are read and evaluated by staff members, and while some editing is done for purposes of clarity, styling, and length, the editors encourage all writers to express their own experience in their own unique way. Articles are selected for publication with the consensus of the editorial staff, and when needed, input from the Editorial Advisory Board.

Grapevine receives approximately 150 manuscript submissions per month via mail, email or downloaded from aagrapevine.org, and whether or not a manuscript or art work is published, the contributor receives a reply from Grapevine's editorial department. A.A. members interested in writing for the magazines can find a list of upcoming topics at www.aagrapevine.org/contribute and/or www.aagrapevine.org/español. Guidelines for writing and submitting artwork are available online, from the Grapevine office, or from your group's Grapevine or La Viña representatives.

La Viña

The Fellowship brought a request for a Spanish-language magazine modeled after Grapevine to the General Service Conference in 1995, which the Conference endorsed. After a plan for the new magazine was approved by the trustees' Finance Committee, A.A. Grapevine, Inc. began working on a bimonthly edition of the magazine. Called La Viña to echo the title of the English magazine, the first issue came off press in June 1996. Early editions drew primarily on translations from the monthly English edition. Nowadays, however, La Viña primarily publishes original material in Spanish, which can be translated into English and appear in the Grapevine as well. Currently, La Viña receives approximately 65 submissions every other month, so there is always a need for members' stories.

The Conference had asked Grapevine to publish La Viña on a trial basis for five years, and when that period expired in 2001, the Conference recommended that Grapevine continue to publish La Viña as a service to the Fellowship with support from the General Service Board. Today, copies of the magazine are printed every other month, and available online. La Viña plays an important role in the Fellowship, providing a lifeline to A.A. for Spanish-speaking alcoholics, fostering unity among Spanish- and English-speaking A.A.s, and introducing readers to general service. Many groups now have a RLV (La Viña representative) and the magazine is widely used as a Twelfth Step tool in correctional facilities, hospitals, and other institutions.

A.A. Grapevine and La Viña Items

A.A. Grapevine, Inc., carries the A.A. message in a variety of media, including books, ebooks, audiobooks, CDs, MP3s trilingual wall calendar, and service items, such as the Serenity Prayer and A.A. Preamble signs. These are all comprised of material previously published in the magazines or from aagrapevine.org.

A Guide to the Grapevine, commonly known as the Workbook, produced in response to a 1986 Conference Advisory Action, and updated in 2014, shares historical information and experience drawn from the work of individual A.A.s and Grapevine committees. It is downloadable from aagrapevine.org. Grapevine and La Viña handbooks outlining what Grapevine and La Viña representatives do are also available.

www.aagrapevine.org

AAGrapevine.org features stories by A.A. members for anyone interested in recovery from alcoholism. In addition, it offers a digital subscription, including access to the Story Archives and 16 digital stories monthly, digital magazine, audio offerings and an online store. It also maintains an extensive calendar of A.A. events, provides information about writing for the magazines and guidelines for submitting art and photographs. It offers Esquina del RLV and other resources available to Grapevine and La Viña representatives. Spanish-language members' stories, tools and resources may be found under aagrapevine. org/español. AAGrapevine.org is independent of G.S.O.'s website, though the two are connected with a hyperlink.

AAGrapevine.org is the place to find the most current information and subscription options for Grapevine, La Viña, and other publications.

A.A. Grapevine Digital (Story) Archive

AAGrapevine.org also provides access to the Digital Archive, now known as the Grapevine's Story Archive, where almost every Grapevine article and letter ever published have been preserved online. With articles written by A.A. members from June 1944, to the present, the digital archive offers a vivid account of A.A. history as well as a view of the Fellowship today. It also makes stories easier to find. Using keywords, visitors can search the archive by location, author, or subject to find the first version of the Traditions, to learn what A.A.s have said about such topics as sponsorship and self-support, and to explore how much—and how little—A.A. has changed. Readers may also browse through the collection by department, topic, or date to find hundreds of jokes and cartoons, along with thousands of articles.

What Does a Grapevine/La Viña Representative Do?

GVRs and RLVs, as they are known, are the link between the group and the A.A. Grapevine office. A.A. members become Grapevine or La Viña reps by volunteering or being elected to the position by their group. They make sure that members are aware of how the magazines support recovery, and how A.A. members can subscribe, write or submit stories. GVRs and RLVs also announce new products. In 1962, an Advisory Action stated that "Retiring delegates will become Grapevine Representatives (GVRs) and recruit other GVRs in their areas with the objective that each group have a GVR."

Once elected district and group GVRs and RLVs may visit aagrapevine.org website to register online. GVR and RLV registration forms can also be downloaded and sent to Office Manager, A.A. Grapevine, Inc., 475 Riverside Dr., New York, NY 10115. They will receive a GVR or RLV kit, which includes a handbook and other materials containing information about the magazines, their history and purpose, and ideas for carrying the A.A. message to other alcoholics. An additional resource is the updated downloadable Guide to the A.A. Grapevine Workbook (see aagrapevine.org). It is anticipated that each A.A. group would have a GVR and a subscription to at least one of the magazines. As awareness of the needs of Spanish-speaking A.A.s throughout the United States has grown, some reps have begun to work with both magazines and refer to themselves as GVR/RLVs.

Most areas have a Grapevine committee, or a combined Grapevine/La Viña committee. Many GVRs/RLVs are encouraged to become active participants in efforts to make Grapevine/La Viña available to other service committees, such as corrections, treatment, literature and cooperation with the professional community.

Literature Published by A.A. Grapevine, Inc.

Magazines

A.A. Grapevine – print   La Viña – print

Online Products

Grapevine Online: Includes Audio Grapevine, Grapevine Story Archive, eight to ten new stories monthly and HTML versions of Grapevine and La Viña print magazines.

Books

ᵉBest of the Grapevine, Vol. 1
ᵉˢ⁺†Best of Bill
ᵉˢ⁺†The Language of the Heart
    I Am Responsible: The Hand of A.A.
ᵉEmotional Sobriety: Vols. 1 & 2
ᵉIn Our Own Words: Stories of Young
    A.A.s in Recovery
ᵉBeginners' Book
ᵉVoices of Long-Term Sobriety
ᵉStep By Step
ᵉ⁺†ʳThe Home Group: Heartbeat of A.A.
ᵉYoung & Sober: Stories of Those
    Who Found A.A. Early
ᵉNo Matter What

ᵉSpiritual Awakenings: Journeys of
    the Spirit Vols. 1 & 2
Thank You for Sharing: Sixty Years of
    Letters to the A.A. Grapevine
Lo Mejor de la Viña
A Rabbit Walks Into a Bar
ᵉ⁺†Happy, Joyous & Free:
    The Lighter Side of Sobriety
ᵉInto Action: How A.A. Members Practice
    the Program in Their Daily Lives
ᵉ⁺†One on One:
    A.A. Sponsorship in Action
ᵉGrapevine Daily Quote Book
ᵉSober and Out
ᵉForming True Partnerships

Compact Discs

Emotional Sobriety, Vols. 1 & 2
Classic Grapevine CDs, Vol. 2
Not for Newcomers Only CD
What It Was Like
La Historia de AA
The Twelve Traditions
Las Doce Tradiciones, Vols. 1 & 2
It Works If We Work It
*Best of Bill Audiobook
Despertares Espirituales, Vols. 1 & 2
Attitude Adjustment
Historias de La Viña Vols. 1, 2 & 3
*The Home Group, Vols. 1 & 2
The Language of the Heart (MP3 CD)

Discounts for bulk orders are also available. Visit our online store at aagrapevine. org for the most up-to-date product listings and order options.

---

*Also available in Spanish.
†Also available in French.
§Also available in Large Print.
e Also available in e-book.

General Guidelines for Reprinting Art and Articles from A.A. Grapevine

Permission to reproduce articles or other A.A. Grapevine or La Viña material, either in print or via electronic media (such as web pages), must be obtained from A.A. Grapevine, Inc. Each article or item must be reprinted in its entirety and carry the following credit line:

Copyright © (Month, Year) A.A. Grapevine, Inc.
Reprinted with permission

Organizations, publications, or websites outside A.A. must add the following:
Permission to reprint A.A. Grapevine, Inc., copyrighted material [in this publication, organization, or website] does not in any way imply affiliation with or endorsement by either Alcoholics Anonymous or AA Grapevine, Inc.

Logo and Artwork

Victor E. and Clara T. are the only Grapevine cartoons that may be reprinted with permission.

A.A. Grapevine, Inc., does not grant permission to reproduce either its logo or registered trademarks (A.A. Grapevine, Inc., AudioGrapevine, A.A. Grapevine Digital Archive, La Viña, A.A. Grapevine, Grapevine, etc.) its artwork or any other cartoons on any other website or in any other publication.

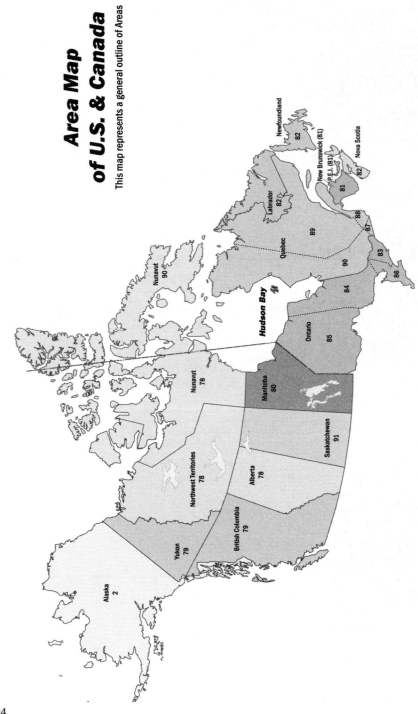

Area Map
of U.S. & Canada

This map represents a general outline of Areas

Newfoundland
82

New Brunswick (81)

P.E.I. (81)

81

Nova Scotia

88

82

87

Labrador
82

83

Quebec
89

86

90

Nunavut
90

Hudson Bay

84

Ontario
85

Nunavut
78

Manitoba
80

Northwest Territories
78

Alberta
78

Saskatchewan
91

Yukon
79

British Columbia
79

Alaska
2

S94

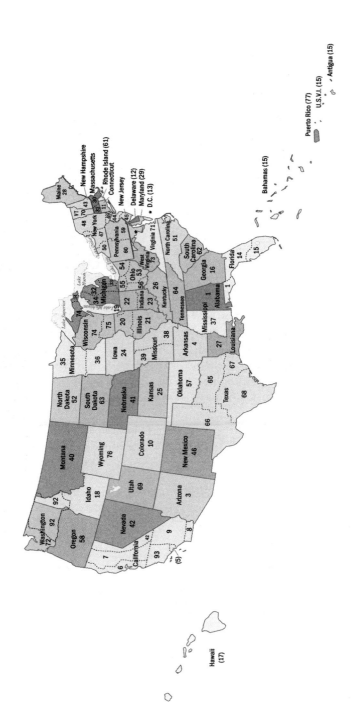

Maine 28
V T
70
New Hampshire
43
Massachusetts
31
Rhode Island (61)
11
30
Connecticut
New Jersey
48
New York
47
44
49
45
Pennsylvania
59
Delaware (12)
Maryland (29)
D.C. (13)
50
60
Virginia 71
North Carolina 51
West Virginia 73
South Carolina 62
54
Ohio
53
55
Michigan
34 32
33
Kentucky 64
Georgia 16
Florida 14
15
Indiana 26
56
22
19
23
Tennessee
Alabama 1
Lake Huron
74
Lake Michigan
75
Illinois 21
Mississippi 37
Wisconsin 74
20
Missouri 38
Arkansas 4
Louisiana 27
Lake Superior
Iowa 24
39
67
Minnesota 35
36
Oklahoma 57
65
Texas 68
North Dakota 52
Nebraska 41
Kansas 25
66
South Dakota 63
Montana 40
Wyoming 76
Colorado 10
New Mexico 46
Idaho 18
Utah 69
Arizona 3
Washington 72
92
92
Oregon 58
Nevada 42
9
8
7
California 6
93
(5)

Bahamas (15)

Puerto Rico (77)
U.S.V.I. (15)
Antigua (15)

Hawaii (17)

S95

Appendix A

Original Conference Charter—1955
(North American Section)

1. *Purpose*: The General Service Conference of Alcoholics Anonymous is the guardian of the World Services and of[1] the Twelve Traditions of Alcoholics Anonymous. The Conference shall be a service body only; never a government for Alcoholics Anonymous.

2. *Composition*: The Conference (North American Section) shall be composed of State and Provincial Delegates, the Trustees of the General Service Board, Directors and staff members of the New York Headquarters and such ex-Trustees or foreign Delegates as the Conference may wish to invite.[2]

Other Sections of the Conference may sometimes be created in foreign lands as the need arises out of language or geographical considerations. The North American Section of the General Service Conference will then become the Senior Section, related to the other Sections by ties of mutual consultation and a cross linking of Delegates.

But no Conference Section shall ever be placed in authority over another. All joint action shall be taken only upon two-thirds vote of the combined Sections. Within its boundaries each Conference ought to be autonomous.[3] Only matters seriously affecting

---

1 Updated by the 1969 Conference to include the words: "the Twelve Steps."

2 Revised by the 1979 Conference to read: "Composition: The Conference (U.S. and Canada) shall be composed of area delegates, the trustees of the General Service Board, directors of A.A. World Services and A.A Grapevine, and staff members of the Grapevine and General Service Office."

3 Updated by the 1987 Conference to read:
"Foreign lands in many cases have created autonomous General Service Conferences of their own, which rely on the Steps and Traditions protected by the Conference (U.S. and Canada) and in other ways often turn to the actions of the Conference for guidance.
"Consultation between Conferences is encouraged. And a formal meeting—the World Service Meeting of delegates from the various Conferences is held once every two years. The US./Canada delegates are chosen from the General Service Board.
"In countries where General Service structure exists, the U.S./Canada Conference will delegate sole right to publish our Conference-approved literature to the General Service Board of the structure.
"Only matters seriously affecting A.A.'s worldwide needs shall be the subject of joint consideration."
Further clarified by the 1988 Conference to read:
"Other countries have created autonomous General Service Conferences of their own, which rely on the Steps and Traditions that are protected by the United States/Canada Conference. In addition, these other Conferences often turn to the actions of the United States/Canada Conference for guidance.
"Consultation between Conferences is encouraged, and a World Service Meeting of delegates from the various

A.A.'s worldwide needs shall be the subject of joint consideration.

3. *Conference Relation to A.A.:* The Conference will act for A.A. in the perpetuation and guidance of its World Services, and it will also be the vehicle by which the A.A. movement can express its views upon all matters of vital A.A. policy and all hazardous deviations from A.A. Tradition. Delegates should be free to vote as their conscience dictates; they should also be free to decide what questions should be taken to the group level, whether for information, discussion or their own direct instruction.

But no change in the A.A. Tradition itself may be made with less than the written consent of two-thirds of all the A.A. groups.[4]

4. *Conference Relation to A.A. Headquarters:* The Conference will replace the founders of Alcoholics Anonymous who formerly functioned as guides and advisors to The General Service Board and its related Headquarters services. The Conference will be expected to afford a reliable cross-section of A.A. opinion for this purpose.

To effectively further this same purpose it will be understood, as a matter of tradition, that a two-thirds vote of a Conference quorum shall be considered binding upon the the General Service Board and its related corporate services. A quorum shall consist of two-thirds of all the Conference members registered.[5]

But no such vote ought to impair the legal rights of the General Service Board and the service corporations to conduct routine business and make ordinary contracts relating thereto.

It will be further understood that, as a matter of tradition, a three-quarters vote of all Conference members may bring about a reorganization of the General Service Board and the Headquarters, if or when such reorganization is deemed essential.

Under such a proceeding, the Conference may request resignations, may nominate new Trustees and may make all other necessary arrangements regardless of the legal prerogatives of the General Service Board.

5. *State and Provincial Assemblies: Composition of:* State and Provincial Assemblies are composed of the elected Representatives of all A.A. groups desiring to participate, in each of the United States and each of the Provinces of Canada.

Each State and Province will always be entitled to one Assembly. But States and

---

Conferences is held once every two years. The United States/Canada delegates to the World Service Meeting are chosen from the General Service Board.

"In countries where a General Service Structure exists, the United States/Canada Conference will delegate sole right to publish our Conference-approved literature to the General Service Board of that structure."

4 Revised by the 1957 Conference as follows: "Bill has suggested that the third article of the Conference Charter, i.e., Conference Relation to A.A. (Second paragraph page 58 of the Third Legacy Manual), be amended to read: "But no change in Article 12 of the Charter or in A.A. Tradition or in the Twelve Steps of A.A. may be made with less than a written consent of three-quarters of the A.A. groups, as described in the resolution adopted by the 1955 Conference and Convention." If this amendment is made, the seventh paragraph on page 57 of the Third Legacy Manual must also be amended to read: "excepting, however that any amendment of Article 12 of the Charter or of A.A.'s Twelve Steps and Twelve Traditions must have the consent of A.A. groups as provided in Article 3 of the Charter." It was recommended that these amendments be made." Subsequently revised by the 1969 Conference to replace the words "A.A. Tradition" with "The Twelve Traditions of A.A."

5 Revised by the 1986 Conference as follows: A quorum shall consist of two-thirds of all the Conference members registered. It will be understood, as a matter of tradition, that a two-thirds vote of Conference members voting shall be considered binding upon the General Service Board and its related corporate services, provided the total vote constitutes at least a Conference quorum.

Provinces of large A.A. populations will be entitled to additional Assemblies, as provided by this Manual of World Service, or by any future amendment thereto.[6]

6. *State and Provincial Assemblies: Purpose of:* State and Provincial Assemblies convene every two years for the election of State and Provincial Committeemen, from which are selected Delegates to the General Service Conference of Alcoholics Anonymous held at New York. Such State or Provincial Assemblies are concerned only with the World Service affairs of Alcoholics Anonymous.

7. *State and Provincial Assemblies: Method of Electing Committeemen and Delegates:* Whenever practicable, Committeemen are elected by written ballot without personal nomination. And Delegates are selected from among such Committeemen by a two-thirds written ballot or by lot, as provided in the Manual of World Service.

8. *State and Provincial Assemblies: Terms of Office for Group Representatives, Committeemen and Delegates:* Unless otherwise directed by the Conference, these terms of office shall all be concurrent and of two years duration each. In half the States and Provinces, Assembly elections will be held in the even years; the remaining half of the Assemblies will elect in the odd years, thus creating rotating Panels One and Two of the Conference as further described in the Manual of World Service.

9. *The General Service Conference Meetings:* The Conference will meet yearly in the City of New York, unless otherwise agreed upon. Special meetings may be called should there be a grave emergency. The Conference may also render advisory opinions at any time by a mail or telephone poll in aid of the General Service Board or its related services.

10. *The General Service Board: Composition, Jurisdiction, Responsibilities:* The General Service Board of Alcoholics Anonymous shall be an incorporated Trusteeship composed of alcoholics and nonalcoholics who choose their own successors, these choices being subject, however, to the approval of the Conference or a committee thereof. Alcoholic out-of-town Trustees are, however, first nominated by their areas or by their State or Provincial Committees after being cleared by the Conference Nominating Committee.[7]

They are then elected to the General Service Board, the Trustees being obligated by tradition so to do.[8]

The General Service Board is the chief Service Arm of the Conference, and is essen-

---

6 Article 5, paragraph 2 reworded by the 1971 Conference to read: "Generally speaking, each state and province will be entitled to one assembly. However, more than one state or province may be joined to another state or province to form one assembly area. But states and provinces of large A.A. populations and/or whose geography presents communication problems may be entitled to additional assemblies, as provided by the A.A. Service Manual, or by any further amendment thereto."
Subsequently, the 1978 Conference made a further amendment to Article 5 as follows:
"Area Assemblies: Composition of: Assemblies, designated as area assemblies, are composed of the elected general service representatives of all A.A. groups desiring to participate, district committee members, and area committee officers in each of the delegate areas of the United States and Canada."

7 The 1970 Conference revised the title indicated here as Alcoholic out-of-town Trustee (later appearing as General Service Trustee-at-Large) to be "Regional General Service Trustee." By 1978, this Board title appeared as Trustee-at-Large.

8 By 1969, the following sentence had been added: "The same procedure is followed for general service trustees in the United States and Canada, except that the Board will specify certain business or professional qualifications." The 1979 Conference substituted the word "will" with "may."

tially custodial in its character.

Excepting for decisions upon matters of policy, finance, or A.A. Tradition, liable to seriously affect A.A. as a whole, the General Service Board has entire freedom of action in the routine conduct of the policy and business affairs of the A.A. General Headquarters at New York and may name suitable committees and elect directors to its subsidiary corporate service entities in pursuance of this purpose.[9]

The General Service Board is primarily responsible for the financial and policy integrity of its subsidiary services: A.A. Publishing, Inc. and A.A. Grapevine, Inc.[10] and for such other service corporations as the Conference may desire to form, but nothing herein shall compromise the Grapevine editor's right to accept or reject material for publication.

The Charter and Bylaws of the General Service Board, or any amendments thereto, should always be subject to the approval of the General Service Conference by a two-thirds vote of all its members.[11]

Except in a great emergency, neither the General Service Board nor any of its related services ought ever take any action liable to greatly affect A.A. as a whole, without first consulting the Conference. It is nevertheless understood that the Board shall at all times reserve the right to decide which of its actions or decisions may require the approval of the Conference.

11. *The General Service Conference: Its General Procedures:* The Conference will hear the financial and policy reports of the General Service Board and its related Headquarters Services. The Conference will advise with the Trustees, Directors and Staff members of the Headquarters upon all matters presented as affecting A.A. as a whole, engage in debate, appoint necessary committees and pass suitable resolutions for the advice or direction of the General Service Board and the Headquarters.

The Conference may also discuss and recommend appropriate action respecting serious deviations from A.A. Tradition or harmful misuse of the name, "Alcoholics Anonymous."

The Conference may draft any needed bylaws and will name its own officers and committees by any method of its own choosing.

The Conference, at the close of each yearly session, will draft a full report of its proceedings to be supplied to all Delegates and Committeemen; also a condensation thereof which will be sent to A.A. Groups throughout the world.

12. *General Warranties of the Conference:* In all its proceedings, the General Service Conference shall observe the spirit of the A.A. Tradition, taking great care that the Conference never becomes the seat of perilous wealth or power; that sufficient operating

---

9 The two service corporations, A.A.W.S., Inc. and the A.A. Grapevine, Inc., although affiliates and not "subsidiaries," of the General Service Board of Alcoholics Anonymous, Inc., are organized as separate, not-for-profit corporations, and, as such, the routine conduct of policy and business affairs and the creation of "suitable committees," respecting each, resides in the respective boards of the two corporations. However, the trustees of the General Service Board, when acting in their capacity as members of the A.A. World Services, Inc., and/or the A.A. Grapevine, Inc., do elect the directors of the two service corporations.

10 See preceding footnote.

11 The approval of the Bylaws by the Conference is a matter of tradition, rather than a legal requirement.

funds, plus an ample reserve, be its prudent financial principle; that none of the Conference members shall ever be placed in a position of unqualified authority over any of the others; that all important decisions be reached by discussion, vote and, whenever possible, by substantial unanimity; that no Conference action ever be personally punitive or an incitement to serious public controversy; that though the Conference may act for the service of Alcoholics Anonymous, it shall never perform any acts of government; and that, like the Society of Alcoholics Anonymous which it serves, the Conference itself will always remain democratic in thought and action.

The principles on which this Charter operates are outlined in "Twelve Concepts" and they should be read.[12]

---

12 The 1981 Conference recommended that this note appear immediately following the Conference Charter.

Appendix B

A Resolution

Offered by Bill W. and Adopted at the
20th Anniversary Convention of A.A., in 1955.
*(This Resolution Authorizes the General Service Conference
to Act for Alcoholics Anonymous
and to Become the Successor to Its Co-Founders.)*

We, the members of the Twentieth Anniversary Convention of Alcoholics Anonymous, here assembled at St. Louis in July of the year 1955, declare our belief that our Fellowship has now come of age and is entirely ready to assume full and permanent possession of the Three Legacies of our A.A. inheritance—the Legacies of Recovery, Unity and Service.

We believe that the General Service Conference of Alcoholics Anonymous, as created in 1951 by our co-founders, Doctor Bob S. and Bill W., and authorized by trustees of the Alcoholic Foundation, has now become entirely capable of assuming the guardianship of A.A.'s Twelve Traditions and of taking over full guidance and control of the world service of our Society, as provided in the "Third Legacy Manual of World Service"[1] recently revised by our surviving co-founder, Bill W.,[2] and of the General Service Board of Alcoholics Anonymous.

We have also heard with approval Bill W.'s proposal that A.A.'s General Service Conference should now become the permanent successor to the founders of Alcoholics Anonymous, inheriting from them all their former duties and special responsibilities, thus avoiding in future time all possible strivings for individual prestige or personal power; and also providing our Society with the means of functioning on a permanent basis.

BE IT THEREFORE RESOLVED: That the General Service Conference of Alcoholics Anonymous should become, as of this date, July 3, 1955, the guardian of the Traditions of Alcoholics Anonymous, the perpetuators of the world services of our Society, the voice of the group conscience of our entire Fellowship, and the sole successors of its co-founders, Doctor Bob and Bill.

---

1 Now called *The A.A. Service Manual.*

2 Bill died January 24, 1971.

AND IT IS UNDERSTOOD: That neither the Twelve Traditions of Alcoholics Anonymous nor the warranties of Article XII of the Conference Charter shall ever be changed or amended by the General Service Conference except by first asking the consent of the registered A.A. groups of the world. [This would include all A.A. groups known to the general service offices around the world.]3 These groups shall be suitably notified of any proposal for change and shall be allowed no less than six months for consideration thereof. And before any such Conference action can be taken, there must first be received in writing within the time allotted the consent of at least three-quarters of all those registered groups who respond to such proposal.

WE FURTHER UNDERSTAND: That, as provided in Article XII of the Conference Charter, the Conference binds itself to the Society of Alcoholics Anonymous by the following means:

That in all its proceedings, the General Service Conference shall observe the spirit of the A.A. Tradition, taking great care that the Conference never becomes the seat of perilous wealth or power; that sufficient operating funds, plus an ample reserve, be its prudent financial principle; that none of the Conference members shall ever be placed in a position of unqualified authority over any of the others; that all important decisions be reached by discussion, vote and, whenever possible, by substantial unanimity; that no Conference action ever be personally punitive, or an incitement to public controversy; that though the Conference may act in the service of Alcoholics Anonymous and may traditionally direct its world services, it shall never enact laws or regulations binding on A.A. as a whole or upon any A.A. group or member thereof, nor shall it perform any other such acts of government; and that, like the Society of Alcoholics Anonymous which it serves, the Conference itself will always remain democratic in thought and action.

(This Resolution was adopted by the Convention by acclamation and, in the Conference, by formal resolution by vote.)

St. Louis, Missouri, July 3, 1955

---

3 Resolution: It was resolved by the 1976 General Service Conference that those instruments requiring consent of three-quarters of the responding groups for change or amendment would include the Twelve Steps of A.A., should any such change or amendment ever be proposed.

Appendix C

Current Conference Charter
(United States and Canada)

1. *Purpose*: The General Service Conference of Alcoholics Anonymous is the guardian of world services and of the Twelve Steps and Twelve Traditions of Alcoholics Anonymous. The Conference shall be a service body only; never a government for Alcoholics Anonymous.

2. *Composition*: The Conference (U.S. and Canada) shall be composed of area delegates, the trustees of the General Service Board, directors of A.A. World Services and A.A. Grapevine, and staff members of the Grapevine and General Service Office.

Other countries have created autonomous General Service Conferences[1] of their own, which rely on the Steps and Traditions that are protected by the United States/Canada Conference. In addition, these other Conferences often turn to the actions of the United States/Canada Conference for guidance.

Consultation between Conferences is encouraged, and a World Service Meeting of delegates from the various Conferences is held once every two years. The United States/ Canada delegates to the World Service Meeting are chosen from the General Service Board.

In countries where a General Service Structure exists, the United States/Canada Conference will delegate sole right to publish our Conference-approved literature to the General Service Board of that structure.

Only matters seriously affecting A.A.'s worldwide needs shall be the subject of joint consideration.

3. *Conference Relation to A.A.*: The Conference will act for A.A. in the perpetuation and guidance of its world services, and it will also be the vehicle by which the A.A. movement can express its view upon all matters of vital A.A. policy and all hazardous deviations from A.A. Tradition. Delegates should be free to vote as their conscience dictates; they should also be free to decide what questions should be taken to the group level, whether for information, discussion, or their own direct instruction.

---

1 The word "Conference," as used in paragraph 2 of the "Current Conference Charter," appears to be synonymous with "General Service Conference," or "General Service Structure," in its application to national A.A. entities outside of the U.S./Canada; and, while the "Charter" may provide guidance to other G.S.O.s, they are still autonomous, and not bound by its mandates, except where the law might require it (e.g., copyright law).

But no change in Article 12 of the Charter or in the Twelve Traditions of A.A. or in the Twelve Steps of A.A. may be made with less than the written consent of three-quarters of the A.A. groups, as described in the Resolution adopted by the 1955 Conference and Convention.[2]

4. *Conference Relation to the General Service Board and its Corporate Services:* The Conference will replace the founders of Alcoholics Anonymous, who formerly functioned as guides and advisers to the General Service Board and its related service corporations. The Conference will be expected to afford a reliable cross section of A.A. opinion for this purpose.

A quorum shall consist of two-thirds of all the Conference members registered.

It will be understood, as a matter of tradition, that a two-thirds vote of Conference members voting shall be considered binding upon the General Service Board and its related corporate services, provided the total vote constitutes at least a Conference quorum. But no such vote ought to impair the legal rights of the General Service Board and the service corporations to conduct routine business and make ordinary contracts relating thereto.

It will be further understood, regardless of the legal prerogatives of the General Service Board, as a matter of tradition, that a three-quarters vote of all Conference members may bring about a reorganization of the General Service Board and the directors and staff members[3] of its corporate services, if or when such reorganization is deemed essential.

Under such a proceeding, the Conference may request resignations, may nominate new trustees, and may make all other necessary arrangements regardless of the legal prerogatives of the General Service Board. The Conference recognizes the principles contained within the Twelve Concepts, particularly the Right of Participation, and the Rights of Petition and Appeal reflected in Concepts IV and V. In keeping with these principles, the Conference may agree to hear Concept V Appeals brought by members of the Conference structure below the Conference level on the inverted triangle.

5. *Area Assemblies, Composition of:* Assemblies, designated as area assemblies, are composed of the elected general service representatives of all A.A. groups desiring to participate, district committee members, and area committee officers in each of the delegate areas of the United States and Canada.

Generally speaking, each delegate area will be entitled to one assembly.[4] But areas of large A.A. populations and/or whose geography presents communication problems will be entitled to additional assemblies, as provided by "The A.A. Service Manual," or by any further amendment thereto.

6. *Area Assemblies, Purpose of:* Area assemblies convene every two years for the election of area committee members, from which are elected delegates to the General Service

---

2 This applies to the original English version only.

3 Employees at G.S.O. are employees of A.A. World Services, Inc., rather than the General Service Board of Alcoholics Anonymous, Inc. In any case, a reorganization of …staff members… would have to comply with applicable laws affecting employees.

4 Paragraph 5 is a carry-over from the original "Charter" and the words "delegate area" replaced the words "State or Province." The sentence originally read, "Each State or Province will always be entitled to one 'Assembly,' where the word "Assembly" meant one Area structure and one Delegate vote at the General Service Conference. States or Provinces with large A.A. populations would be entitled to additional "Assemblies."

Conference of Alcoholics Anonymous. Such area assemblies are concerned only with the world service affairs of Alcoholics Anonymous.[5]

7. *Area Assemblies, Methods of Electing Area Committee Members and Delegates:* Whenever practicable, committee members are elected by written ballot without personal nomination. And delegates are selected from among such committee members by a two-thirds written ballot or by lot, as provided in "The A.A. Service Manual."

8. *Area Assemblies, Terms of Office for Group General Service Representatives, Area Committee Members and Delegates:* Unless otherwise directed by the Conference, these terms of office shall all be concurrent and of two years' duration each. In approximately half the areas, assembly elections will be held in the even years; the remaining assemblies will elect in the odd years, thus creating rotating Panels of the Conference, as further described in "The A.A. Service Manual."

9. *The General Service Conference Meetings:* The Conference will meet yearly in the City of New York, unless otherwise agreed upon. Special meetings may be called should there be a grave emergency. The Conference may also render advisory opinions at any time by a mail or telephone poll in aid of the General Service Board or its related services.

10. *The General Service Board: Composition, Jurisdiction, Responsibilities:* The General Service Board of Alcoholics Anonymous shall be an incorporated trusteeship, composed of alcoholics and nonalcoholics who elect their own successors, these choices being subject, however, to the approval of the Conference or a committee thereof. Candidates for alcoholic regional trustee are, however, first selected by the areas in the region. Then, at the General Service Conference, voters consisting of delegates from the region involved, plus an equal number of voters—one-half to come from the Conference Committee on Trustees and one-half to come from the trustees' Nominating Committee— make a selection of a nominee by two-thirds written ballot or by lot. This nominee is then elected to the General Service Board, the trustees being obligated by tradition to do so. For trustees-at-large in the U.S. and Canada, the Board may specify certain business or professional qualifications. The procedure is then as follows. Each Conference area may select one candidate via Third Legacy procedure. Resumes of all candidates will be reviewed for eligibility by the trustees' Nominating Committee. At the General Service Conference, delegates from each region will caucus prior to the nomination, using Third Legacy procedure, to reduce the number of candidates to one for each region in the U.S. and two for each region in Canada. A maximum of six candidates for trustee-at-large, U.S., and a maximum of four candidates for trustee-at-large, Canada, will be presented to the voting members of the Conference for nomination. Voting members of the Conference will be all delegates from the nominating country (U.S. or Canada) and all members of the trustees' Nominating Committee. These nominees are then elected to the General Service Board, the trustees being obligated by tradition to do so.

---

5 Areas assemblies still meet every two years in order to elect a delegate to the General Service Conference, but they typically meet far more frequently in order to conduct on-going area business.

The General Service Board is the chief service arm of the Conference, and is essentially custodial in its character.

Excepting for decisions upon matters of policy, finance, or A.A. Tradition, liable to seriously affect A.A. as a whole, the General Service Board has entire freedom of action in the routine conduct of the policy and business affairs of the A.A. service corporations and may name suitable committees and elect directors to its subsidiary corporate service entities in pursuance of this purpose.[6]

The General Service Board is primarily responsible for the financial and policy integrity of its subsidiary services: A.A. World Services Inc., and A.A. Grapevine, Inc.,[7] and for such other service corporations as the Conference may desire to form, but nothing herein shall compromise the Grapevine editor's right to accept or reject material for publication.

The Charter and Bylaws of the General Service Board, or any amendments thereto, should always be subject to the approval of the General Service Conference by a two-thirds vote of all its members.[8]

Except in a great emergency, neither the General Service Board nor any of its related services ought ever take any action liable to greatly affect A.A. as a whole, without first consulting the Conference. It is nevertheless understood that the board shall at all times reserve the right to decide which of its actions or decisions may require the approval of the Conference.

11. *The General Service Conference, Its General Procedures:* The Conference will hear the financial and policy reports of the General Service Board and its related corporate services. The Conference will advise with the trustees, directors, and staff members upon all matters presented as affecting A.A. as a whole, engage in debate, appoint necessary committees, and pass suitable resolutions[9] for the advice or direction of the General Service Board and its related services.

The Conference may also discuss and recommend appropriate action respecting serious deviations from A.A. tradition or harmful misuse of the name "Alcoholics Anonymous."

The Conference may draft any needed bylaws and will name its own officers and committees by any method of its own choosing.

The Conference at the close of each yearly session will draft a full report of its proceedings, to be supplied to all delegates and committee members; also a condensation thereof which will be sent to A.A. groups throughout the world.

12. *General Warranties of the Conference:* In all its proceedings, the General Service Conference shall observe the spirit of the A.A. Tradition, taking great care that the

---

6 The two service corporations, A.A.W.S., Inc. and the A.A. Grapevine, Inc., although affiliates and not "subsidiaries," of the General Service Board of Alcoholics Anonymous, Inc., are organized as separate, not-for-profit corporations, and, as such, the routine conduct of policy and business affairs and the creation of "suitable committees," respecting each, resides in the respective boards of the two corporations. However, the trustees of the General Service Board, when acting in their capacity as Members of the A.A. World Services, Inc., and/or The Grapevine, Inc., do elect the directors of the two service corporations.

7 See previous footnote.

8 The approval of the Bylaws by the Conference is a matter of tradition, rather than a legal requirement.

9 "Suitable resolutions" are now termed "Conference Advisory Actions."

Conference never becomes the seat of perilous wealth or power; that sufficient operating funds, plus an ample reserve, be its prudent financial principle; that none of the Conference members shall ever be placed in a position of unqualified authority over any of the others; that all important decisions be reached by discussion, vote, and, whenever possible, by substantial unanimity; that no Conference action ever be personally punitive or an incitement to public controversy, that though the Conference may act for the service of Alcoholics Anonymous, it shall never perform any acts of government; and that, like the Society of Alcoholics Anonymous which it serves, the Conference itself will always remain democratic in thought and action.

A RESOLUTION

Offered by Bill W. and Adopted at the
20th Anniversary Convention of A.A., in 1955.
*(This Resolution Authorizes the General Service Conference
to Act for Alcoholics Anonymous
and to Become the Successor to Its Co-Founders.)*

We, the members of the Twentieth Anniversary Convention of Alcoholics Anonymous, here assembled at St. Louis in July of the year 1955, declare our belief that our Fellowship has now come of age and is entirely ready to assume full and permanent possession of the Three Legacies of our A.A. inheritance—the Legacies of Recovery, Unity and Service.

We believe that the General Service Conference of Alcoholics Anonymous, as created in 1951 by our co-founders, Doctor Bob S. and Bill W., and authorized by trustees of the Alcoholic Foundation, has now become entirely capable of assuming the guardianship of A.A.'s Twelve Traditions and of taking over full guidance and control of the world service of our Society, as provided in the "Third Legacy Manual of World Service"[10] recently revised by our surviving co-founder, Bill W.,[11] and of the General Service Board of Alcoholics Anonymous.

We have also heard with approval Bill W.'s proposal that A.A.'s General Service Conference should now become the permanent successor to the founders of Alcoholics Anonymous, inheriting from them all their former duties and special responsibilities, thus avoiding in future time all possible strivings for individual prestige or personal power; and also providing our Society with the means of functioning on a permanent basis.

BE IT THEREFORE RESOLVED: That the General Service Conference of Alcoholics Anonymous should become, as of this date, July 3, 1955, the guardian of the Traditions of Alcoholics Anonymous, the perpetuators of the world services of our Society, the voice of the group conscience of our entire Fellowship, and the sole successors of its co-founders, Doctor Bob and Bill.

---

10 Now called "The A.A. Service Manual."
11 Bill died January 24, 1971.

AND IT IS UNDERSTOOD: That neither the Twelve Traditions of Alcoholics Anonymous nor the warranties of Article XII of the Conference Charter shall ever be changed or amended by the General Service Conference except by first asking the consent of the registered A.A. groups of the world. [This would include all A.A. groups known to the general service offices around the world.][12] These groups shall be suitably notified of any proposal for change and shall be allowed no less than six months for consideration thereof. And before any such Conference action can be taken, there must first be received in writing within the time allotted the consent of at least three-quarters of all those registered groups who respond to such proposal.

WE FURTHER UNDERSTAND: That, as provided in Article XII of the Conference Charter, the Conference binds itself to the Society of Alcoholics Anonymous by the following means:

That in all its proceedings, the General Service Conference shall observe the spirit of the A.A. Tradition, taking great care that the Conference never becomes the seat of perilous wealth or power; that sufficient operating funds, plus an ample reserve, be its prudent financial principle; that none of the Conference members shall ever be placed in a position of unqualified authority over any of the others; that all important decisions be reached by discussion, vote and, whenever possible, by substantial unanimity; that no Conference action ever be personally punitive, or an incitement to public controversy; that though the Conference may act in the service of Alcoholics Anonymous and may traditionally direct its world services, it shall never enact laws or regulations binding on A.A. as a whole or upon any A.A. group or member thereof, nor shall it perform any other such acts of government; and that, like the Society of Alcoholics Anonymous which it serves, the Conference itself will always remain democratic in thought and action. (This Resolution was adopted by the Convention by acclamation and, in the Conference, by formal resolution by vote.)

St. Louis, Missouri, July 3, 1955

---

12 Resolution: It was resolved by the 1976 General Service Conference that those instruments requiring consent of three-quarters of the responding groups for change or amendment would include the Twelve Steps of A.A., should any such change or amendment ever be proposed.

Appendix D

Conference Panels

In any one year, about half of the A.A. groups are busy electing G.S.R.s and half of all area assemblies are electing qualified delegates to the annual Conference meeting, depending on whether the area is an "odd" or "even" panel. A panel is a numerical designation that refers to a group of delegates elected to begin serving at the General Service Conference in a particular year.

The Conference started in 1951 (an odd year, Panel 1) and included 37 delegates.

The following year (an even year, Panel 2) there were 38 delegates added. Since then, there have been additional areas added to states and provinces—total count, 93—with about half elected in an odd year and half in an even year. You can look at the table below and easily determine whether your area is odd or even.

Each panel is numbered for the Conference at which the Area's delegate will first serve. For example, delegates attending the 63rd General Service Conference as their first Conference are Panel 63 delegates.

The two-year cycle frequently applies to area committee officers and committee members, as well.

DELEGATES ELECTED FOR 'ODD' YEARS

State or Province	Number of Delegates	Area No.	Area Represented
Alabama	One	1	Alabama/Northwest Fla.
Arkansas	One	4	Arkansas
British Columbia/ Yukon Territory	One	79	British Columbia/ Yukon Territory
California	Three Odd Years (Total 6)	93	Central
		6	Northern Coastal
		5	Southern
Colorado	One	10	Colorado
Connecticut	One	11	Connecticut
District of Columbia	One	13	D.C.
Florida	Two	14	Northern
		15	Southern/Bahamas/Virgin Islands/Antigua/St. Maarten/Cayman Islands

State or Province	Number of Delegates	Area No.	Area Represented
Hawaii	One	17	Hawaii
Illinois	Two Odd Years (Total 3)	19	Chicago
		21	Southern
Indiana	One Odd Years (Total 2)	22	Northern
Iowa	One	24	Iowa
Louisiana	One	27	Louisiana
Massachusetts	One Odd Years (Total 2)	30	Eastern
Michigan	Two Odd Years (Total 3)	33	Southeastern
		32	Central
Minnesota	One Odd Years (Total 2)	36	Southern
Missouri	Two	38	Eastern
		39	Western
Montana	One	40	Montana
Nevada	One	42	Nevada
New Jersey	One Odd Years (Total 2)	44	Northern
New York	Two Odd Years (Total 4)	49	Southeastern
		47	Central
North Carolina	One	51	North Carolina
North Dakota	One	52	North Dakota
Nova Scotia/Nfld./ Labrador	One	82	Nova Scotia/Nfld./ Labrador
Ohio	Two Odd Years (Total 4)	53	Central/Southeastern
		54	Northeastern
Oklahoma	One	57	Oklahoma
Ontario	Two Odd Years (Total 4)	83	Eastern
		85	Northwestern
Pennsylvania	Two	59	Eastern
		60	Western
Quebec	Two Odd Years (Total 4)	88	Southeastern
		89	Northeastern
Saskatchewan	One	91	Saskatchewan
Texas	Two Odd Years (Total 4)	65	Northeastern
		67	Southeastern
Utah	One	69	Utah
Virginia	One	71	Virginia/Cuba
Washington	One Odd Years (Total 2)	72	Western Washington
West Virginia	One	73	West Virginia
Wisconsin	One Odd Years (Total 2)	75	Southern Wisconsin

DELEGATES ELECTED FOR 'EVEN' YEARS

State or Province	Number of Delegates	Area No.	Area Represented
Alaska	One	2	Alaska
Alberta/ N.W.T.	One	78	Alberta/ N.W.T.
Arizona	One	3	Arizona

California	Three Even Years (Total 6)	9	Mid-Southern
		7	Northern Interior
		8	San Diego/Imperial
Delaware	One	12	Delaware
Georgia	One	16	Georgia
Idaho	One	18	Idaho
Illinois	One Even Years (Total 3)	20	Northern
Indiana	One Even Years (Total 2)	23	Southern
Kansas	One	25	Kansas
Kentucky	One	26	Kentucky
Maine	One	28	Maine
Manitoba	One	80	Manitoba
Maryland	One	29	Maryland
Massachusetts	One Even Years (Total 2)	31	Western
Michigan	One Even Years (Total 3)	34	Western
Minnesota	One Even Years (Total 2)	35	Northern
Mississippi	One	37	Mississippi
Nebraska	One	41	Nebraska
New Brunswick/P.E.I.	One	81	New Brunswick/P.E.I.
New Hampshire	One	43	New Hampshire
New Jersey	One Even Years (Total 2)	45	Southern
New Mexico	One	46	New Mexico
New York	Two Even Years (Total 4)	50	Western
		48	Hudson/Mohawk/Berkshire
Ohio	Two Even Years (Total 4)	55	N.W. Ohio
		56	S.W. Ohio
Ontario	Two Even Years (Total 4)	84	Northeast
		86	Western
Oregon	One	58	Oregon
Puerto Rico	One	77	Puerto Rico
Quebec	Two Even Years (Total 4)	87	Southwestern
		90	Northwestern
Rhode Island	One	61	Rhode Island
South Carolina	One	62	South Carolina
South Dakota	One	63	South Dakota
Tennessee	One	64	Tennessee
Texas	Two Even Years (Total 4)	68	Southwestern/
		66	Northwestern
Vermont	One	70	Vermont
Washington	One Even Years (Total 2)	92	Washington East
Wisconsin	One Even Years (Total 2)	74	N. Wis./Upper Pen. Mich.
Wyoming	One	76	Wyoming

Appendix E

BYLAWS of The General Service Board of Alcoholics Anonymous, Inc.

As Bill W. explains in the introduction to this manual, the General Service Board (the trustees) was originally the Alcoholic Foundation, with bylaws as broad as the continent. When the corporate name was changed to General Service Board of A.A., new bylaws were needed which would reflect more clearly the scope and direction of Alcoholics Anonymous. The new bylaws, adopted in 1957, are the work of the late Bernard B. Smith, noted international lawyer, long a nonalcoholic trustee, chair of the board from 1951 to 1956. "Bern" Smith composed the bylaws out of his great love and respect for our Fellowship. They contain both the Twelve Steps and the Twelve Traditions. They are good reading for all A.A.s and friends of A.A.

(Adopted April 22, 1957, by the General Service Board following consideration by the General Service Conference of A.A.; amended 1962, 1966, 1968, 1970, 1971, 1972, 1978, 1985, 1991, 1992, 1994, 2006, 2007, 2008, and 2015.)

The General Service Board of Alcoholics Anonymous, Inc., now has but one purpose, that of serving the Fellowship of Alcoholics Anonymous. It is in effect an agency created and now designated by the Fellowship of Alcoholics Anonymous to maintain services for those who should be seeking, through Alcoholics Anonymous, the means for arresting the disease of alcoholism through the application to their own lives, in whole or in part, of the Twelve Steps which constitute the recovery program upon which the Fellowship of Alcoholics Anonymous is founded. These Twelve Steps are as follows:

1. We admitted we were powerless over alcohol—that our lives had become unmanageable.
2. Came to believe that a Power greater than ourselves could restore us to sanity.
3. Made a decision to turn our will and our lives over to the care of God as *we understood Him.*
4. Made a searching and fearless moral inventory of ourselves.
5. Admitted to God, to ourselves, and to another human being the exact nature of our wrongs.
6. Were entirely ready to have God remove all these defects of character.
7. Humbly asked Him to remove our shortcomings.

8. Made a list of all persons we had harmed, and became willing to make amends to them all.

9. Made direct amends to such people wherever possible, except when to do so would injure them or others.

10. Continued to take personal inventory and when we were wrong promptly admitted it.

11. Sought through prayer and meditation to improve our conscious contact with God *as we understood Him,* praying only for knowledge of His will for us and the power to carry that out.

12. Having had a spiritual awakening as the result of these steps, we tried to carry this message to alcoholics, and to practice these principles in all our affairs.

The General Service Board of Alcoholics Anonymous (hereinafter referred to as either the "General Service Board" or the "Board") claims no proprietary right in the recovery program, for these Twelve Steps, as all spiritual truths, may now be regarded as available to all mankind. However, because these Twelve Steps have proven to constitute an effective spiritual basis for life which, if followed, arrests the disease of alcoholism, the General Service Board asserts the negative right of preventing, so far as it may be within its power so to do, any modification, alteration, or extension of these Twelve Steps, except at the instance of the Fellowship of Alcoholics Anonymous in keeping with the Charter of the General Service Conference of Alcoholics Anonymous as the same may from time to time be amended (hereinafter referred to as the "Charter").

Members of the General Service Conference of Alcoholics Anonymous are hereinafter referred to as "Conference delegates."

The General Service Board in its deliberations and decisions shall be guided by the Twelve Traditions of Alcoholics Anonymous, hereinafter referred to as the "Traditions," which are as follows:

1. Our common welfare should come first; personal recovery depends upon A.A. unity.

2. For our group purpose there is but one ultimate authority—a loving God as He may express Himself in our group conscience. Our leaders are but trusted servants; they do not govern.

3. The only requirement for A.A. membership is a desire to stop drinking.

4. Each group should be autonomous except in matters affecting other groups or A.A. as a whole.

5. Each group has but one primary purpose—to carry its message to the alcoholic who still suffers.

6. An A.A. group ought never endorse, finance or lend the A.A. name to any related facility or outside enterprise, lest problems of money, property and prestige divert us from our primary purpose.

7. Every A.A. group ought to be fully self-supporting, declining outside contributions.

8. Alcoholics Anonymous should remain forever nonprofessional, but our service centers may employ special workers.

9. A.A., as such, ought never be organized; but we may create service boards or committees directly responsible to those they serve.

10. Alcoholics Anonymous has no opinion on outside issues; hence the A.A. name ought never be drawn into public controversy.

11. Our public relations policy is based on attraction rather than promotion; we need always maintain personal anonymity at the level of press, radio, and films.

12. Anonymity is the spiritual foundation of all our Traditions, ever reminding us to place principles before personalities.

The General Service Board shall use its best efforts to insure that these Twelve Traditions are maintained, for it is regarded by the Fellowship of Alcoholics Anonymous as the custodian of these Traditions and, accordingly, it shall not itself nor, so far as it is within its power so to do, permit others to modify, alter, or amplify these Traditions, except in keeping with the provisions of the Charter.

The General Service Board also shall be guided by the spirit of the Twelve Concepts of Alcoholics Anonymous, hereinafter referred to as the "Concepts" which, in their short form, are as follows:

1. Final responsibility and ultimate authority for A.A. World Services should always reside in the collective conscience of our whole Fellowship.

2. The General Service Conference of A.A. has become, for nearly every practical purpose, the active voice and the effective conscience of our whole Society in its world affairs.

3. To insure effective leadership, we should endow each element of A.A.—the Conference, the General Service Board and its service corporations, staffs, committees, and executives—with a traditional "Right of Decision."

4. At all responsible levels, we ought to maintain a traditional "Right of Participation," allowing a voting representation in reasonable proportion to the responsibility that each must discharge.

5. Throughout our structure, a traditional "Right of Appeal" ought to prevail, so that minority opinion will be heard and personal grievances receive careful consideration.

6. The Conference recognizes that the chief initiative and active responsibility in most world service matters should be exercised by the trustee members of the Conference acting as the General Service Board.

7. The Charter and bylaws of the General Service Board are legal instruments, empowering the trustees to manage and conduct world service affairs. The Conference Charter is not a legal document; it relies upon tradition and the A.A. purse for final effectiveness.

8. The trustees are the principal planners and administrators of overall policy and finance. They have custodial oversight of the separately incorporated and constantly active services, exercising this through their ability to elect all the directors of these entities.

9. Good service leadership at all levels is indispensable for our future functioning and safety. Primary world service leadership, once exercised by the founders, must necessarily be assumed by the trustees.

10. Every service responsibility should be matched by an equal service authority, with the scope of such authority well defined.

11. The trustees should always have the best possible committees, corporate service direc-

tors, executives, staffs and consultants. Composition, qualifications, induction procedures, and rights and duties will always be matters of serious concern.

12. The Conference shall observe the spirit of the A.A. tradition, taking care that it never becomes the seat of perilous wealth or power; that sufficient operating funds and reserve be its prudent financial principle; that it place none of its members in a position of unqualified authority over others; that it reach all important decisions by discussion, vote, and, whenever possible, by substantial unanimity; that its actions never be personally punitive nor an incitement to public controversy; that it never perform acts of government, and that, like the Society it serves, it will always remain democratic in thought and action.

The membership of the General Service Board shall consist of the trustees. Each trustee shall automatically become a member upon qualifying as a trustee, and shall automatically cease to be a member upon ceasing to be a trustee of the General Service Board. The sole reason for constituting trustees members is in order to comply with the laws of the State of New York, which require a membership corporation to be composed of members. Accordingly, except where distinctions must be made under these bylaws or as a matter of law, the words "member" and "trustee" shall be employed in these bylaws collectively.

As a condition of election as a member and election as a trustee of the General Service Board, each person shall before qualifying to serve as a member and trustee, execute an appropriate instrument addressed to the General Service Board of Alcoholics Anonymous, stating that such person agrees to comply with and be bound by all the terms and provisions of these bylaws.

Member trustees are divided into two categories, viz., nonalcoholics and ex-alcoholics. The use of the term "entire membership" herein refers to the total number of member trustees entitled to vote that the General Service Board would have if there were no vacancies. The number of member trustees constituting the entire membership shall be twenty-one. Except as otherwise provided in these bylaws, the nonalcoholic member trustees shall be seven (7) in number and are referred to in these bylaws as Class A member trustees. Except as otherwise provided in these bylaws, the ex-alcoholic member trustees shall be fourteen (14) in number and are referred to in these bylaws as Class B member trustees.

Class A member trustees shall be persons who are not and have not been afflicted by the disease of alcoholism and who express a profound faith in the recovery program upon which the Fellowship of Alcoholics Anonymous is founded. Class A member trustees shall be ineligible to serve for more than two successive three-year terms, to be confirmed annually, except that in order to provide the Board with a sufficient degree of flexibility, the chair of the General Service Board may recommend to the member trustees that a Class A member trustee be permitted to serve for a third successive three-year term and the member trustees, acting as members, have the authority to permit a Class A member trustee to serve a third successive three-year term if in their judgment such service is in the best interest of the Fellowship. A Class A member trustee who, at the expiration of the maximum period of time he or she is eligible to serve as a member trustee (namely, three successive three-year terms), is serving or newly elected as chair, shall continue to serve as a Class A member trustee during his or her term as chair, even if such service during his or her term as chair will expand the number of Class A member trustees then serving to eight (8), and upon the date that the member trustee ceases to serve as chair, such member trustee shall cease to be a member trustee. The foregoing limitation with respect to the maximum term of service of Class A member trustees shall not be applicable to those Class A member trustees who were serving as such during the 1993 General Service Conference.

Except as otherwise provided in these bylaws, there shall be fourteen (14) Class B member trustees. These Class B member trustees are designated as ex-alcoholic, only because in the common speech of man an ex-alcoholic is an individual who at one time imbibed alcoholic beverages excessively and uncontrollably, but who does not now imbibe at all. For the purposes of these bylaws, an ex-alcoholic shall be referred to as an "alcoholic" which means within the terminology of the Fellowship of Alcoholics Anonymous those individuals who have arrested their drinking and are living so far as possible within the concepts of the Twelve Steps which constitute the recovery program.

While in these bylaws we refer to "member trustees" in order to comply with the laws of the State of New York, members shall elect the trustees. All member trustees shall be elected or re-elected at an annual meeting of the members of the General Service Board. Except as otherwise provided in these bylaws, Class B member trustees, shall be ineligible to serve for more than four successive annual terms, following which, such member trustee shall be ineligible for any further service as a member trustee. A Class B member trustee who, at the expiration of the maximum period of time he or she is eligible to serve as a member trustee as set forth above, is serving or newly elected as chair, shall continue to serve as a Class B member trustee during his or her term as chair, even if such service during his or her term as chair will expand the number of Class B member trustees then serving to fifteen (15), and upon the date that the member trustee ceases to serve as chair, such member trustee shall cease to be a member trustee. Class B trustees shall be divided into three categories: eight (8) shall be subclassified as "regional trustees"; four (4) shall be subclassified as "general service trustees"; and two (2) shall be subclassified as trustees-at-large. One (1) trustee-at-large shall be from Canada and one (1) from the United States. Class B regional trustees are expected to contribute their time basically during the four periods of the years, viz., with respect to the first, third, and fourth quarterly meetings of the trustees of the General Service Board, each three-day period ending on the day of the respective quarterly meeting; and, with respect to the second quarterly meeting of the trustees of the General Service Board, regional trustees are expected to attend the second quarterly meeting, which occurs on the Saturday immediately following the annual General Service Conference, as well as the week-long General Service Conference. In addition, Class B regional trustees are expected to advise the Board with respect to regional views and opinions regarding policy matters. Class B general service trustees, in addition to providing services at the same time as Class B regional trustees, are expected to provide continued service to the Board during all of the times of the year. Although the trustees are divided into two classes, viz., Class A and Class B, and, although Class B trustees are further subcategorized as "regional trustees," general service trustees," and "trustees-at-large," the nature of the fiduciary responsibilities of each trustee to the General

Service Board is uniform, under the laws of New York State, and these bylaws, regardless of such distinctions.

In the event that any member trustee shall resign, die, retire, be removed, become disqualified, or shall be otherwise unable to serve, the trustees may, at any regular or special meeting of the Board of Trustees, elect a new member trustee to fill such vacancy, or, alternatively, permit such a vacancy to continue until the next annual meeting of the members of the General Service Board. A third alternative, with respect to Class B regional member trustee vacancies occasioned by resignation, death, retirement, removal, or disqualification, is to permit the vacancy to remain unfilled for the remainder of the four year commitment, and allow regional coverage to be provided by the trustee-at-large or the regional trustee from an adjacent region, unless a region decides that a new regional member trustee should be elected.

Any member trustee elected by the Board of Trustees to fill a vacancy shall hold office until the next annual meeting of the members of the General Service Board and until the election and qualification of his or her successor. In the event that any such vacancy occurs, and the Board elects to permit the vacancy to continue until the next annual meeting of the members of the General Service Board, a nominee shall be selected in accordance with the Nominating Committee's procedures for determining trustee nominees, and such nominee shall commence service as a member trustee when, and if, elected and qualified at the next annual meeting of members, in the usual course of business. Any Class A member trustee elected by the members of the General Service Board to fill such a vacancy shall serve a three-year term and shall be eligible to serve for the same number of terms as any other Class A trustee. Any period of time served by a Class A member trustee by virtue of being elected by the Board of Trustees to fill a vacancy in between annual meetings of the members shall not count in determining a Class A trustee's total term of service. However, when the vacancy being filled is that of a Class B regional trustee, the maximum term of service of such successor member trustee shall be limited to that number of one-year terms which will result in the term of service of the successor member trustee ending at the same time as the term of the replaced member trustee would have ended if no vacancy had occurred and the replaced member trustee had served four successive one-year terms. A Class B successor member trustee who, at the expiration of the maximum period of time he or she is eligible to serve as a member trustee as set forth above, is serving or newly elected as chair, shall continue to serve as a Class B member trustee during his or her term as chair, even if such service during his or her term as chair will expand the number of Class B member trustees then serving to fifteen (15), and upon the date that the member trustee ceases to serve as chair, such member trustee shall cease to be a member trustee.

Notwithstanding the foregoing, Class B member trustees, as well as Class A member trustees, are expected, subject only to the laws of the State of New York and to these bylaws, at the request of the Conference of Alcoholics Anonymous, to resign their trusteeships and memberships, even though their terms of office as member trustees may not have expired.

The General Service Board, by a vote of at least ¾ of the total Board of Trustees, may remove a trustee member for cause, as determined in their sole discretion; and the member trustees, when acting in their capacity as members of the Corporation, by similar ¾ vote of the entire membership, may remove a trustee with or without cause, if it is determined that such removal is in the best interests of Alcoholics Anonymous as a whole.

Proposed new member trustees to the General Service Board shall be nominated by a nominating committee designated by the chair. No person shall become a member trustee of the General Service Board until all Conference delegates have been polled by mail or at an annual meeting of the Conference of Alcoholics Anonymous, as the Board of Trustees may determine. If a majority of the Conference delegates disapprove the election of such proposed member trustee, such person shall not be eligible as a member trustee, and the member trustees shall, unless there is a 100% vote of member trustees present at a meeting of members to the contrary, have no power to elect such person as a member trustee. If, however, a majority of the Conference delegates do not disapprove the election of such proposed member trustee, such person may be elected as a member and trustee of the General Service Board upon a vote of a majority of the member trustees at a meeting of the members.

The Board of Trustees shall have all the powers provided for in these bylaws and as are vested in a Board of Directors under the laws of the State of New York.

The members of the Board, subject to the laws of the State of New York, are expected to exercise the powers vested in them by law in a manner consonant with the faith that permeates and guides the Fellowship of Alcoholics Anonymous, inspired by the Twelve Steps of A.A., in accordance with the Twelve Traditions, and in keeping with the Charter of the Conference of Alcoholics Anonymous.

The General Service Board may set up new corporate bodies to serve the purposes of Alcoholics Anonymous, provided the General Service Board shall own all of the capital stock of such corporate bodies, and if such corporate body is a membership corporation, its structure shall be in keeping with that of the General Service Board of Alcoholics Anonymous. Manifestly, the General Service Board is expected to refrain from forming any new corporate body if a majority of the Conference delegates shall disapprove of its formation.

In order that the General Service Board may more effectively serve the purposes for which it is formed, the Board of Trustees shall, at its 2nd quarterly meeting, or at any other meeting, if a vacancy shall occur, elect a chair, a first vice-chair, second vice-chair, secretary, and a treasurer. The chair shall have those duties generally attributable by law and custom to a president under the laws of the State of New York, with such other greater or lesser duties as may from time to time be determined by the Board of Trustees. No employee of the General Service Board may serve as the chair. The term of the chair shall hereafter be not more than four (4) successive annual terms. The foregoing limitation with respect to the term of chair shall not be applicable to the chair serving as such at the expiration of the year 1966. A member trustee who, at the expiration of the maximum period of time he or she is eligible to serve as a member trustee as set forth above, is serving or newly elected as chair, shall continue to serve as a member trustee during his or her term as chair, even if such service during his or her term as chair will expand the number of member trustees then serving on the Board to twenty-two (22), and upon the date that the member trustee ceases to serve as chair, such member trustee shall cease to be a member trustee. Similarly, an individual who has served the maximum period of time he or she is eligible to serve as a member trustee may be elected as chair and shall serve as a member trustee during his or her term as chair, even if such service during his or her term as chair will expand the number of member trustees then serving on the Board to twenty-two (22), and upon the date that the member trustee ceases to serve as chair, such member trustee shall cease to be a member trustee. The first and second vice-chairs shall in their respective order perform the duties of the chair in the event of the chair's absence or disability.

The Chair of the General Service Board shall appoint the Assistant Treasurer of the Board, the Assistant Secretary of the Board, and shall appoint all other officers, if any, other than those elected by the Board of Trustees pursuant to these bylaws, each subject to approval by the Board of Trustees at the 2nd quarterly Board meeting, or at any other meeting of the Board when necessary to fill an existing vacancy; and the Chair shall also appoint members of the committees of the corporation, subject to approval by the Board of Trustees, at the 3rd quarterly Board meeting, or at any other meeting of the Board when necessary to fill an existing vacancy.

In order to render unto the law that which the law requires, the chair shall be president, and the first and second vice-chairs shall be the first and second vice-presidents respectively, but they shall at no time employ such titles, except as may be required for the execution of legal documents or by reason of other provisions of the law.

The secretary, assistant secretary, treasurer, and assistant treasurer shall similarly perform those duties generally attributed by law and custom to such offices with such other greater or lesser duties as may from time to time be determined by the Board of Trustees.

The second quarterly meeting of the Trustees of the Board shall take place on Saturday, immediately following the close of the General Service Conference. The agenda shall provide for a temporary adjournment of the Board meeting so that the annual meeting of members for the election of trustees may be convened. As required by the Not-For-Profit Corporation Law (the "NPCL"), during the annual meeting of members, the Board of Trustees shall present to members an annual report for the most recently ended fiscal year of the General Service Board (the Board has adopted the calendar year as its fiscal year). The annual report shall be certified by the General Service Board's independent public accountant or otherwise verified as provided in Section 519 of the NPCL, and shall contain at a minimum all information required to be included therein by the NPCL. The meeting of the Board of Trustees shall be reconvened, following the adjournment of the annual meeting of members.

The first, third and fourth quarterly meetings of the Board of Trustees shall take place on the fifth Monday following the close of a calendar quarter, with the proviso that special meetings may be convened at the request of one-third of the Board of Trustees or at the request of the chair. The chair may also postpone a regular meeting to such date as the chair may determine, not later, however, than one month prior to the date of the next scheduled meeting, and at the request of the majority of the Board of Trustees, one or more regular meetings may be eliminated. All meetings of members and trustees shall take place in the City and County of New York, unless at a meeting of the Board, the trustees shall decide to hold a future meeting or meetings outside of the City of New York. The actual place and time of day of each meeting shall be determined by the chair.

At least ten days', but not to exceed fifty days', notice of the date, time and place of all meetings of members shall be given by first class mail, facsimile, email or hand delivery, signed by the chair or, at the chair's request, by the secretary or assistant secretary. Notice of a special meeting of members also shall state the purpose of the meeting. At least ten days', but not to exceed fifty days', notice of the date, time and place of all meetings of the Board of Trustees shall be given by first class mail, facsimile, email or hand delivery, signed by the chair or, at the chair's request, by the secretary or assistant secretary. The chair, at the time of the sending of notices, shall determine the order in which matters shall be dealt with at all meetings, and the chair, or a majority of the member trustees present at any meeting, may always decide to modify such order.

Whenever in the judgment of one-third of the member trustees present at a meeting a decision to take any action involves a matter of principle or basic policy and in the judgment of at least one-third of the member trustees a delay in arriving at a decision will not adversely affect the Fellowship of Alcoholics Anonymous, the matter shall be submitted to a mail vote of Conference delegates, and if a majority of the Conference delegates votes against the taking of such action, then the Board of Trustees will be expected to refrain from deciding to take such action.

Whenever a mail vote is taken of Conference delegates, at least two weeks' notice shall be given, and the vote shall be determined in keeping with an analysis of such vote by the chair and secretary, or in their absence, by a vice-chair and assistant secretary, at the end of such two-week period. An announcement of the result of such vote shall thereupon be mailed by the secretary or assistant secretary to Conference delegates and to member trustees.

At all meetings of member trustees, whether meetings of the members or the Board of Trustees, two-fifths of the member trustees shall be sufficient to constitute a quorum for the conduct of the affairs of the General Service Board, and the vote of a majority of the member trustees present at any meeting at which there is a quorum shall, except as otherwise may be provided by these bylaws or by statute, constitute a decision of the membership or of the Board of Trustees, as the case may be. If at any meeting there is less than a quorum present, a majority of those present may adjourn the meeting to a time to be fixed by those present, without further notice to any absent member trustee.

The Board may, by resolution adopted by a majority of the entire Board, designate from among its members such Committees of the Board as it may deem appropriate from time to time, including, among others, a nominating committee. Such Committees shall be formed in keeping with the needs of service by resolution of the Board, with such powers as the Board may regard as then necessary, except as limited by applicable law. Committees other than Committees of the Board shall be committees of the corporation, and, as provided by the law, the members of such committees shall be appointed or elected in the same manner as officers of the corporation, and, generally, the provisions of law applicable to officers shall apply to such committee members.. Committees may be created, discharged, eliminated, replaced, their powers expanded or limited, as the Board may from time to time by appropriate resolution determine. The law provides that no committee shall be empowered to act on the following: (1) the submission to members of any action requiring members' approval under the NPCL; (2) the filling of vacancies in the Board of Trustees or in any committee; (3) the fixing of compensation of the directors for serving on the Board or on any committee (if applicable); (4) the amendment or repeal of the bylaws or the adoption of new bylaws; (5) the amendment or repeal of any resolution of the Board which by its terms shall not be so amendable or repealable.

No member of the General Service Board shall at any time have any right, title or interest in and to the funds or property of the General Service Board. Should at any time in the future the General Service Board be dissolved, all of the remaining assets and property of the Corporation shall, after paying or making provision for the payment of all the liabilities of the Corporation and for the necessary expenses thereof, be applied as determined by the Board of Trustees and as approved by a Justice of the Supreme Court of the State of New York, for the charitable or educational purposes for which the Corporation is organized by distributing such property and assets for the furtherance of the work of institutions with similar purposes and objects which shall qualify under Section 501(c)(3) of the Code or corresponding section of any future Federal tax code. In the event of voluntary dissolution, such institutions shall be selected in the discretion of the trustees, subject to approval of the plan of dissolution and distribution of assets upon an order of the Justice of the Supreme Court of the State of New York. In no event shall any of such assets be distributed to any member, trustee, director, or officer, or any private individual.

The Corporation may, to the fullest extent authorized by law, indemnify any present or former officers or trustees of the Corporation or the personal representatives thereof, made or threatened to be made a party in any civil or criminal action or proceeding by reason of the fact that he or she, his or her testator or intestate is or was a trustee or officer of the Corporation, or served with any other corporation, partnership, joint venture, trust, employee-benefit plan, or other enterprise in any capacity at the request of the Corporation, against judgments, fines (including excise taxes assessed on such a person in connection with service to an employee-benefit plan), amounts paid in settlement and reasonable expenses, including attorneys' fees, actually and necessarily incurred as a result of such action or proceeding or any appeal therein.

Expenses (including attorneys' fees) incurred in defending a civil or criminal action or proceeding may, to the fullest extent authorized by law, be paid by the Corporation in advance of the final disposition of such action or proceeding upon receipt of an undertaking by or on behalf of such trustee or officer to repay such amount as, and to the extent, the person receiving the advancement is ultimately found not to be entitled to indemnification or, where indemnification is granted, to the extent the expenses so advanced by the Corporation exceed the indemnification to which he or she is entitled. The foregoing right of indemnification and advancement of expenses shall not be deemed exclusive of any other rights to which any person, his or her testator or intestate may be entitled apart from this provision provided that no indemnification may be made to or on behalf of any trustee or officer if a judgment or other final adjudication adverse to the trustee or officer establishes that his or her acts were committed in bad faith or were the result of active and deliberate dishonesty and were material to the cause of action so adjudicated, or that he or she personally gained in fact a financial profit or other advantage to which he or she was not legally entitled. Nothing contained in this provision shall affect any rights to indemnification to which corporate personnel other than the trustees and officers may be entitled by contract or otherwise under the law.

The Certificate of Incorporation of the General Service Board and these bylaws may be amended by the affirmative vote of 75% of all the members of the Board of Trustees. When amending the Certificate of Incorporation, or when considering an amendment to the bylaws that affects the rights of corporate members, as such, the trustees must act in their capacity as members of the corporation. In keeping with the spirit and principles of the Fellowship of Alcoholics Anonymous, the Board is expected, although not legally required, to submit any amendment or amendments of the Certificate of Incorporation and of these bylaws to Conference delegates, either by mail or at the annual meeting of the Conference of Alcoholics Anonymous as the Board of Trustees may determine, and if a majority of such delegates disapproves of such amendment or amendments, the member trustees are expected to refrain from proceeding therewith, except when such amendment or amendments are otherwise required by law. Where, however, an amendment or amendments to the Certificate of Incorporation are submitted to Conference delegates and are not disapproved as aforesaid, such amendment or amendments shall require the affirmative vote of only a majority of the members present at a meeting of members provided that the votes cast in favor of such action are at least equal to the quorum. Where an amendment or amendments to the bylaws are submitted to Conference delegates and are not disapproved as aforesaid, the amendment or amendments shall require the affirmative vote of only a majority of member trustees present at a meeting, provided that when considering an amendment to the bylaws that affects the rights of corporate members, as such, the member trustees must act in their capacity as members of the corporation.

Index

These are the changes made to the 2016-2018 edition of *The A.A. Service Manual/Twelve Concepts for World Service,* and the origin of those changes.

Page	Changes	Source of Change
Copyright Page	Update	Publishing Dept.
Table of Contents and Index	Update pagination and/or add new entries, as needed.	Publishing Dept.
Various pages	Update any page reference (e.g. "See page_") affected by shifts in pagination.	Publishing Dept.
S10	Update footnote #8	Publishing Dept.
S18	Update Treatment and Accessibilities Committees — G.S.C. Chart	Publishing Dept.
S19	Add Definition of *The A.A. Service Manual/Twelve Concepts for World Service* to Glossary of Terms.	Publishing Dept.
S22	Add language from existing language to The Third Legacy Procedure Chart after 4th ballot.	Publishing Dept.
S34	Revise text in the section, **District Information.**	Publishing Dept.
S41, S76, S77, S80, S87-S93	Remove/Revise text regarding A.A. Grapevine.	Grapevine Board
S61, S62	Revise name to read, TREATMENT and ACCESSIBILITIES	Publishing Dept.
S67	Update schedule of regional elections.	Publishing Dept.
S72, S73	Insert section describing "Local Forums."	66th G.S.C.
S80	Update G.S.O. Structure Chart, as needed.	G.S.O. General Manager
S84-86, S90	Update publication lists.	Publishing Dept.
Concepts Copyright page	Update, as needed.	Publishing Dept.
58	Remove text from the Concept Eleven essay from Twelve Concepts for World Service.	66th G.S.C.
59	That endnote 10 be revised to read, "Due to an Advisory Action of the 66th A.A. General Service Conference, two paragraphs have been removed from the published version of Concept XI essay. However, these paragraphs are available, upon request, from G.S.O. Archives."	66th G.S.C.
Footnotes Pages 26, 33, 59, 73	Update, as needed.	Publishing Dept.
73	Remove endnote 4	66th G.S.C.

TWELVE CONCEPTS FOR WORLD SERVICE

by Bill W.

*As adopted by the 12th Annual
General Service Conference of Alcoholics Anonymous
on April 26, 1962*

Published by
GENERAL SERVICE OFFICE
of
ALCOHOLICS ANONYMOUS®

475 Riverside Drive
New York, NY 10115

Mail address: P.O. Box 459
Grand Central Station
New York, NY 10163

1st Printing 1962
24th Printing 1993
25th Printing 1996
26th Printing 1997
27th Printing 1999
28th Printing 2001
29th Printing 2002
30th Printing 2003
31st Printing 2004
32nd Printing 2005
33rd Printing 2006
34th Printing 2007
35th Printing 2008
36th Printing 2009
37th Printing 2010
38th Printing 2011
39th Printing 2012
40th Printing 2013
41st Printing 2014
42nd Printing 2015
43rd Printing 2016

PREFACE

The "Twelve Concepts for World Service" were written by Bill W. in 1962. His introduction to that first printing, following this preface, explains its purpose, as relevant today as at that time.

Over the years the size of the Fellowship and the responsibilities of its service entities have grown immensely. Therefore, some details of the original text have become outdated and were changed in editions of the Concepts since that time, and a number of bracketed inserts were added.

Following the recommendations of an ad hoc committee of the A.A. General Service Board, the 1985 General Service Conference recommended that future publication of the Concepts in "The A.A. Service Manual" and the booklet "Twelve Concepts for World Service" be in the original 1962 version, with required factual changes provided as numbered footnotes at the end of each chapter. The only exceptions are certain footnotes written by Bill W. in the years following the first appearance of the Concepts: these are marked by asterisks that appear on the same pages as the text they refer to.

A "short form" of the Concepts was approved by the 1971 General Service Conference, and in 1974 it was approved for inclusion in *The A.A. Service Manual*. It now appears in the Bylaws of the General Service Board, printed in the manual, and also precedes the introduction to the Twelve Concepts.

General Service Office
September 1985

The Twelve Concepts (Short Form)

I   Final responsibility and ultimate authority for A.A. world services should always reside in the collective conscience of our whole Fellowship

II   The General Service Conference of A.A. has become, for nearly every practical purpose, the active voice and the effective conscience of our whole Society in its world affairs

III   To insure effective leadership, we should endow each element of A.A.—the Conference, the General Service Board and its service corporations, staffs, committees, and executives—with a traditional "Right of Decision"

IV   At all responsible levels, we ought to maintain a traditional "Right of Participation," allowing a voting representation in reasonable proportion to the responsibility that each must discharge

V   Throughout our structure, a traditional "Right of Appeal" ought to prevail, so that minority opinion will be heard and personal grievances receive careful consideration

VI   The Conference recognizes that the chief initiative and active responsibility in most world service matters should be exercised by the trustee members of the Conference acting as the General Service Board

VII   The Charter and Bylaws of the General Service Board are legal instruments, empowering the trustees to manage and conduct world service affairs. The Conference Charter is not a legal document; it relies upon tradition and the A.A. purse for final effectiveness

VIII   The trustees are the principal planners and administrators of overall policy and finance. They have custodial oversight of the separately incorporated and constantly active services, exercising this through their ability to elect all the directors of these entities

IX   Good service leadership at all levels is indispensable for our future functioning and safety. Primary world service leadership, once exercised by the founders, must necessarily be assumed by the trustees

X   Every service responsibility should be matched by an equal service authority, with the scope of such authority well defined

XI   The trustees should always have the best possible committees, corporate service directors, executives, staffs, and consultants. Composition, qualifications, induction procedures, and rights and duties will always be matters of serious concern

XII   The Conference shall observe the spirit of A.A. tradition, taking care that it never becomes the seat of perilous wealth or power; that sufficient operating funds and reserve be its prudent financial principle; that it place none of its members in a position of unqualified authority over others; that it reach all important decisions by discussion, vote, and, whenever possible, by substantial unanimity; that its actions never be personally punitive nor an incitement to public controversy; that it never perform acts of government, and that, like the Society it serves, it will always remain democratic in thought and action

The Twelve Concepts (Long Form)

I   The final responsibility and ultimate authority for A.A. world services should always reside in the collective conscience of our whole Fellowship.

II   When, in 1955, the A.A. groups confirmed the permanent charter for their General Service Conference, they thereby delegated to the Conference complete authority for the active maintenance of our world services and thereby made the Conference—excepting for any change in the Twelve Traditions or in Article 12 of the Conference Charter—the actual voice and the effective conscience for our whole Society.

III   As a traditional means of creating and maintaining a clearly defined working relation between the groups, the Conference, the A.A. General Service Board and its several service corporations, staffs, committees and executives, and of thus insuring their effective leadership, it is here suggested that we endow each of these elements of world service with a traditional "Right of Decision."

IV   Throughout our Conference structure, we ought to maintain at all responsible levels a traditional "Right of Participation," taking care that each classification or group of our world servants shall be allowed a voting representation in reasonable proportion to the responsibility that each must discharge.

V   Throughout our world service structure, a traditional "Right of Appeal" ought to prevail, thus assuring us that minority opinion will be heard and that petitions for the redress of personal grievances will be carefully considered.

VI   On behalf of A.A. as a whole, our General Service Conference has the principal responsibility for the maintenance of our world services, and it traditionally has the final decision respecting large matters of general policy and finance. But the Conference also recognizes that the chief initiative and the active responsibility in most of these matters should be exercised primarily by the Trustee members of the Conference when they act among themselves as the General Service Board of Alcoholics Anonymous.

VII   The Conference recognizes that the Charter and the Bylaws of the General Service Board are legal instruments: that the Trustees are thereby fully empowered to manage and conduct all of the world service affairs of Alcoholics Anonymous. It is further understood that the Conference Charter itself is not a legal document: that it relies instead upon the force of tradition and the power of the A.A. purse for its final effectiveness.

VIII   The Trustees of the General Service Board act in two primary capacities: (a) With respect to the larger matters of over-all policy and finance, they are the principal planners and administrators. They and their primary committees directly manage these affairs. (b) But with respect to our separately incorporated and constantly active services, the relation of the Trustees is mainly that of full stock ownership and of custodial oversight which they exercise through their ability to elect all directors of these entities.

IX   Good service leaders, together with sound and appropriate methods of choosing them, are at all levels indispensable for our future functioning and safety. The primary world service leadership once exercised by the founders of A.A. must necessarily be assumed by the Trustees of the General Service Board of Alcoholics Anonymous.

X Every service responsibility should be matched by an equal service authority— the scope of such authority to be always well defined whether by tradition, by resolution, by specific job description or by appropriate charters and bylaws.

XI While the Trustees hold final responsibility for A.A.'s world service administration, they should always have the assistance of the best possible standing committees, corporate service directors, executives, staffs, and consultants. Therefore the composition of these underlying committees and service boards, the personal qualifications of their members, the manner of their induction into service, the systems of their rotation, the way in which they are related to each other, the special rights and duties of our executives, staffs, and consultants, together with a proper basis for the financial compensation of these special workers, will always be matters for serious care and concern.

XII General Warranties of the Conference: in all its proceedings, the General Service Conference shall observe the spirit of the A.A. Tradition, taking great care that the Conference never becomes the seat of perilous wealth or power; that sufficient operating funds, plus an ample reserve, be its prudent financial principle; that none of the Conference Members shall ever be placed in a position of unqualified authority over any of the others; that all important decisions be reached by discussion, vote, and, whenever possible, by substantial unanimity; that no Conference action ever be personally punitive or an incitement to public controversy; that, though the Conference may act for the service of Alcoholics Anonymous, it shall never perform any acts of government; and that, like the Society of Alcoholics Anonymous which it serves, the Conference itself will always remain democratic in thought and action.

CONTENTS

Introduction

The "Twelve Concepts for World Service" to be described in this Manual are an interpretation of A.A.'s world service structure. They reveal the evolution by which it has arrived in its present form, and they detail the experience and reasoning on which our operation stands today. These Concepts therefore aim to record the "why" of our service structure in such a fashion that the highly valuable experience of the past, and the lessons we have drawn from that experience, can never be forgotten or lost.

Quite rightly, each new generation of A.A. world servants will be eager to make operational improvements. Unforeseen flaws in the present structure will doubtless show up later on. New service needs and problems will arise that may make structural changes necessary. Such alterations should certainly be effected, and these contingencies squarely met.

Yet we should always realize that change does not necessarily spell progress. We are sure that each new group of workers in world service will be tempted to try all sorts of innovations that may often produce little more than a painful repetition of earlier mistakes. Therefore it will be an important objective of these Concepts to forestall such repetitions by holding the experiences of the past clearly before us. And if mistaken departures are nevertheless made, these Concepts may then provide a ready means of safe return to an operating balance that might otherwise take years of floundering to rediscover.

There will also be seen in these Concepts a number of principles which have already become traditional to our services, but which have never been clearly articulated and reduced to writing. For example: the "Right of Decision" gives our service leaders a proper discretion and latitude; the "Right of Participation" gives each world servant a voting status commensurate with his (or her) responsibility, and "Participation" further guarantees that each service board or committee will always possess the several elements and talents that will insure effective functioning. The "Right of Appeal" protects and encourages minority opinion; and the "Right of Petition" makes certain that grievances can be heard, and properly acted upon. These general principles can of course be used to good effect throughout our entire structure.

In other sections, the Concepts carefully delineate those important traditions, customs, relationships and legal arrangements that weld the General Service Board into a working harmony with its primary committees and with its corporate arms of active service — A.A. World Services, Inc. and The A.A. Grapevine, Inc. This is the substance of the structural framework that governs the internal working situation at A.A.'s World Headquarters.

Concern has been expressed lest the detailed portrayal of our internal structure might not later harden down into such a firm tradition or gospel that necessary changes would be impossible to make. Nothing could stray further from the intent of these Concepts. The future advocates of structural change need only make out a strong case for their recommendations — a case convincing to both the Trustees and to the Conference. This is no more than would be required for the transaction and passage of any other important piece of A.A. business. Save for an exception or two, it is noteworthy that the Conference Charter itself can be easily amended.

Perhaps one more precaution ought to be observed when a proposed structural change is to be specially far-reaching. In such an event, the alteration should for an appropriate period be labeled as "experimental." On final approval, an alteration of this character could be entered into a special section of this Manual which might be entitled "AMENDMENTS." This would leave the original draft of the Twelve Concepts intact as an evidential record of our former experience. Then it could always be clearly seen by our future service workers just what did happen and why.

In other chapters great emphasis is laid on the need for a high order of personal leadership, on the desirability of careful induction methods for all incoming personnel, and upon the necessity for the best possible personal relations between those who work in our services. The Concepts try to design a structure in which all may labor to good effect, with a minimum of friction. This is accomplished by so relating our servants to their work and to each other that the chances of personal conflict will be minimized.

In the A.A. services we have always had to choose between the authoritarian setup, whereby one group or one person is set in unqualified authority over another, and the democratic concept which calls for "checks and balances" that would prevent unqualified authority from running unrestrained. The first approach is that of the "institutional" or authoritarian type. The second is the method of "constitutional" governments and many large business corporations in their upper echelons.

Well knowing our own propensities for power driving, it is natural and even imperative that our service concepts be based on the system of "checks and balances." We have had to face the fact that we usually try to enlarge our own authority and prestige when we are in the saddle. But when we are not, we strenuously resist a heavy-handed management wherein someone else holds the reins. I'm the more sure of this because I possess these traits myself.

Consequently ideas like the following pervade the Concepts: "No group or individual should be set in *unqualified* authority over another," "Large, active and *dissimilar* operations should be separately incorporated and managed, each with its own staff, equipment and working capital," "We ought to avoid undue concentration of money or personal influence in any service group or entity," "At each level of service, authority should be equal to responsibility," "Double-headed executive direction should be avoided." These and other similar provisions define working relations that can be friendly and yet efficient. They would especially restrain our tendency to concentrate money and power, this being nearly always the underlying (though not always the conscious) motivation of our recurrent passion for the "consolidation" of world service entities.

Because of the large range of topics which had to be included, these Concepts have been difficult to organize and write. Since each Concept is really a *group of related principles,* the kind of abbreviated statements used in A.A.'s "Twelve Steps and Twelve Traditions" have not been possible. However, these Concepts do represent the best summation that I am able to make after more than twenty years experience in the creation of our service structure and in the conduct of A.A.'s world affairs. Like the earlier written "Twelve Steps and Twelve Traditions," and the Conference Charter, these service principles are also the outcome of long reflection and extensive consultation.

It is much to be hoped that these Twelve Concepts will become a welcome addition to our "Third Legacy Manual of A.A. World Service," and that they will prove to be a reliable working guide in the years that lie ahead.

Concept I

The final responsibility and the ultimate authority for A.A. world services should always reside in the collective conscience of our whole Fellowship.

The A.A. groups today hold ultimate responsibility and final authority for our world services — those special elements of over-all service activity which make it possible for our Society to function as a whole. The groups assumed that responsibility at the St. Louis International Convention of 1955. There, on behalf of Dr. Bob, the Trustees and A.A.'s old-time leaders, I made the transfer of world service responsibility to our entire Fellowship.

Why, and by what authority was this done? There were reasons of stark necessity for it, and there were further reasons which have to do with A.A.'s fundamental structure and tradition.

By the year 1948 our necessities had become clear enough. Ten years earlier — in 1938 — helped by dedicated friends, Dr. Bob and I had commenced work upon a world service structure. Our first step was the creation of a trusteeship for A.A. as a whole. We called this body The Alcoholic Foundation; and in 1954 it was renamed The General Service Board of Alcoholics Anonymous.

This trusteeship was designed to inaugurate and maintain all of those special services for A.A. as a whole that could not well be performed by single groups or areas. We envisioned the writing of a uniform A.A. literature, the development of a sound public relations policy, and a means of handling the large numbers of pleas for help that might follow in the wake of national and international publicity. We thought in terms of aiding new groups to form and of furnishing them with counsel based upon the experience of the older and already successful groups. We thought there would be a need for a monthly magazine and also for translations of our literature into other languages.

By 1950 nearly all of these dreams for world service had come true. In the dozen years following the creation of The Foundation, A.A. membership had jumped from 50 to 100,000. The A.A. Traditions had been written and adopted. A confident unity had pretty much replaced fear and doubt and strife. Our services had unquestionably played a large and critical role in this unfoldment. World service, therefore, had taken on crucial meaning for A.A.'s future. If these vital agencies were to collapse or bog down, our unity within and the carrying of our message to innumerable alcoholics without, would suffer serious and perhaps irreparable damage. Under all conditions and at any sacrifice, we would have to sustain those services and the flow of life blood that they were pumping into the world arteries of our Fellowship. Among the A.A. groups it had been proven that we could survive great strain and stress. But could we stand heart failure at our world center?

And so we asked ourselves: What further precautions could we take that would definitely guard us against an impairment or a collapse? Nevertheless the period 1945 to 1950 was one of such exuberant success that many A.A.'s thought that our future was completely guaranteed. Nothing, they believed, could possibly happen to our Society as a whole, because God was protecting A.A. This attitude was in strange contrast to the extreme vigilance with which our members and groups had been looking after themselves. They had quite prudently declined to charge Providence with the entire responsibility for their own effectiveness, happiness, and sobriety.

When, at A.A.'s Service Headquarters, some of us began to apply this tested principle of "stop, look, and listen" to A.A.'s world affairs, it was widely thought that we must be foolish worriers who lacked faith. Many said, "Why change? Things are going fine!" "Why call in delegates from all over the country? That means expense and politics, and we don't want either." And the clincher was always, "Let's keep it simple."

Such reactions were natural enough. The average member, preoccupied with his group life and his own "twelfth stepping," knew almost nothing of A.A.'s world services. Not one member in a thousand could tell who our Trustees were. Not one in a hundred had the least idea what had been done for A.A.'s general welfare. Tens of thousands already owed their chance at sobriety to the little noticed activity of our Trustees and general services. But few realized that this was true.

Among the Trustees themselves, a sharp division of opinion was developed. For a long time most of them had strongly opposed calling together a representative conference of A.A. delegates, to whom they would become accountable. They thought that the risks were immense and that politics, confusion, expense, and fruitless strife surely would result. It was true that the woes of much lesser undertakings, such as local A.A. services and clubs, had sometimes been great. Hence the conviction was widespread that calamity would be in the making if ever a conference representing all of A.A. were assembled. These arguments were not without merit; they were difficult to contest.

However, in 1948, there occurred an event that shook us all. It became known that Dr. Bob was suffering from a fatal illness. As nothing else could, this news drove home the hard fact that he and I were almost the sole links between our virtually unknown Trustees and the movement they served. The Trustees always had relied heavily upon Dr. Bob and me for advice. They had taken a firm grip on money expenditures, but they necessarily turned to us every time that A.A. policy questions arose. Then, too, the groups of that time did not really rely much on the Trustees for the management of their service affairs; they were still looking to Dr. Bob and me. So here was a society whose total functioning was still largely dependent upon the credit and the confidence which, for the time being, its founders happened to enjoy.

The fact had to be faced that A.A.'s founders were perishable. When Dr. Bob and I had gone, who would then advise the Trustees; who could link our little-known Board to our thousands of groups? For the first time it was seen that only a representative conference could take the place of Dr. Bob and me. This gap simply had to be filled without delay. Such a dangerous open end in our affairs could not be tolerated. Regardless of trouble or expense, we had to call an A.A. General Service Conference and deliver our world services into its permanent keeping. It took little imagination to see that future collapse would be the certain penalty if we did not act boldly and decisively. Thus propelled by events, we did take the necessary action. Now that the Conference is in its second decade, we find that our former fears of the troubles a Conference might involve were largely groundless. The results of the Conference have exceeded our highest expectations. It now stands proven that the A.A. groups can and will take the final responsibility for their world services.

There were other reasons for this basic shift of ultimate responsibility and authority to A.A. as a whole. These reasons center around Tradition Two, which declares, "For our group purpose, there is but one ultimate authority — a loving God as He may express Himself in our group conscience. Our leaders are but trusted servants; they do not govern."

Tradition Two, like all the A.A. Traditions, is the voice of experience, based upon the trials of thousands of groups in our pioneering time. The main principles of Tradition Two are crystal clear: the A.A. groups are to be the final authority; their leaders are to be entrusted with delegated responsibilities only.

Tradition Two had been written in 1945, and our Trustees had then authorized its publication. But it was not until 1951 that the first experimental General Service Conference was called to see whether Tradition Two could be successfully applied to A.A. as a whole, including its Trustees and founders. It had to be found out whether the A.A. groups, by virtue of this Conference, could and would assume the ultimate responsibility for their world service operation. It took five years more for all of us to be convinced that Tradition Two was for everybody. But at St. Louis in 1955, we knew that our General Service Conference — truly representing the conscience of A.A. world-wide — was going to work and work permanently.

Perhaps many of us are still vague about the "group conscience" of Alcoholics Anonymous, about what it really is.

Throughout the entire world today we are witnessing the breakdown of "group conscience." It has always been the hope of democratic nations that their citizens would always be enlightened enough, moral enough, and responsible enough to manage their own affairs through chosen representatives. But in many self-governing countries we are now seeing the inroads of ignorance, apathy, and power-seeking upon democratic systems. Their spiritual resources of right purpose and collective intelligence are waning. Consequently many a land has become so helpless that the only answer is dictatorship.

Happily for us, there seems little prospect of such a calamity in A.A. The life of each individual and of each group is built around our Twelve Steps and Twelve Traditions. We very well know that the penalty for extensive disobedience to these principles is death for the individual and dissolution for the group. An even greater force for A.A.'s unity is the compelling love that we have for our fellow members and for the principles upon which our lives today are founded.

Therefore we believe that we see in our Fellowship a spiritualized society characterized by enough enlightenment, enough responsibility and enough love of man and of God to insure that our democracy of world service will work under all conditions. We are confident that we can rely upon Tradition Two, our group conscience and its trusted servants. Hence it is with a sense of great security that we old-timers have now fully vested in A.A.'s General Service Conference the authority for giving shape — through the labors of its chosen Delegates, Trustees, and service workers — to the destiny that we trust God in His wisdom is holding in store for all of us.

Concept II

When, in 1955, the A.A. groups confirmed the permanent charter for their General Service Conference, they thereby delegated to the Conference complete authority for the active maintenance of our world services and thereby made the Conference — excepting for any change in the Twelve Traditions or in Article 12 of the Conference Charter — the actual voice and the effective conscience for our whole Society.

It is self-evident that the thousands of A.A. groups and the many thousands of A.A. members, scattered as they are all over the globe, cannot *of themselves* actually manage and conduct our manifold world services. The group conscience is out there among them, and so are the needed funds. The power of the groups and members to alter their world service structure and to criticize its operation is virtually supreme. They have all of the final responsibility and authority that there is. The operation is really theirs; they really own it. This has been true ever since the groups took over from the founders and old-timers at St. Louis in 1955.

But an ultimate authority and responsibility in the A.A. groups for world services — if that is all there were to it — could not amount to anything. Nothing could be accomplished on that basis alone. In order to get effective action, the groups must delegate the actual operational authority to chosen service representatives who are fully empowered to speak and to act for them. The group conscience of A.A. could not be heard unless a properly chosen Conference were fully trusted to speak for it respecting most matters of world service. Hence the principle of amply delegated authority and responsibility to "trusted servants" must be implicit from the top to the bottom of our active structure of service. This is the clear implication of A.A.'s Tradition Two.

Even from the beginning, large delegations of service authority had to be the rule. It will be recalled how, in 1937, the Akron and New York Groups authorized Dr. Bob and me to create over-all services which could spread the A.A. message world-wide. Those two fledgling groups gave to us the authority to create and manage world services. Following their action, we held both the final responsibility and the immediate authorization to get this project underway and keep it going. On our own, however, we knew we could do little, and so we had to find trusted servants who in turn would help us. As time went by, we found that we had to delegate to these friends a very large part of our own authority and responsibility. That process of delegation was as follows:

First of all, Dr. Bob transferred nearly all of his immediate responsibility for the creation of world service to me. In New York we stood a better chance of finding friends and funds, and we saw that our world service center consequently would have to be located in that city. I started the search for trusted nonalcoholic friends who could help, and in 1938 The Alcoholic Foundation was formed as a small trusteeship of A.A. members and our nonalcoholic friends.

At first the Trustees of our new Foundation took jurisdiction over money matters only. Little by little, however, they were obliged to assume many other responsibilities, because I alone could not discharge these on any permanent basis. Hence I gave the Trustees added responsibility and corresponding authority as fast as possible.

For example, in 1940, a year after the book "Alcoholics Anonymous" was published, we all saw that this great new asset had to be put in trust for our whole Fellowship. Therefore the stock ownership of Works Publishing, Inc.* (a publishing corporation which I had helped to separately organize) was turned over to the Board of Trustees.

Nearly all the income from the A.A. book was then needed to finance the over-all service office that we had set up for A.A. The Trustees, therefore, presently took over the primary management of office operation, because they were now responsible for the funds upon which its support depended. Consequently, so far as financial decisions were concerned, I became an adviser only. Another sizable chunk of my original authority was thus delegated. When, in 1941, the A.A. groups began to send contributions to The Alcoholic Foundation for the support of our over-all service office, the Trustees' control of our world service monies became complete.

After some time it became apparent that A.A.'s public relations, a vital matter indeed, could not continue to be entrusted to me alone. Therefore the A.A. groups were asked to give the Trustees of the Foundation complete control in this critical area. Later on, the Trustees took jurisdiction over our national magazine, "The A.A. Grapevine," which had been separately organized by another group of volunteers.

Thus it went with every one of our world services. I still functioned in an advisory capacity in our Headquarters operation, but the Board of Trustees was in full legal charge of all our affairs. As Dr. Bob and I looked to the future, it was clear that ample delegation to the Board was the only possible way.

Notwithstanding these delegations, Dr. Bob and I did quite properly feel that we still held an ultimate responsibility to A.A., and to the future, for the proper organization and structuring of our A.A. world services. If anything were to go wrong with them, we would be held accountable, because the groups still looked to us, rather than to their then little-known Trustees, for leadership in A.A.'s world affairs.

In the course of these developments the great difference between *ultimate* and *immediate* service authority became apparent.

---

* Works Publishing, Inc. was later renamed A.A. Publishing, Inc. Today A.A. Publishing is a division of A.A. World Services, Inc.

As early as 1945 it began to be evident that the co-founders' ultimate responsibility and authority for services should never be wholly vested in a Board of Trustees. Certainly our Trustees must be given a large share of the active and immediate responsibility. But the ultimate and final responsibility which Dr. Bob and I still possessed simply could not be transferred to a self-appointing Board which was relatively unknown among A.A.'s as a whole. But where, then, would our ultimate responsibility for world services finally be lodged? And what would become of my own leadership in world service matters? A.A.'s history now shows where the ultimate authority finally went. At St. Louis it went from Dr. Bob and me to the A.A. groups themselves.

But the groups' acceptance of ultimate service authority and responsibility was not enough. No matter what authority the groups had, they could not meet their new responsibilities until they had actually delegated most of the active ones. It was precisely in order to meet this need that the General Service Conference of Alcoholics Anonymous was given the general responsibility for the maintenance of A.A.'s world services and so became the service conscience for A.A. as a whole.

Exactly as Dr. Bob and I earlier had found it necessary to delegate a large part of our active authority to the Trustees, so have the A.A. groups since found it necessary to delegate these same powers to their General Service Conference. The final say — the ultimate sanction in matters of large importance — has not been given to the Trustees alone. By the Conference Charter, confirmed at St. Louis, this authority is now delegated to the A.A. groups and thence to their Conference, a body which is a representative cross section of our entire Fellowship.

Therefore the General Service Conference of A.A. — plus any later formed sections — has become for nearly every practical purpose the active voice and the effective conscience of our whole Society in its world affairs.

In making this momentous transfer, we old-timers deeply hope that we have avoided those pitfalls into which societies have so often fallen because their originators have failed, during their lifetimes, to properly delegate and distribute their own authority, responsibility and leadership.

Concept III

As a traditional means of creating and maintaining a clearly defined working relation between the groups, the Conference, the A.A. General Service Board and its several service corporations, staffs, committees and executives, and of thus insuring their effective leadership, it is here suggested that we endow each of these elements of world service with a traditional "Right of Decision."

Within the framework of their general responsibilities, whether these be defined by charter, by resolution, or by custom, it should be the traditional right of all world service boards, committees, and executives to decide which problems they will dispose of themselves and upon which matters they will report, consult, or ask specific directions. We ought to trust our world servants with these discretions, because otherwise no effective leadership can be possible. Let us consider in detail, therefore, why the need for a "right of decision" in our leadership is imperative, and let us examine how this principle can be applied practically in all levels of our structure of world service.

We have seen how the A.A. groups, under the concept of the "group conscience," are today holding the ultimate authority and the final responsibility for world services. We have also noted how, by reason of the Conference Charter and the "trusted servant" provision of Tradition Two, the groups have delegated to their General Service Conference full authority to manage and conduct A.A.'s world affairs.

The Conference and General Service Board Charters in broad terms define the responsibility of the Conference to act on behalf of A.A. as a whole. In these two documents a necessarily large area of delegated service authority and responsibility has been staked out. These instruments, in a general way, describe the relation between the groups, the Conference, the Trustees and the active service units. These broad definitions and descriptions are an indispensable frame of reference, and we could not function without them.

Nevertheless it has long been evident that these highly important Charter provisions cannot *by themselves* ensure smooth functioning and proper leadership at the several different levels of service which are involved. This has become crystal clear, and we need not seek very far for the reasons.

For example: knowing that theirs is the final authority, the groups are sometimes tempted to instruct their Delegates exactly how to vote upon certain matters in the

11

Conference. Because they hold the ultimate authority, there is no doubt that the A.A. groups have the *right* to do this. If they insist, they *can* give directives to their Delegates on any and all A.A. matters. But good management seldom means the full exercise of a stated set of ultimate rights.

For example, were the groups to carry their instruction of Delegates to extremes, then we would be proceeding on the false theory that group opinion in most world service matters would somehow be much superior to Conference opinion. Practically speaking, this could almost never be the case. There would be very few questions indeed that "instructed" Delegates could better settle than a Conference acting on the spot with full facts and debate to guide it. Of course it is understood that complete *reporting* of Conference actions is always desirable. So is full *consultation* with Committee Members and Group Representatives. Nevertheless the "instructed" Delegate *who cannot act on his own conscience* in a final Conference vote is not a "trusted servant" at all; he is just a messenger.

Now the Conference Charter does not actually solve typical problems like this. It is a broad document which can be variously construed. Under one interpretation, the groups can instruct the Delegates all they like. Under another, the Delegates and Trustees actually can ignore such instructions, whenever they believe that to be desirable. How, then, shall we practically understand and reconcile such a condition?

Let us look at two more illustrations: the Conference, as will be later demonstrated, is in a state of nearly complete practical authority over the Trustees, despite the legal rights of the Board. Suppose the Conference Delegates began to use this ultimate power of theirs unwisely? Suppose they began to issue hasty and flat directives to the Trustees on matters respecting which the Trustees would be far more knowledgeable than the Delegates? What then?

This same kind of confusing problem used to beset the relations between the Trustees and their wholly-owned active service corporations, entities which are nowadays partly directed by non-Trustee volunteers and paid service workers. But the Board of Trustees certainly does own these outfits. Therefore the Trustees can hire and fire; their authority is final. Yet if the Trustees were constantly to exert their really full and absolute authority, if they were to attempt to manage these operating entities *in detail*, then the volunteers and Staff members working in them would quickly become demoralized; they would be turned into buck-passers and rubber stamps; their choice would be to rebel and resign, or to submit and rot.

Therefore some traditional and practical principle has to be devised which at all levels *will continuously balance the right relation between ultimate authority and delegated responsibility*. How, then, are we going to accomplish this?

There are three possible attitudes that we might take toward such a state of affairs. We could, for instance, throw away all corporate charters, bylaws, job definitions, and the like. This would leave it entirely to each group of trusted servants to figure out what its authority and responsibility really is. But such an absence of any chartered structure would be absurd; nothing but anarchy could result.

Then of course we could take the opposite tack. Refusing to give our leadership any worthwhile discretion at all, we could add to our present Charters great numbers of rules, regulations, and bylaws that would attempt to cover every conceivable action or contingency. That would be altogether too much red tape—more than we A.A.'s could stand. The right A.A. solution for this problem is to be found, however, in the latter part of Tradition Two, which provides for "trusted servants." This really means that we ought to trust our responsible leaders *to decide*, within the understood framework of their duties, *how they will interpret and apply their own authority and responsibility to each particular problem or situation as it arises.* This sort of leadership discretion should be the essence of *"The Right of Decision,"* and I am certain that we need not have the slightest fear of granting this indispensable privilege at nearly every level of world service.

There will always be plenty of ultimate authority to correct inefficiency, ineffectiveness, or abuse. If the Conference does not function well, the groups can send in better Delegates. If the Trustees get badly out of line, the Conference can censure them, or even reorganize them. If the Headquarters' services go sour, the Trustees can elect better directors and hire better help. These remedies are ample and direct. But for so long as our world services function reasonably well—and there should always be charity for occasional mistakes—then "trust" must be our watchword, otherwise we shall wind up leaderless.

These are the reasons for my belief that we should forthwith invest in all of our service bodies and people a traditional "Right of Decision." In our structure of world service this "Right of Decision" could be practically applied as follows:

A. Excepting its Charter provisions to the contrary, the Conference always should be able to decide which matters it will fully dispose of on its own responsibility, and which questions it will refer to the A.A. groups (or more usually, to their Committee Members or G.S.R.'s) for opinion or for definite guidance.
    Therefore it ought to be clearly understood and agreed that our Conference Delegates are *primarily* the world servants of A.A. as a whole, that only in a secondary sense do they represent their respective areas. Consequently they should, on final decisions, be entitled to cast their votes in the General Service Conference *according to the best dictates of their own judgment and conscience at that time.*

B. Similarly the Trustees of the General Service Board (operating of course within the provisions of their own Charter and Bylaws) should be able at all times to decide when they will act fully on their own responsibility and when they will ask the Conference for its guidance, its approval of a recommendation, or for its actual decision and direction.

C. Within the scope of their definitely defined or normally implied responsibilities, all Headquarters service corporations, committees, staff or executives should also be possessed of the right to decide when they will act wholly on their own and when they will refer their problems to the next higher authority.

This "Right of Decision" should never be made an excuse for failure to render proper reports of all significant actions taken; it ought never be used as a reason for constantly exceeding a clearly defined authority, nor as an excuse for persistently failing to consult those who are entitled to be consulted before an important decision or action is taken.

Our entire A.A. program rests squarely upon the principle of mutual trust. We trust God, we trust A.A., and we trust each other. Therefore we cannot do less than trust our leaders in service. The "Right of Decision" that we offer them is not only the practical means by which they may act and lead effectively, but it is also the symbol of our implicit confidence.

Concept IV

Throughout our Conference structure, we ought to maintain at all responsible levels a traditional "Right of Participation," taking care that each classification or group of our world servants shall be allowed a voting representation in reasonable proportion to the responsibility that each must discharge.

The principle of "Participation" has been carefully built into our Conference structure. The Conference Charter specifically provides that the Trustees, the Directors of our service corporations, (A.A. World Services, Inc. and The A.A. Grapevine, Inc.) together with their respective executive staffs, shall always be voting members of the General Service Conference itself.

Exactly the same concept is borne in mind when our General Service Board elects the Directors of its wholly-owned active service corporations, A.A. World Services, Inc. and The A.A. Grapevine, Inc. If it wished, the General Service Board could elect none but its own Trustees to these corporate directorships. But a powerful tradition has grown up to the effect that this never ought to be done.

For example, A.A. World Services, Inc. (which also includes the A.A. Publishing division) currently has seven directors, only two of whom are Trustees.[1] The other five non-Trustee directors comprise three volunteers, both expert in office management and publishing, and two directors who are paid staff members: the general manager and his assistant. The general manager is traditionally the president of A.A. World Services, Inc. and his assistant is a vice president. For communication linkage, the editor or a staff member of the Grapevine or his nominee is invited to attend A.A. World Services, Inc. meetings.

Therefore the active management of A.A. World Services, Inc. and its publishing division is composed of Trustees whose mission is to see that these projects are properly managed; of volunteer experts who contribute their advice and professional experience; and of two paid office executives who are charged with getting most of the work done. It will be seen that each member of every classification, is a director, and so has a legal vote; that each corporate officer bears a title which, both practically and legally, denotes what his (or her) actual status and responsibility is.

Such a typical corporate business management easily permits a proper degree of voting "participation." Every skilled element to do the allotted job is present. No class is set in absolute authority over another. This is the corporate or "participating" method of doing business, as distinguished from structures so common to many institutional, military and governmental agencies wherein high-level people or classes of people often are set in absolute authority, one over the other.

We should also note that the seven[2] A.A. Grapevine directors are elected on the same principle as those of A.A. World Services, Inc. Here too we see Trustees, volunteer experts and paid staff members acting in concert as the active managers of that operation. And a world service nominee should be present at all GV meetings, both corporate and editorial.

The General Service Board, furthermore, rigorously abides by the principle of "Participation" whenever its chairman makes appointments to the Board's principal standing committees. Numbers of non-Trustees and paid staff workers are customarily chosen for these important posts. As with the active service corporations, the same elements are nearly always present in these committees, viz., representatives of the General Service Board, non-Trustee experts, and one or more staff members who must do most of the leg work. All can vote, and therefore all can truly "participate." When the time comes to ballot, there are no "superiors," no "inferiors," and no "advisers."

To this highly effective and unifying principle of "Participation" at all responsible levels, there is one regrettable but necessary exception. Members holding paid staff positions cannot become Trustees. This cannot be permitted because such a practice would interfere with the four-year rotation of the A.A. Trustees. And if ever the General Service Board had to be reorganized by the Conference, paid A.A. Trustees might prove to be a vested interest most difficult to dislodge.

Nevertheless our Trustees of today traditionally invite paid executives, staff members, accountants, and any others whose reports or advice may be required, to attend each quarterly meeting of the General Service Board. Thus the Trustees are put into direct communication with these workers who are thus made to feel that they are wanted and needed. Although they do not vote, these workers may freely participate in debate.

The preservation of the principle of "Participation" in our service structure is, to those of us who already understand its application and benefits, a matter of the highest importance to our future. Experience suggests, however, that some of each new generation of Delegates and Trustees will inevitably try to weaken, modify or toss out the principle of corporate "participation." Every year, a few Delegates will question the "right" of the corporate directors, staffs and even of the Trustees to vote in Conference. New volunteer corporate directors will ask why any paid woman staff member should also be a director and thereby have a vote as good as their own. Every now and then a move will be made to abolish A.A. World Services, Inc. and The A.A. Grapevine, Inc. It will be urged that these separate corporations ought to become "departments" or "committees" of the General Service Board, mainly managed by Trustees. To my view, it is so vital that we preserve this traditional "Right of Participation" in the face of every tendency to whittle it down that we should here bring some of our pioneering experience to bear upon the problem.

In its early days the A.A. Headquarters was run on authoritarian and institutional lines. At that time the Trustees saw no reason to delegate their managerial powers or to work in voting participation with any others outside their own body. The result was often grievous trouble and misunderstanding, and it was out of this rough going that the principle of "Participation" finally emerged. This lesson was learned the hard way, but it *was* learned.

We have seen how Dr. Bob and I had placed our Board of Trustees in full legal possession of all of our service assets. This had included our book literature, our funds, our public relations, and our A.A. General Service Office. This is how our early Trustees came to have all of the authority there was. But most of the actual responsibility for the conduct of A.A.'s Headquarters nevertheless fell on me, my assistant, and her staff. On the one hand we had Trustees who possessed complete authority, and on the other hand there were founders and office managers who had great responsibility but practically no authority. It was a kind of schizophrenia, and it caused real trouble.

It was natural for the Trustees, who had all of the authority and all of the money, to feel that theirs was the duty to directly manage the office and to actively superintend practically everything that was done. To accomplish this, two Trustee committees were formed, a policy and an administrative committee. We at the office had no membership on these committees and hence no real "participation." Of course I could go to Trustee meetings to persuade or advise, and the same was true of the committee meetings. But my assistant, who really carried the greater part of the office load, couldn't get inside a Trustees meeting, and she was called into committee meetings only to make suggestions and reports, answer questions and receive orders. Sometimes these committees issued us conflicting directives.

The situation was complicated by yet another wheel in the management machine. Our publishing company (then Works Publishing, Inc.) was of course wholly owned by the Board of Trustees. Except in one important particular, Works Publishing, Inc. had, however, become a pure "dummy." It had nothing to do with the active management except to issue checks for office and publishing expenses. An old A.A. friend of mine, its Trustee-treasurer, signed those checks. Once, when he was a bit out of sorts, he tore up all of our paychecks because my assistant had issued them a couple of days early so that the gals in the back office could buy Easter bonnets. Right then and there we began to wonder how much *absolute* authority over money and people any one of us drunks could handle. Also, how much of this type of coercion we alkies on the receiving end could sit and take. In any case it had become dead sure that our Headquarters could not be run by two executive committees and a dummy corporation, each able to issue point-blank nonparticipating directives.

The point may be made that nowadays we drunks can "dish it out" or "take it" better than we used to. Even so, I would sure hate to see us ever go back to a nonparticipating setup. Now that we have more service people involved and more money to handle, I am afraid the result would be much the same and maybe worse. There was really nothing exceptional about the incident of the torn-up checks. Every time an absolute authority is created it always invites this same tendency toward over-domination respecting all things, great and small.

It was years before we saw that we could never put all authority in one group and virtually all responsibility in another and then expect efficiency of operation, let alone real harmony. Of course, no one is against the idea of final authority. We are only against its misapplication or misuse. "Participation" can usually stop this sort of demoralizing non-sense before it starts.

Let us look at another aspect of this participation problem. The final authority for services must lie in the A.A. groups; but suppose the groups, sensing their great power, should try to over-exercise it by sending in Delegates irrevocably instructed as to how to vote on most questions. Would the Delegates feel that they were participants, trusted servants? No, they would feel like agents and order-takers.

The Delegates themselves, of course, could also give the Trustees this same treatment. The Delegates' power is so great that they could soon make the Trustees feel like rubber stamps, just as the Trustees unknowingly did to workers at Headquarters. If, therefore, the Conference ever begins to refuse the Trustees vote in it, and if the Trustees ever again refuse to let corporate service volunteers and staff members vote at the level of their own corporate and Conference work, we shall have thrown all past experience to the winds. The principle of allowing a proper voting participation would have to be painfully relearned.

One argument for taking away the Trustee and service worker vote in the Conference is this: it is urged that there is danger if we allow service people and Trustees to vote on their own past performance; for example, their annual reports. To a certain extent this argument is sound. As a matter of tradition, there is no doubt that Trustees and service workers alike should refrain from voting on reports on their own past activities.

But those who would *do away entirely* with the votes of Trustees and service work-ers in the Conference overlook the point that such reports of past performance constitute only a fraction of the business of that body. The Conference is far more concerned with policies, plans, and actions which are to take effect in the future. To take away the votes of Trustees and service workers on such questions would obviously be unwise. Why should our Conference be deprived of the votes of such knowledgeable people as these?*

Perhaps someone will object that, on close votes in the Conference, the combined Trustees and service worker ballots may decide a particular question. But why not? Certainly our Trustees and service workers are no less conscientious, experienced and wiser than the Delegates. Is there any good reason why their votes are undesirable? Clearly there is none. Hence we ought to be wary of any future tendency to deny either our Trustees or our service people their Conference votes, except in special situations that involve past performances, job qualifications or money compensation, or in case of a sweeping reorganization of the General Service Board itself, occasioned by misfunction of the Board. However, this should never be construed as a bar to Trustee vote on structural changes. It is also noteworthy that

---

* There is another very practical reason for not giving Conference Delegates absolute voting authority over trustees, service directors, and staff members. It should be borne in mind that our delegates can never be like a Congress in constant session, having its own working committees, elected leaders, etc. Our delegates cannot possibly function in this manner for the simple reason that they meet for a few days only, once a year. Hence they cannot have an extensive firsthand acquaintance with many of the problems on which they are expected to vote. This is all the more reason for allowing the sometimes better-informed minority of trustees and Headquarters people the balloting privilege in all cases where no self-interest is involved.

in actual practice our Trustees and Headquarters people have never yet voted in a "bloc." Their differences of opinion among themselves are nearly always as sharp and considerable as those to be found among the Delegates themselves.

There is another good reason for "participation," and this one has to do with our spiritual needs. All of us deeply desire to *belong*. We want an A.A. relation of brotherly partnership. It is our shining ideal that the "spiritual corporation" of A.A. should never include any members who are regarded as "second class." Deep down, I think this is what we have been struggling to achieve in our world service structure. Here is perhaps the principal reason why we should continue to ensure "participation" at every important level. Just as there are no second-class A.A.'s, neither should there be any second-class world service workers, either.

The "Right of Participation" is therefore a corrective of ultimate authority because it mitigates its harshness or misuse. It also encourages us who serve A.A. to accept the necessary disciplines that our several tasks require. We can do this when we are sure that we belong, when the fact of our "participation" assures us that we are truly the "trusted servants" described in A.A.'s Tradition Two.

---

[1] Currently A.A.W.S. has nine directors, of which four are trustees.
[2] Currently seven.

Concept V

Throughout our world service structure, a traditional "Right of Appeal" ought to prevail, thus assuring us that minority opinion will be heard and that petitions for the redress of personal grievances will be carefully considered.

In the light of the principle of the "Right of Appeal," all minorities—whether in our staffs, committees, corporate boards or among the Trustees—should be *encouraged* to file minority reports whenever they feel a majority to be in considerable error. And when a minority considers an issue to be such a grave one that a mistaken decision could seriously affect A.A. as a whole, it should then charge itself with the actual *duty* of presenting a minority report to the Conference.

In granting this traditional "Right of Appeal," we recognize that minorities frequently can be right; that even when they are partly or wholly in error they still perform a most valuable service when, by asserting their "Right of Appeal," they compel a thorough-going debate on important issues. The well-heard minority, therefore, is our chief protection against an uninformed, misinformed, hasty or angry majority.

The traditional "Right of Appeal" should also permit any person in our service structure, whether paid or unpaid, to petition for the redress of a personal grievance, carrying his complaint, if he so desires, directly to the General Service Board. He or she should be able to do this without prejudice or fear of reprisal. Though in practice this will be a seldom exercised right, its very existence will always tend to restrain those in authority from unjust uses of their power. Surely our workers should cheerfully accept the necessary direction and disciplines that go with their jobs, but all of them should nevertheless feel that they need not silently endure unnecessary and unfair personal domination.

Concerning both "Appeal" and "Petition," I am glad to say that in A.A.'s world services these valuable practices and rights have always been put to good use. Therefore I am committing them to writing only by way of helping to confirm and enlarge their future applications.

The *Rights of "Appeal" and "Petition"* of course aim at the total problem of protecting and making the best possible use of minority feeling and opinion. This has always been, and still is, a central problem of all free governments and democratic societies. In Alcoholics Anonymous individual freedom is of enormous importance. For instance, any alcoholic is a member of A.A. the moment he says so; we cannot take away his right to belong. Neither can we force our members to believe anything or pay anything. Ours is indeed a large charter of minority privileges and liberties.

When we look at our world services, we find that here we have also gone to great lengths in our trust of minority groups. Under Tradition Two, the *group conscience* is the final authority for A.A. world service, and it will always remain so respecting all the larger issues that confront us. Nevertheless the A.A. groups have recognized that for world service purposes the "group conscience of A.A." *as a totality* has certain limitations. It cannot act directly in many service matters, because it cannot be sufficiently informed about the problems in hand. It is also true that during a time of great disturbance the group conscience is not always the best possible guide because, temporarily, such an upset may prevent it from functioning efficiently or wisely. When, therefore, the group conscience cannot or should not act directly, *who does act for it?*

The second part of Tradition Two provides us with the answer when it describes A.A. leaders as "trusted servants." These servants must always be in readiness to do for the groups what the groups obviously cannot or should not do for themselves. Consequently the servants are bound to use their own information and judgment, sometimes to the point of disagreeing with uninformed or biased group opinion.

Thus it will be seen that in world service operations A.A. often trusts a small but truly qualified minority—the hundred-odd members of its General Service Conference—to act as A.A.'s group conscience in most of our service affairs. Like other free societies, we have to trust our servants, knowing that in the unusual event that they should fail their responsibilities, we shall still have ample opportunity to recall and replace them.

The foregoing observations illustrate, in a general way, A.A.'s concern for the freedom and protection of individual members and the whole membership's willingness to trust able and conscientious servants to function in their several capacities, for us all. As the longtime recipients of this kind of trust, I am sure that many of A.A.'s old-timers would like me to record their gratitude along with my own.

By 1951, when the General Service Conference was put into experimental operation, these attitudes of trust already were an essential part of A.A. life. In drafting the Charter for our Conference, therefore, we naturally infused that document with provisions which would insure protection and respect for minorities. This is exemplified, for instance, in our "Third Legacy" method of selecting Delegates. Unless the majority candidate can poll a two-thirds vote of his State or Provincial Assembly, he must place his name in a hat with one or more of the choices of the Assembly minority. By thus drawing lots, the minority candidates have an equal chance with the majority's choice.

Strictly speaking, a democracy operates on the will of the majority, no matter how slim that majority may be. So when making special concessions to the feelings and the often-demonstrated wisdom of minorities, we occasionally may deny democracy's cherished principle of final decision by a simple majority vote. Nevertheless we actually have found that our Third Legacy method of electing Delegates has much *strengthened* the *spirit* of democracy among us. Unity has been cemented, cooperation has been increased, and when the Delegate is finally chosen, no discontented minority can trail in his wake. To increase the actual *spirit of democracy* by special deference to minority opinion is, we think, better than to follow blindly the rule which always insists on an unqualified dominance by a slight majority vote.

Consider another example: our respect for the minority position, plus a desire for unity and certainty, often prompts A.A.'s General Service Conference to debate at length on important questions of policy, provided there is no need for an immediate or early decision. On many occasions the Conference has insisted on a continuing discussion even in certain cases when a two-thirds majority easily could have been obtained. Such a traditional voluntary practice is evidence of real prudence and courteous deference to minority views. Unless it has been absolutely unavoidable, the Conference has usually refused to take important decisions on anything less than a two-thirds vote.

This same kind of consideration for the minority position can be found in the Charter provision that no Conference vote can be considered binding on the Trustees of the General Service Board unless it equals two-thirds of a Conference quorum. This gives the Trustees a power of veto in cases where the majority is not great. By reason of this provision the Trustees, if they wish, can insist on further debate and so check any tendency to haste or emotionalism. In practice the Trustees seldom exercise this option. More often they go along with a simple majority of the Delegates, especially when prompt action on less critical matters is clearly needed. But the choice is always theirs whether to veto a simple majority or to act with it. Here again is a recognition of the constructive value of a trusted minority.

If to such a generous recognition of minority privileges we now add the traditional Rights of "Appeal" and "Petition," I believe we shall have granted to all minorities, whether of groups or of individuals, the means of discharging their world service duties confidently harmoniously and well.

More than a century ago a young French nobleman named De Toqueville came to America to look at the new Republic. Though many of his friends had lost their lives and fortunes in the French Revolution, De Toqueville was a worshipful admirer of democracy. His writings on government by the people and for the people are classics, never more carefully studied than at the present time.

Throughout his political speculation De Toqueville insisted that the greatest danger to democracy would always be the "tyranny" of apathetic, self-seeking, uninformed or angry majorities. Only a truly dedicated citizenry, quite willing to protect and conserve minority rights and opinions, could, he thought, guarantee the existence of a free and democratic society. All around us in the world today we are witnessing the tyranny of majorities and the even worse tyranny of very small minorities invested with absolute power. De Toqueville would have neither, and we A.A.'s can heartily agree with him.

We believe that the spirit of democracy in our Fellowship and in our world service structure will always survive, despite the counter forces which will no doubt continue to beat upon us. Fortunately we are not obliged to maintain a government that enforces conformity by inflicting punishments. We need to maintain only a structure of service that holds aloft our Traditions, that forms and executes our policies thereunder, and so steadily carries our message to those who suffer.

Hence we believe that we shall never be subjected to the tyranny of either the majority or the minority, provided we carefully define the relations between them and forthwith tread the path of world service in the spirit of our Twelve Steps, our Twelve Traditions, and our Conference Charter—in which I trust that we shall one day inscribe these traditional Rights of "Appeal" and "Petition."

Concept VI

On behalf of A.A. as a whole, our General Service Conference has the principal responsibility for the maintenance of our world services, and it traditionally has the final decision respecting large matters of general policy and finance. But the Conference also recognizes that the chief initiative and the active responsibility in most of these matters should be exercised primarily by the Trustee members of the Conference when they act among themselves as the General Service Board of Alcoholics Anonymous.

Just as the A.A. groups find themselves unable to act decisively respecting world service affairs unless they delegate a great amount of active authority and responsibility to their Conference, so must the Conference in turn delegate a liberal administrative authority to the General Service Board, in order that its Trustees may act freely and effectively in the absence of the Conference itself.

This critical need for Trustee liberty of action raises several important questions.* Next to the Conference, A.A.'s Board of Trustees should be the most influential group of world servants that we have, and therefore we shall have to consider carefully the kind and degree of authority, responsibility, leadership, and legal status the Trustees must possess in order to function at top effectiveness over the years to come. We shall need to review and perhaps amend somewhat our present methods of choosing Trustees. We shall need to define clearly the several kinds of professional and financial skills that will always be required for a balanced trusteeship. Only by so doing can we permanently insure the Board's capability of future leadership.

In order to avoid continuous confusion, it will also be necessary to show precisely how the Trustees ought to be related to the Conference and just how they in turn should relate themselves to their active service corporations, A.A. World Services, Inc. (including its division of A.A. Publishing) and the A.A. Grapevine, Inc., our monthly magazine. In a general way these relations already are indicated in our Conference Charter, and to some extent they have been discussed on preceding pages. Nevertheless there still remains a real

---

* See Concept VIII for a definition of the Trustees' powers and activities.

need to interpret and spell them out in detail. Of course there is no desire to freeze these relations into a rigid pattern. However satisfactory and right our present arrangements seem, the future may reveal flaws that we do not yet envision. New conditions may require refinements or even considerable alterations. For this reason our service Charter is capable in most respects of being readily amended by the Conference itself.

It ought to be recalled, however, that all of our present arrangements, including the status of A.A.'s Trustees, are based on a great amount of experience, which it is the purpose of these writings to describe and make clear. When this is done, we shall not be hampered later on by such a lack of understanding that we could be tempted into hasty or unwise amendments. Even if we do someday make changes that happen to work out poorly, then the experience of the past will not have been lost. These articles can then be relied upon as a point of safe return.

Let us therefore make a more specific examination of the need of a wide latitude of administrative freedom for the Trustees of the General Service Board.

As we have seen, the Conference Charter (and also the Charter of the General Service Board, and its Bylaws) has already staked out a large area of freedom of action for our Trustees. And we have re-inforced these Charter provisions by granting to all world service bodies, including of course our Trustees, the traditional Rights of "Decision," "Participation," and "Appeal." A careful review of these legal and traditional rights can leave little doubt what the actual administrative responsibilities of the Trustees are; nor can there be any question that their authority in this area is large indeed.

Why should our Trustees be given this very wide latitude of judgment and action? The answer is that we A.A.'s are holding them mainly responsible for all our service activities: A.A. World Services, Inc. (including A.A. Publishing) and The A.A. Grapevine, Inc. These entities (as of 1960) have combined gross receipts approaching one-half million dollars annually.[1] Our Trustees are also responsible for A.A.'s world-wide public relations. They are expected to lead in the formulation of A.A. policy and must see to its proper execution. They are the active guardians of our Twelve Traditions. The Trustees are A.A.'s bankers. They are entirely responsible for the investment and use of our substantial reserve funds. The very wide range of their activities will be still further seen under "Concept XI," wherein the work of their five[2] standing committees is described.

While the Trustees must always operate under the close observation, guidance and sometimes the direction of the Conference, it is nevertheless true that nobody but the Trustees and their wholly-owned service corporations could possibly pass judgment upon and handle the very large number of transactions now involved in our total world service operation. In view of this very large responsibility, they must therefore be given a correspondingly large grant of authority and leadership with which to discharge it. We should quite understand, too, that the conduct of our world services is primarily a matter of policy and business. Of course our objective is always a spiritual one, but this service aim can only be achieved by means of an effective business operation. Our Trustees must function almost exactly like the directors of any large business corporation. They must have ample authority to really manage and conduct A.A.'s business.

This is the basic corporate concept on which our structure of world service rests. We have deliberately chosen the corporate form rather than the institutional or governmental model, because it is well known that the corporation is a far superior vehicle when it comes to the administration of policy and business.

From top to bottom, our whole service structure indeed resembles that of a large corporation. The A.A. groups are the stockholders; the Delegates are their representatives or proxies at the "annual meeting"; our General Service Board Trustees are actually the directors of a "holding company." And this holding company, the General Service Board, actually owns and controls the "subsidiaries" which carry on our active world services.

This very real analogy makes it even more clear that, just like any other board of directors, our Trustees must be given large powers if they are to effectively manage the principal world affairs of Alcoholics Anonymous.

---

[1] The 2015 revenue of the General Service Board, A.A. World Services, Inc. and A.A. Grapevine, Inc. was approximately 23 million dollars.

[2] There are now eleven standing committees.

Concept VII

The Conference recognizes that the Charter and the Bylaws of the General Service Board are legal instruments: that the Trustees are thereby fully empowered to manage and conduct all of the world service affairs of Alcoholics Anonymous. It is further understood that the Conference Charter itself is not a legal document: that it relies instead upon the force of tradition and the power of the A.A. purse for its final effectiveness.

This concept may appear to be contradictory; it may look like the collision of an irresistible force with an immovable object. On the one hand we see a Board of Trustees which is invested with complete legal power over A.A.'s funds and services, while on the other hand we find that A.A.'s General Service Conference is clothed with such great traditional influence and financial power that, if necessary, it could overcome the legal rights of the Board of Trustees. It can therefore give the Trustees directives and secure compliance with them—practically speaking.

This means that the practical power of the Conference will nearly always be superior to the legal power of the Trustees. This superior power in the Conference flows from the powerful traditional influence of the Charter itself. It derives from the large majority of group-chosen Delegates in the Conference. And finally, in any great extremity, it would rest upon the undoubted ability of the Delegates to deny the General Service Board the monies with which to operate—viz., the voluntary contributions of the A.A. groups themselves. Theoretically, the Conference is an advisory body only, but practically speaking it has all of the ultimate rights and powers that it may ever need.

When we reflect that our Trustees have no salaried financial interest in their posts, we can be quite sure that such a Board would never think of legally contesting the clear and sustained will of the Conference Delegates and the A.A. areas they represent. If someday the chips were really down, there would be little chance of a stalemate. The Conference would find itself in complete control of the situation. As the conscience of A.A., the Delegates would find themselves in ultimate authority over our General Service Board and also its corporate arms of active world service.

The history of this development is interesting and important. When in 1950 the Conference Charter was drawn, this question of where the final authority ought to rest was a very moot matter. Would the Conference have the last word, or would the Trustees? By then we knew for sure that complete and final authority over our funds and services should never continue to reside in an isolated Board of Trustees who had an unqualified right to appoint their own successors. This would be to leave A.A. world services in the hands of a paternalistic group, something entirely contradictory to the "group conscience" concept of Tradition Two. If the Trustees were to be our permanent service administrators and the guardians of A.A.'s Twelve Traditions, it was evident that they must somehow be placed in a position where they would necessarily have to conform to our Traditions, and to the desires of our Fellowship.

To accomplish this objective we considered all kinds of devices. We thought of incorporating the Conference itself, thus placing it in direct legal authority over the Board. This would have meant that all Conference members would have had to have a legal status. It would have been much too cumbersome an arrangement, involving really the incorporation of our whole Fellowship, an idea which the Conference itself later repudiated.

We also considered the idea of country-wide elections for all Trustees. But this procedure would have produced a political shambles, rather than the top flight managerial talent the Board had to have. So that notion was abandoned.

We next inquired whether the Conference itself could not both nominate and directly elect our Trustees. But how could several scores of Delegates do this? They would come from all over the country. They would not be too well acquainted with each other. Their terms would be short and their meetings brief. How, then, could such a body nominate and elect alcoholic and nonalcoholic Trustees of a top managerial caliber? Clearly there could be no reliable method for doing this. Very reluctantly, we had to drop this idea.

It thus became obvious that new Trustee choices—subject to Conference approval—would still have to be left pretty much to the Trustees themselves. Only they would be capable of understanding what the Board needed. Except in a time of reorganization, this method of selection would have to continue—certainly as to the larger part of the Board's membership. Otherwise the Board could not be held accountable for management results. We might wind up with no effective management at all. For these reasons, the Conference was given the right to reject, but not to elect, new Trustee candidates.[1]

It was out of these considerations that our present Conference Charter was developed, a structure which clearly gives the Conference a final and ultimate authority but which nevertheless legally preserves the right of the Trustees to function freely and adequately, just as any business board of directors must. This arrangement is in strict conformity with the "trusted servant" provision of Tradition Two, which contemplates that our servants, within the scope of their duties, should be trusted to use their own experience and judgment. Trusted servants at all A.A. levels are expected to exercise leadership, and leadership is not simply a matter of submissive housekeeping. Of course leadership cannot function if it is constantly subjected to a barrage of harassing directives.

Up to the present time our experience shows that this balance of powers between the Trustees and the Conference is thoroughly workable. We have taken great pains to reserve final authority to the Conference by practical and traditional means. By legal means we have delegated ample functional and discretionary authority to the Trustees. We believe this balance can be maintained indefinitely, because the one is protected by tradition and the other by law.

Now we come to another interesting question often raised by new General Service Board Trustees. They say, "We Trustees have certain rights and duties which are legally established by our Charter. Are we not violating this Charter when we accept a Conference opinion or directive? We should have a perfect legal right to say 'no' to anything and everything that the Conference wants."

Our Trustees certainly do have this absolute legal authority, but there is nothing in their Charter that *compels* them to use *all* of their authority *all* of the time. They are quite at liberty to accept advice or even direction from anyone at all. They can simply refrain from using their absolute legal right to say "no" when it would be much wiser, all things considered, to say "yes." Just as the Conference should avoid the overuse of its traditional authority, so should the Trustees avoid overuse of their legal rights. The President of the U.S., for example, has an absolute legal right to veto congressional legislation. Yet ninety-nine percent of the time he does not do it, because (a) he likes a piece of legislation or (b) he does not like the legislation but believes a veto would nevertheless be unwise or impossible of success. Whether or not he will exercise his veto is determined by circumstances. It is just like that with A.A.'s Board of Trustees.

Clearly, then, our Board of Trustees does reserve a veto power over any Conference action; this is legally necessary and right in principle, even though the veto will seldom be used. At certain times, however, the Trustees' veto could be of important and constructive use.

Here, for instance, are three typical examples in which it would be the duty of the Trustees to veto Conference action:

1. If, in a time of haste or heavy stress, the Conference should take an action or issue a directive to the Trustees in clear violation of its own Charter, or that of the General Service Board; or if the Conference were to pass any measure so ill-considered or so reckless as to seriously injure, in the judgment of the Trustees, A.A.'s public relations or A.A. as a whole, it would then be the duty of the Trustees to ask for a Conference reconsideration. In event of a Conference refusal to reconsider, the Trustees could then use their legal right of veto. And, if desirable, they could appeal the issue directly to the A.A. groups themselves.

2. Although traditionally the Trustees never should substantially exceed a Conference-approved budget without consulting the Conference, they should *feel entirely free to reduce the Conference budget figure* during any fiscal year, even though such an action might curtail or cancel special plans or projects initiated and directed by the Conference itself.

3. If, by reason of unforeseen conditions, any particular plan, project or directive of the Conference should become impractical or unworkable during a fiscal year, the Trustees should without prejudice, be able to use their right of veto and cancellation.

If, therefore, in the years ahead, the Conference will always bear in mind the actual rights, duties, responsibilities and legal status of the General Service Board, and if the

Trustees in their deliberations will constantly realize that the Conference is the real seat of ultimate service authority, we may be sure that neither will be seriously tempted to make a "rubber stamp" out of the other. We may expect that in this way grave issues will always be resolved and harmonious cooperation will be the general rule.

---

[1] Trustee elections are now held during Conference week for regional and at-large trustees; to that extent the Conference now chooses trustees according to the procedure described in the "Service Manual."

Concept VIII

The Trustees of the General Service Board act in two primary capacities: (a) With respect to the larger matters of over-all policy and finance, they are the principal planners and administrators. They and their primary committees directly manage these affairs. (b) But with respect to our separately incorporated and constantly active services, the relation of the Trustees is mainly that of full stock ownership and of custodial oversight which they exercise through their ability to elect all directors of these entities.

Since our Trustees bear the primary responsibility for the good conduct of all our world service affairs, this discussion deals with the basic concepts and methods by which they can best discharge their heavy obligations. Long experience has now proved that our Board as a whole must devote itself almost exclusively to the larger and more serious questions of policy, finance, group relations, public relations and leadership that constantly confront it. In *these more critical matters,* the Board must of course function with great care and deliberation. Here the Board is expected skillfully to *plan, manage, and execute.*

It follows, therefore, that the close attention of the Board to such large problems must not be subject to constant distraction and interference. Our Trustees, as a body, cannot be burdened with a mass of lesser matters; they must not concern themselves with the endless questions and difficulties which arise daily, weekly and monthly in the routine conduct of the World Service Office and of our publishing enterprises. In these areas the Board cannot possibly manage and conduct in detail; it must delegate its executive function.

Here the Board's attitude has to be that of custodial oversight; it cannot be the executive. Hence the Trustees are the guarantors of the good management of A.A. World Services, Inc. and The A.A. Grapevine, Inc. They discharge their custodial obligation by electing the directors of these services, a part of whom must always be Trustees. By this means, the executive direction of these functions is securely lodged in the active service corporations themselves rather than in the General Service Board. Each corporate service entity should possess its own charter, its own working capital, its own executive, its own employees, its own offices and equipment. Except to mediate difficult situations and to see that the service corporations operate within their budgets and within the general framework of A.A. and Headquarters policy, the Board will seldom need to do more, so far as routine service operations are concerned.

This arrangement is in line with modern corporate business practice. The General Service Board is in effect a holding company, charged with the custodial oversight of its wholly-owned and separately incorporated subsidiaries, of which each has, for operating purposes, a separate management. We have demonstrated to our satisfaction that this corporate basis of operation is superior to any other.

This lesson, as we have observed before, has been learned the hard way. When discussing "Participation" in Concept IV, we saw that earlier attempts to manage the A.A. General Service Office and A.A. Publishing Company through a multiplicity of Trustee committees did not work well. These were really efforts to make our services into departments of the old Alcoholic Foundation (now the General Service Board). It was found difficult to define the powers of these several Trustee service committees respecting each other and respecting the work at hand. Responsibility and authority rarely could be kept in balance. Point-blank directives, rather than participating decisions, were the rule. In these committees nobody held titles that fully denoted what individual responsibilities actually were; and, naturally enough, those who handled money and signed checks assumed the greater authority. The control of money, therefore, too often determined A.A. policy, regardless of the views of the workers and volunteers at the office who sometimes understood these matters better.

But the moment we consolidated our service office function into a single and permanent corporate structure wherein officers and directors had legally defined titles and duties and responsibilities—the moment such a corporation was provided with its own working capital, employees and facilities—the moment its directors could legally vote in proportion to their actual responsibilities—the moment we were able in this way to define clearly executive authority—from that moment we began to see great improvement. More harmonious and effective conduct of our business has been the result ever since.

We finally learned what the business world well knows: that we could not, at the level of top management, run a large, active and full-fledged business entity with loose-jointed committees and departments. For example, how could our Trustees function today if they were to become a mere "committee" or "department" of the General Conference instead of the legally chartered and carefully defined body that they necessarily are?

Neither can our General Service Board be made into an operating corporation. Any corporation conducting a large and active business always must have a single executive head who is familiar with every department, who is actually on the job most of the time, and who therefore can directly co-ordinate the several departments and mediate their differences. This would mean (if we tried it) that the General Service Board "divisions" would have to report to the General Service Board Chairman, as their chief executive. But unless he was *an executive in fact,* and constantly available to them, how could they do so? In the very nature of our particular setup, our Board Chairman can never be such an executive. He is usually a nonalcoholic and could not give the required time. Nor, as a Trustee, could he be paid a salary for the work that would be required of him as the top executive of all our services.

Suppose, however, that the Trustees engaged a full-time manager who would actively conduct all three of our service enterprises as departments of the Board. An immediate difficulty would be that such a person could never be a Trustee and could therefore never act as the Chairman of the General Service Board. He would therefore have no real status. He would become a man of all work under the absentee direction of the Board Chairman. Consider, too, the fact that half of our Board of Trustees normally live out of town[1] and the further fact that we cannot well ask our nonalcoholic Trustees to give the active services close and continuous supervision. Altogether, these are weighty reasons why we should never turn the General Service Board into an operating corporation.

Nor would we be much better off if we formed one big subsidiary service corporation, wholly-owned by the General Service Board and designed to encompass under a single top executive all of our active services, including The A.A. Grapevine. This plan would also create executive difficulties because it would overconcentrate executive authority. And finally, an individual executive having the many diverse talents required would be hard to find and hard to replace.

A further consideration is that we have always rigorously avoided any great money or executive concentration by placing our reserve funds with the Trustees and by dividing our total working capital between the A.A. World Services, Inc. and The A.A. Grapevine, Inc., each entity having its separate executive. There is always a powerful connection between money and authority. Whenever we concentrate money, we shall inevitably create the temptation for the exercise of too much executive authority, an undesirable condition for us. Therefore we should strenuously avoid placing too much money or too much authority in any one service entity. These are potent reasons for maintaining separate incorporations for each of our active services.

However, experience dating from our earliest days strongly suggests that future Trustees and service workers, in the supposed interests of accounting simplicity, tax savings, and hoped-for efficiency, will be periodically tempted to go in for concentrations and consolidations of one kind or another. Should this be again attempted, we know that the risk of making an administrative shambles out of the total operation will be great indeed.

These observations are not intended to bar any future needful change. It is urged only that we avoid unnecessary repetitions of those painful experiences and mistakes of the past which sometimes resulted from too much concentration of money and authority. It can only be left on the record that we still see no workable way to convert the Board of Trustees into an active, "all-purpose" service corporation.

---

[1] In 2016, 90% of the trustees live "out of town."

Concept IX

Good service leaders, together with sound and appropriate methods of choosing them, are at all levels indispensable for our future functioning and safety. The primary world service leadership once exercised by the founders of A.A. must necessarily be assumed by the Trustees of the General Service Board of Alcoholics Anonymous.

No matter how carefully we design our service structure of principles and relationships, no matter how well we apportion authority and responsibility, the operating results of our structure can be no better than the personal performance of those who must man it and make it work. Good leadership cannot function well in a poorly designed structure. But weak leadership can hardly function at all, even in the best of structures. But once we have created a basically sound structure, that job is finished, except for occasional refinements.

With *leadership* we shall have a continuous problem. Good leadership can be here today and gone tomorrow. Furnishing our service structure with able and willing workers has to be a continuous activity. It is therefore a problem that in its very nature cannot be permanently solved. We must continuously find the right people for our many service tasks. Since our future effectiveness must thus depend upon ever-new generations of leaders, it seems desirable that we now proceed to define what a good service leader should be; that we carefully indicate in each level of service, especially in our Board of Trustees, what special skills will always be required; and that we review our present methods of finding and choosing that leadership.

First let's remember that the base for our service structure rests on the dedication and ability of several thousand General Service Representatives (G.S.R.'s), several hundred area Committee Members, and nearly a hundred Delegates. These are the direct agents of the A.A. groups; these are the indispensable linkage between our Fellowship and its world service; these are the primary representatives of A.A.'s group conscience. Without their support and activity we could not operate permanently at all.

When making their choices of G.S.R.'s, the A.A. groups should therefore have such facts well in mind. It ought to be remembered *that it is only the G. S. R.'s* who, in Group Assembly meetings (or in caucus) can name Committee Members and finally name the Delegates. Hence great care needs to be taken by the groups as they choose these Representatives. Hit-or-miss methods should be avoided. Groups who name no G.S.R.'s should be encouraged to do so. In this area a degree of weakness tends to persist. The needed improvement seems to be a matter of increased care, responsibility and education. As the G. S. R.'s meet in their Assemblies to name Delegates, an even greater degree of care and dedication will be required. Personal ambitions will have to be cast aside, feuds and controversy forgotten. "Who are the best qualified people that we can name?" This should be the thought of all.

Thus far our Third Legacy method of naming Delegates by a two-thirds vote or by lot has proved highly satisfactory. This system of choosing has greatly reduced political friction; it has made each Delegate feel that he or she is truly a world servant rather than just the winner of a contest. In Committee Members and Delegates alike, our Third Legacy methods have generally produced people of a high level of dedication and competence. In this area of service we are in good shape. Our Area Assemblies need only to continue to act with care and in selfless good spirit.

It should be reported that some members still doubt whether choice by lot is ever a good idea. They say that the best man does not always win. In answer it must be pointed out that each time we have abandoned the "two-thirds vote or lot" in naming Delegates, there has been a sense of defeat and disturbance in the minority camp which is nowhere nearly offset by the advantage of naming the supposedly best man. Indeed the second-best man can often be as good a Delegate as the Assembly's first choice; he may even be a better Delegate.

We now come to the principal theme of this particular Concept: How can we best strengthen the composition and the leadership of the future Board of Trustees, the Board which in years to come will have to exercise A.A.'s primary leadership in world service administration, the trusteeship which will in fact have to assume most of my former duties and responsibilities in connection with A.A.'s world services?

As previously noted, the actual transference of authority and responsibility from me to the Trustees has been going on for a long time. I am still around and still serving as an adviser, and I have also been finishing a few remaining chores (for example, the development of these Concepts) which were left over from the 1955 St. Louis Convention. But the time approaches when I shall have to withdraw from nearly all world service activity. This is why I feel a great interest now in doing everything possible to strengthen the administrative composition and A.A. leadership of our General Service Board, so that future Trustees may be better able to cope with the problems and dangers which time will no doubt bring.

My admiration for what A.A.'s alcoholic and nonalcoholic Trustees have done for us all is boundless. During the time of our infancy and adolescence, nothing could have been structurally better than the setup we have had. Looking at this record, many A.A.'s naturally feel that what was good for the past will surely be good for the future; that any change in the induction methods, in the Trustee ratio of alcoholics to nonalcoholics, or in the present composition of our Board will prove dangerous rather than beneficial.

But change has been pressing upon us right along, and it is still doing so. For example, our Board operated in all the years between 1938 and 1951 without the support of a Conference. But it was finally and reluctantly realized that this relatively unseen and unknown Board could not continue without a permanent linkage to A.A., something that

Dr. Bob and I could not give it forever. We did not like to face this change, but we had to. The trusteeship had to be securely anchored to A.A. or it eventually would have collapsed. The Conference simply *had* to come into being.

This change profoundly altered the position of the Trustees. Their former authority was modified; they were firmly linked to A.A. and were thus made directly accountable to our Fellowship. Nobody today questions the wisdom of that momentous change, because everybody can now see that it has provided an essential protection for the service effectiveness and security of A.A.'s future. Experience has refuted the idea that changes which are needed to meet altered conditions are necessarily unwise.

We now stand on the edge of still another great change. Though we have already solved the problem of the Trustee's authority, their responsibility and their linkage to A.A., *we have by no means solved, in my belief, the question of the Board's future role in service leadership.* Hence it is my deep conviction that the administrative and A.A. leadership strength of the Board should be considerably increased; that these and other improvements can place it in a much better position, practically and psychologically; that such changes are truly necessary to meet the conditions which will be certain to follow when my own world service leadership has been terminated.

Students of history recognize that the transference of the original leadership of a society to its successors in leadership is always a critical turning point. This difficult question of leadership, this problem of transference, must now be faced.

✶ ✶ ✶ ✶ ✶

Let us finally consider what specific personal qualities a world service leader ought to have. For whatever use it may be to future generations of our trusted servants, I here offer a discussion on this subject published in a 1959 issue of "The A.A. Grapevine."

LEADERSHIP IN A.A.: EVER A VITAL NEED

No society can function well without able leadership in all its levels, and A.A. can be no exception. It must be said, though, that we A.A.'s sometimes cherish the thought that we can do without much personal leadership at all. We are apt to warp the traditional idea of "principles before personalities" around to such a point that there would be no "personality" in leadership whatever. This would imply rather faceless automatons trying to please everybody, regardless.

At other times we are quite as apt to demand that A.A.'s leaders must necessarily be people of the most sterling judgment, morals, and inspirations; big doers, prime examples of all, and practically infallible.

Real leadership, of course, has to function in between these entirely imaginary poles of hoped-for excellence. In A.A. certainly no leader is faceless, and neither is any leader perfect. Fortunately our Society is blessed with any amount of *real* leadership—the active people of today and the potential leaders of tomorrow as each new generation of able members swarms in. We have an abundance of men and women whose dedication, stability, vision, and special skills make them capable of dealing with every possible service assignment. We have only to seek these folks out and trust them to serve us.

Somewhere in our literature there is a statement to this effect: "Our leaders do not drive by mandate, they lead by example." In effect, we are saying to them, "Act for us, but don't boss us."

A leader in A.A. service is therefore a man (or woman) who can personally put principles, plans and policies into such dedicated and effective action that the rest of us want to back him up and help him with his job. When a leader power-drives us badly, we rebel; but when he too meekly becomes an order-taker and he exercises no judgment of his own—well, he really isn't a leader at all.

Good leadership originates plans, policies, and ideas for the improvement of our Fellowship and its services. But in new and important matters, it will nevertheless consult widely before taking decisions and actions. Good leadership will also remember that a fine plan or idea can come from anybody, anywhere. Consequently, good leadership will often discard its own cherished plans for others that are better, and it will give credit to the source.

Good leadership never passes the buck. Once assured that it has, or can, obtain sufficient general backing, it freely takes decisions and puts them into action forthwith, provided of course that such actions be within the framework of its defined authority and responsibility.

A "politico" is an individual who is forever trying to "get the people what they want." A statesman is an individual who can carefully discriminate when and *when not* to do this. He recognizes that even large majorities, when badly disturbed or uninformed, can, once in a while, be dead wrong. When such an occasional situation arises, and something very vital is at stake, it is always the duty of leadership, even when in a small minority, to take a stand against the storm, using its every ability of authority and persuasion to effect a change.

Nothing, however, can be more fatal to leadership than opposition for opposition's sake. It never can be "Let's have it our way or no way at all." This sort of opposition is often powered by a visionless pride or a gripe that makes us want to block something or somebody. Then there is the opposition that casts its vote saying, "No, we don't like it." No real reasons are ever given. This won't do. When called upon, leadership must always give its reasons, and good ones.

Then, too, a leader must realize that even very prideful or angry people can sometimes be dead right, when the calm and the more humble are quite mistaken.

These points are practical illustrations of the kinds of careful discrimination and soul-searching that true leadership must always try to exercise.

Another qualification for leadership is "give and take," the ability to compromise cheerfully whenever a proper compromise can cause a situation to progress in what appears to be the right direction. Compromise comes hard to us "all-or-nothing" drunks. Nevertheless we must never lose sight of the fact that progress is nearly always characterized by a *series of improving compromises.* We cannot, however, compromise always. Now and then it is truly necessary to stick flat-footed to one's conviction about an issue until it is settled. These are situations for keen timing and careful discrimination as to which course to take.

Leadership is often called upon to face heavy and sometimes long-continued criticism. This is an acid test. There are always the constructive critics; our friends indeed. We ought never fail to give them a careful hearing. We should be willing to let them modify our opinions or change them completely. Often, too, we shall have to disagree and then stand fast without losing their friendship.

Then there are those whom we like to call our "destructive" critics. They power-drive, they are "politickers," they make accusations. Maybe they are violent, malicious. They pitch gobs of rumors, gossip, and general scuttle-butt to gain their ends—all for the good of A.A., of course! But in A.A. we have at last learned that these folks, who may be a trifle sicker than the rest of us, need not be really destructive at all, depending very much on how we relate ourselves to them.

To begin with, we ought to listen carefully to what they say. Sometimes they are telling the whole truth; at other times, a little truth. More often, though, they are just rationalizing themselves into nonsense. If we are within range, the whole truth, the half truth, or no truth at all can prove equally unpleasant to us. That is why we have to listen so carefully. If they have got the whole truth, or even a little truth, then we had better thank them and get on with our respective inventories, admitting we were wrong. If it is nonsense, we can ignore it. Or we can lay all the cards on the table and try to persuade them. Failing this, we can be sorry they are too sick to listen, and we can try to forget the whole business. There are few better means of self-survey and of developing genuine patience, than the work-outs these usually well-meaning but erratic brother members afford us. This is always a large order and we shall sometimes fail to make good on it ourselves. But we must keep trying.

Now we come to the all-important attribute of *vision.* Vision is, I think, the ability to make good estimates, both for the immediate and for the more distant future. Some might feel this sort of striving to be a sort of heresy, because we A.A.'s are constantly telling ourselves, "One day at a time." But that valuable principle really refers to our mental and emotional lives and means chiefly that we are not foolishly to repine over the past nor wishfully to day-dream about the future.

As individuals and as a fellowship, we shall surely suffer if we cast the whole job of planning for tomorrow onto a fatuous idea of Providence. God's real Providence has endowed us human beings with a considerable capacity for foresight, and He evidently expects us to use it. Therefore we must distinguish between wishful fantasy about a happy tomorrow and the present use of our powers of thoughtful estimate. This can spell the difference between future progress and unforeseen woe.

Vision is therefore the very essence of prudence, an essential virtue if ever there was one. Of course we shall often miscalculate the future in whole or in part, but that is better than to refuse to think at all.

The making of estimates has several aspects. We look at past and present experience to see what we think it means. From this we derive a tentative idea or policy. Looking first at the nearby future, we ask how our idea or policy might work. Then we ask how our policies or ideas might apply under the several differing conditions that could arise in the longer future. If an idea looks like a good bet, we try it on—experimentally when that is possible. Later we revalue the situation and ask whether our estimate is working out. At about this stage we may have to take a critical decision. Maybe we have a policy or plan that still looks fine and is apparently doing well. Nevertheless we ought to ponder carefully what its longtime effect will be. Will today's nearby advantages boomerang into large liabilities for tomorrow? The temptation will almost always be to seize the nearby benefits and quite forget about the harmful precedents or consequences that we may be setting in motion.

These are no fancy theories. We have found that we must use these principles of estimate constantly, especially at world service levels where the stakes are high. In public relations, for example, we must estimate the reaction both of A.A. groups and the general public, both short-term and long-term. The same thing goes for our literature. Our finances have to be estimated and budgeted. We must think about our service needs as they relate to general economic conditions, group capability, and willingness to contribute. On many such problems often we must try to think months and years ahead.

As a matter of fact, all of A.A.'s Twelve Traditions were at first questions of estimate and vision for the future. Years ago for example we slowly evolved an idea about A.A. being self-supporting. There had been trouble here and there about outside gifts. Then still more trouble developed. Consequently we began to devise a policy of "no outside gifts." We began to suspect that large sums of this kind would tend to make us irresponsible and could divert us from our primary aim. Finally we saw that for the long pull, outside money could really ruin us. At this point, what had been just an idea or general policy crystallized firmly into an A.A. tradition. We saw that we must sacrifice the quick, nearby advantage for long-term safety.

We went through this same process on anonymity. A few public breaks had looked good. But finally the vision came that many such breaks eventually could raise havoc among us. So it went: first a tentative idea, then an experimental policy, then a firm policy, and finally a deep conviction—a vision for tomorrow.

Such is our process of estimating the future and responsible world leadership must be proficient in this vital activity. It is an essential ability, especially in our Trustees. Most of them, in my view, should be chosen on the basis that they have already demonstrated an aptness for foresight in their own business or professional careers.

We shall be in continual need of these same attributes—tolerance, responsibility, flexibility, and vision—among our leaders of A.A. services at all levels. The principles of leadership will be the same whatever the size of the operation.

Maybe this seems like an attempt to stake out a specially privileged and superior type of A.A. member. But it really is not so. We simply are recognizing that our talents vary greatly. The conductor of an orchestra is not necessarily good at finance or foresight. And it is quite unlikely that a fine banker could be a great musical performer. So when we talk about A.A. leadership we only declare that we ought to select that leadership on the basis of obtaining the best talent we can find.

While this article was first thought of in connection with our world service leadership, it is possible that some of its suggestions can be useful to anyone who takes an active part in our Society.

This is true particularly in the area of Twelfth Step work, in which nearly all of us are actively engaged. Every sponsor is necessarily a leader. The stakes are about as big as they could be. A human life and usually the happiness of a whole family hang in the balance. What the sponsor does and says, how well he estimates the reactions of his prospects, how well he times and makes his presentation, how well he handles criticisms, and how well he leads his prospect on by personal spiritual example—these qualities of leadership can make all the difference, often the difference between life and death.

We thank God that Alcoholics Anonymous is blessed with so much leadership in all of its affairs.

Concept X

Every service responsibility should be matched by an equal service authority—the scope of such authority to be always well defined whether by tradition, by resolution, by specific job description or by appropriate charters and bylaws.

Nearly all societies and governments of today exhibit serious deviations from the very sound principle that *each operational responsibility* must be accompanied by *a corresponding authority* to discharge it.

This is why we have been at such pains in preceding discussions to define the several authorities and responsibilities of the A.A. groups, the Conference, the Trustees, and our active service corporations. We have tried to make sure that authority in each of these levels is equal to responsibility. Then we have tried to relate these levels one to another in such a way that this principle is maintained throughout.

An outstanding characteristic of every good operational structure is that it guarantees harmonious and effective function by relating its several parts and people in such a way that none can doubt what their respective responsibilities and corresponding authorities actually are. Unless these attributes are well defined; unless those holding the final authority are able and willing properly to delegate and maintain a suitable operational authority; unless those holding such delegated authority feel able and willing to use their delegated authority freely as trusted servants; and unless there exists some definite means of interpreting and deciding doubtful situations—then personal clashes, confusion, and ineffectiveness will be inevitable.

The matter of responsibility and its necessary and co-equal authority is of such urgent importance that we might profitably recapitulate what has already been said, meanwhile taking a bird's-eye-view of our entire structure to better envision how this principle does, and always must, apply in our every activity and attitude.

The first characteristic that any working structure must have is a point, or succession of points, where there is an ultimate responsibility and therefore an ultimate authority. We have already seen how, for A.A.'s world services, this kind of final responsibility and authority resides in the A.A. groups themselves. And they in turn have apportioned some of their ultimate authority to the Conference and the Trustees.

We have observed how the Conference Delegates, directly representing the groups, are actually in a position of ultimate authority over the Trustees. We have seen further how the Trustees are in ultimate authority over the General Service Board's wholly-owned service corporations — A.A. World Services, Inc. and The A.A. Grapevine, Inc. Likewise we know that the directors of these corporations are in ultimate authority over their officers who, on their part, are in like authority over their staffs.

The principle of ultimate authority runs clear through our structure. This is necessary, because all of our service affairs and activities have to head up *somewhere* for final responsibility. Ultimate authority is also needed so that each worker or each classification of servants knows where and who the final boss is.

If however, ultimate authority is not carefully qualified by delegated authority, we then have the reverse result. Were there no delegated authority, the groups would be directing their Delegates on every important vote, the Delegates would similarly turn the Trustees into a timid committee which would receive point-blank direction on just about everything; the Trustees would then install themselves as the sole directors of the service entities and would commence to run them by directives. The corporate executives would become small czars, pushing the working staffs about. In short, such a misuse of ultimate authority would add up to a dictatorship wherein nearly every classification of A.A. servants would have large responsibilities but no real or certain authority, and hence no capability of effective decision and leadership with which to operate. Big or little tyrannies and buck-passing would be the inevitable penalties.

Therefore it becomes clear that ultimate authority is something which cannot be used indiscriminately. Indeed ultimate authority should practically never be used in full, *except in an emergency.* That *emergency* usually arises when delegated authority has gone wrong, when it must be reorganized because it is ineffective, or because it constantly exceeds its defined scope and purpose. For example, if the groups are dissatisfied with the Conference, they can elect better Delegates or withhold funds. If the Delegates must, they can censure or reorganize the Trustees. The Trustees can do the same with the service corporations. If a corporation does not approve of the operations of its executives or staff, any or all of them can be fired.

These are the *proper* uses of *ultimate authority,* because they rightly discharge a truly ultimate responsibility. The *influence* of ultimate authority must always be felt, but it is perfectly clear that *when delegated authority is operating well it should not be constantly interfered with.* Otherwise those charged with operating responsibility will be demoralized because their authority to do their work will be subject to arbitrary invasion, and because their actual responsibility will be made greater than their real authority.

How have we *structurally* tried to restrain the natural human tendency of those in ultimate authority to usurp and take over the needed operational or delegated authority? Well, this has been a large order, and several structural devices have been required. Let us review them, noting how they apply.

In our structure we have tried to create at each level accurate definitions of authority and responsibility. We have done this (a) by legal means, (b) by traditional means, and (c) by principles under which doubtful and seemingly or really conflicting situations can be interpreted and readily resolved.

Take the Conference Charter. It is not a legal instrument, but practically speaking it is the substance of a contract between the A.A. groups and their Conference. The Charter makes clear in a general way that the A.A. groups have delegated some of their ultimate authority and all needed operational authority to the Conference, which includes the Trustees and the active services. It is further suggested, in these present articles, that each Conference member on a final vote be entitled to cast his ballot according to the dictates of his own conscience; that the Conference itself also be granted, under the traditional "Right of Decision," the privilege of choosing which matters it will decide by itself and which it will refer back to the groups for their discussion, guidance or direction. These are the traditional definitions which can check the natural tendency of the groups to over-instruct Delegates. This gives the Conference an authority equal to its real responsibility.

Consider next the position of the Trustees. In previous articles we have made it clear that although the Conference has the ultimate authority, the Trustees at most times must insist on their legal right to actively administer our service affairs. Their legal right has been further strengthened and its use encouraged by the traditional "Right of Decision." In these articles we also recognize that the Trustees have a legal right of "veto" over the Conference when, in rare cases, they feel this should be used. By these means we have guaranteed the Trustees an administrative authority equal to their actual responsibility. This has of course been done without denying in any way the ultimate authority of the Conference, or of the Delegates, should it be really necessary to give the Trustees directives or censures, or to reorganize the Board. It should also be noticed that the position of the Trustees is still further strengthened by their "voting participation" in the Conference and by the recognition that they are A.A.'s primary world service administrators.

Much care has also been taken to guarantee the Directors of A.A. World Services, Inc. and the A.A. Grapevine, Inc. an ample operating authority that fully matches their responsibility for the routine conduct of our active services. The Charter provisions of their corporations legally protect their rights; the tradition that the Trustees must elect non-Trustee experts to these boards strengthens them further. Besides, the traditional "Right of Decision" adds still more substance to their position. In these Concepts the perils of turning the General Service Board back into a "departmentalized" operating corporation have also been emphasized.

These are the extraordinary precautions we have taken to maintain the operating authority and integrity of the active services themselves. These safeguards are necessary because the General Service Board owns these corporations. Therefore the authority of the Trustees over them is not only ultimate, it is absolute the moment the Trustees want to make it that way. They can elect new boards of directors at any time; they control the corporate budget; they can withhold operating funds. All these powers are needed and right. Nevertheless, so long as things go well, it is highly important that the Trustees do not unnecessarily interfere with, or usurp the operating authority of these entities. Hence the care we have taken in constructing these definitions of delegated authority.

To a considerable degree, the standing committees of the General Service Board—Policy, Finance, Public Relations, and the like—have a similar latitude. Under the principle of the "Right of Decision," each primary committee may choose what business it will dispose of on its own and what matters it will refer to the Board. The position of these committees is also fortified by the appointment of a generous proportion of non-Trustee members. Here, too, we try to make the authority of these committees equal to their responsibility.[1]

Now we come to the matter of conflicting authorities and to the question of how these conflicts are to be resolved. Most routine conflicts in the active services are easily settled, because we have provided ready communication between all service corporations and the committees of the General Service Board. For example: at every meeting of The Grapevine Boards or staff, a representative of A.A. World Services, Inc. is present, and vice versa. The General Policy Committee always contains one or more members of the Finance and Budgetary Committee, and vice versa. Such interlocking provides easy communication. Each entity knows what the other is doing. This practical arrangement irons out many conflicts of authority—but not all.

Suppose, for example, that the framing and execution of an important A.A. policy is involved. In such a case the General Policy Committee naturally assumes the primary jurisdiction, taking on the job of planning and of making recommendations to the Board of Trustees.

Let us suppose, however, that a considerable sum of money will be needed. In such a case the plan also will have to be placed before the Finance and Budgetary Committee. If this committee agrees that the expenditure is warranted and is in line with the over-all budget, it tells the Policy Committee to go ahead and make its recommendation to the Trustees. But if the Finance and Budgetary Committee objects, then it must file its objection with the Trustees, who will settle the issue. Or if they think it necessary, the Trustees will refer the matter to the Conference.

The principle of primary and a secondary jurisdiction also works the other way round. If the Finance Committee, for example, proposes a large expenditure that may strongly affect A.A. feeling and policy, it must be sure to check with the Policy Committee, even though the main jurisdiction still lies with the Budget and Finance people.

In all matters of joint or conflicting authority, therefore, a senior jurisdiction must be established. The junior jurisdiction must be heard and, regardless of the question involved, there must be an understood point or body where a final settlement can be had. It is understood that lesser conflicts are not to be loaded upon the Trustees for final decision. But it should always be clear *where* the *point* of *final decision* is *located*.

A condition to be avoided at all costs is *double-headed* business or policy management. Authority can never be divided into equal halves. Nowhere does such split authority or double-headed management so bedevil a structure as in its executive departments. The vital need of avoiding double-headed executive management will be fully discussed under Concept XI.

In addition to the methods we use to make delegated authority equal to delegated responsibility, we have two more guarantees — the "Right of Appeal" and the "Right of Petition." As we know, a bare majority is apt to constitute itself as a pseudo-ultimate authority on many occasions when it should not do so. Likewise, executives are apt to over-boss their assistants. Therefore we use the concepts of appeal and petition to insure that every minority, and every worker doing a job, has an authority and a status commensurate with the responsibility involved.

To sum up: Let us always be sure that there is an abundance of final or ultimate authority to correct or to reorganize; but let us be equally sure that all of our trusted servants have a clearly defined and adequate authority to do their daily work and to discharge their clear responsibilities.

All of this is fully implied in A.A.'s Tradition Two. Here we see the "group conscience" as the *ultimate* authority and the "trusted servant" as the *delegated* authority. One cannot function without the other. We well know that only by means of careful definitions and mutual respect can we constantly maintain a right and harmonious working balance.

---

[1] In the years since Bill wrote on the General Policy Committee (see also p. 50), its functions have changed markedly. Now known as the General Sharing Session, it meets three times a year for about two hours on the Saturday preceding the General Service Board meeting, and considers the long-range plans of board committees and other topics of special interest. Its membership comprises all the trustees, the A.A.W.S. and Grapevine directors and staffs, and the appointed members of the board committees.

Concept XI

While the Trustees hold final responsibility for A.A.'s world service administration, they should always have the assistance of the best possible standing committees, corporate service directors, executives, staffs and consultants. Therefore the composition of these underlying committees and service boards, the personal qualifications of their members, the manner of their induction into service, the systems of their rotation, the way in which they are related to each other, the special rights and duties of our executives, staffs and consultants, together with a proper basis for the financial compensation of these special workers, will always be matters for serious care and concern.

The longtime success of our General Service Board will rest not only on the capabilities of the Trustees themselves; it will depend quite as much upon the competent leadership and harmonious association of those non-Trustee committee members, corporate service directors, executives and staff members who must actively carry on A.A.'s world services. Their quality and dedication, or their lack of these characteristics, will make or break our structure of service. Our final dependency on them will always be great indeed.

Far more than most of the Trustees, these servants will be in direct contact with A.A. world-wide, and their performance will be constantly on view. They will perform most of the routine labor. They will carry on most of our services. They will travel widely and will receive most visitors at the Headquarters. They will often originate new plans and policies. Some of them will eventually become Trustees. Because this group will form the visible image of world service, most A.A.'s will measure our service values by what they see and feel in them. Members of this group will not only *support* the world leadership of the Trustees; in the nature of the case they will be bound to *share* world leadership with them.

Fortunately we already have a sound internal structure of service in which a very competent group of non-Trustee servants are now working. Only a few refinements and changes will still be needed in A.A. World Services, Inc. and at The A.A. Grapevine, Inc., the latter being a comparatively recent comer to our service scene. The main outlines of this underlying structure are now defined, and the effectiveness of this arrangement has been well proven. Of what, then, does our underlying structure of service consist?

It is composed of the following elements: the five[1] standing committees of the General Service Board, plus our two active service corporations, A.A. World Services, Inc. (including its A.A. publishing division) and The A.A. Grapevine, Inc. Let's have a look at each of these operations.

The standing committees of the General Service Board are Nominating, Finance and Budgetary, Public Information, Literature, and General Policy—the titles clearly denoting the direct administrative responsibilities of the General Service Board. These committees are appointed yearly by the General Service Board Chairman, and each committee, as we have seen, includes a suitable proportion of Trustees, non-Trustee experts in the work to be done, a Headquarters executive and a staff worker.

The Nominating Committee: This committee aids the Trustees in discharging their prime obligation to see that all vacancies—whether within their own ranks or among key service directors, executives, staff members—are properly filled with members and workers of the greatest possible competence, stability and industry.

The recommendations of this committee to a large extent will determine the continuous success of our services. Its members will have the primary voice in choosing our future Trustees and non-Trustee workers. Careful deliberation, painstaking investigation and interviewing, refusal to accept casual recommendations, preparation well in advance of lists of suitable candidates—these will need to be the principal attitudes and activities of this committee. All temptation to haste or snap judgment will need to be faithfully and constantly resisted.

Another problem that future committees may have to face is the subtle tendency toward deterioration in the caliber of personnel due to the very natural and usually unconscious tendency of those who suggest nominees to select individuals of somewhat less ability than themselves. Instinctively we look for associates rather like ourselves, only a little less experienced and able. For example, what executive is likely to recommend an assistant who is a great deal more competent than he is? What group of staff members will suggest a new associate whose capabilities are a great deal above their own average? The reverse is the more likely. Government bureaus, institutions and many commercial enterprises suffer this insidious deterioration. We have not yet experienced it to any extent, but let us be sure that we never do. All of us need to be on guard against this ruinous trend, especially the Nominating Committee, whose first and last duty is to choose only the best obtainable for each vacant post.

The Finance and Budgetary Committee: The main responsibility of this body is to see that we do not become money-crippled or go broke. This is the place where money and spirituality *do* have to mix, and in just the right proportion. Here we need hard-headed members with much financial experience. All should be realists, and a pessimist or two can be useful. The whole temper of today's world is to spend more than it has, or may ever have. Many of us consequently are infected with this rosy philosophy. When a new and promising A.A. service project moves into sight, we are apt to cry, "Never mind the money, let's get at it." This is when our budgeteers are expected to say "Stop, look and listen." This is the exact point where the "savers" come into a constructive and healthy collision with the "spenders." The primary function of this committee, therefore, is to see that our Headquarters operation is always solvent and that it stays that way, in good times and bad.

This committee must conservatively estimate each year's income. It needs to develop plans for increasing our revenues. It will keep a cold and watchful eye on needless cost, waste and duplication. It will closely scrutinize the yearly budgets of estimated income and expense submitted by A.A. World Services, Inc. and The A.A. Grapevine, Inc. It will recommend amendments of the estimates when necessary. At mid-year it will ask for budget revisions if earlier estimates have gone too much wrong. It will scrutinize every new and considerable expenditure asking "Is this necessary or desirable now? Can we afford it, all considered?"

This committee, in good times, will insist that we continue to set aside substantial sums to our Reserve Fund. It will pursue an investment policy in that fund which will guarantee the immediate availability of at least two-thirds of it at any time, without loss, thereby enabling us to meet hard times or even a calamity.

This is not to say that our Finance and Budgetary Committee constantly says "no" and fearfully hoards our money. I can remember an earlier day when we were so intent on building up the Reserve Fund out of book earnings that we let the office services run down badly for sheer lack of enough help to cope with our fast growth. Confidence was thereby lost out in the groups, and contributions suffered severely; they dropped by tens of thousands a year. By the time the office had been reorganized and confidence restored, we had used all our current book earnings and a large part of our Reserve Funds besides. This sort of false and unimaginative economy can prove very costly—in spirit, in service and in money.

Future committees, therefore, will ponder the difference between real prudence (which is neither fear nor hoarding and which may indeed require us sometimes to run temporary deficits) and that kind of persistent recklessness which could someday result in the severe contraction or collapse of our vital services.

The safe course will usually lie midway between reckless budget-slashing and imprudent spending.

The Public Information Committee: This one, too, is of top importance. Of course most of its members should be experts in the field of public relations. But emphasis should also be laid on the fact that sheer commercial expertness will not be quite enough. Because of A.A.'s traditional conservatism, reflected in the maxim "Attraction rather than promotion," it is evident that the professional members of the committee should be capable of adapting their business experience to A.A.'s needs. For instance, the techniques used to sell a big time personality or a new hair lotion would not be for A.A. The committee should always include a certain number of A.A.'s who, because of long experience, really do have "A.A. sense," that is, a thorough grasp of our total picture and what it needs public relation-wise. At the same time let us not overlook the need for high professional skill. Dealing with the huge complex of public communications as it exists today is not a job wholly for amateurs. Skill in this area implies much technical experience, diplomacy, a sense of what is dangerous and what is not, the courage to take calculated risks, and a readiness to make wise but tradition-abiding compromises. These are the skilled talents we shall always need.

We are trying our best to reach more of those 25 million alcoholics who today inhabit the world. We have to reach them directly and indirectly. In order to accomplish this it will be necessary that understanding of A.A. and public good will towards A.A. go on growing everywhere. We need to be on even better terms with medicine, religion, employers, governments, courts, prisons, mental hospitals, and all those conducting enterprises in the alcohol field. We need the increasing good will of editors, writers, television and radio channels. These publicity outlets—local, national and international—should be opened wider and wider, always forgoing, however, high pressure promotion tactics. It is to, and through, all these resources that we must try to carry A.A.'s message to those who suffer alcoholism and its consequences.

This accounts for the importance in which we hold the work and the recommendations of our Public Information Committee. It is a critical assignment; a single large public blunder could cost many lives and much suffering because it would turn new prospects away. Conversely, every real public relations success brings alcoholics in our direction.

The Literature Committee: This body is charged with the revision of existing books and pamphlets; also with the creation of fresh pamphlet material to meet new needs or changing conditions. Broadly speaking, its mission is to see that an adequate and comprehensive view of A.A. in its every aspect is held up in writing to our members, friends, and to the world at large. Our literature is a principal means by which A.A. recovery, unity and service are facilitated. Tons of books and pamphlets are shipped each year. The influence of this material is incalculable. To keep our literature fully abreast of our progress is therefore an urgent and vital work.

The Literature Committee constantly will have to solve new problems of design, format and content. Here our policy is to aim at only the best; we firmly believe that cheap looking, cheap selling, and poorly conceived literature is not in A.A.'s best interest from any standpoint, whether effectiveness, economy or any other.

Like other General Service Board Committees, this one must be expert in the work to be done. A key figure in its operation will necessarily be a paid writer and consultant. The creative work—that is, the initial form and draft and the final development of new undertakings—will be for this specialist to make. The role of the other committeemen will be of constructive criticism and amendment of the consultant's effort. Here, too, we should remember that the committee must certainly include persons of wide A.A. experience. This matter of getting the "A.A. feel" into all our writings is absolutely vital. What we say so well by word of mouth we must also communicate in print.

The Literature Committee consequently will find it desirable to test carefully each new creation by asking a number of A.A.'s who are sensitive to A.A. feeling and reaction, to offer their criticism and suggestions. If the new material is to affect the nonalcoholic world, especially the fields of medicine and religion, a consultation should be held with those nonalcoholic Trustees or other qualified friends who are knowledgeable in these areas.

The General Policy Committee: Perhaps this is the most important of all of the General Service Board Committees, and it is regarded as the senior one. It can take jurisdiction of practically all problems or projects which involve A.A. policy, public information, or A.A. Traditions that may arise in the other committees or service corporations.[2]

Several years ago it became evident that the mass of business coming before the quarterly Trustees meetings had become too big to handle. We therefore had to devise a committee that could filter all these matters, disposing of the lesser and fully examining the larger. The object was to break the jam at Trustees meetings and to present the Board with carefully discussed recommendations, including minority reports, on the more serious issues. Thus the attention of the General Service Board could be accurately focused on what it really had to do. This committee, with ample time at its disposal, could also strengthen our process of planning and policy formation. It could avert blunders, both large and small, due to haste.

This was our original concept, and it has worked wonderfully well. Because this committee is designed to be super-sensitive to A.A. opinion and reaction, its hard core is composed of (a) the "out-of-town" A.A. Trustees, one of whom is traditionally named chairman, (b) two staff members of the World Service Office, (c) the president of the A.A. World Services, Inc., who is also general manager of the World Office, (d) the president of The A.A. Grapevine, Inc., who is the editor, and (e) those Trustees and service directors known to be long experienced with our Fellowship.

All other Trustees, committee members and directors and staffs are invited to attend meetings—the Trustees because they can thus get a preview of the questions that will confront them at their own meeting to follow—the committeemen and directors because in this way they will get a comprehensive picture of what other Headquarters units have been doing.

This is a large committee and it operates "town meeting-style," requiring four to six hours each Sunday afternoon preceding the Monday quarterly meeting of the General Service Board. A carefully worked out agenda is always prepared. The committee issues to the Trustees a full report of its recommendations, together with any minority views. Its report also shows the actual disposition of minor matters. This General Policy Committee has greatly strengthened our Headquarters unity. All participants get the feeling that they are "on the team." The size of the meeting is no obstacle. Many minds, plenty of time, and real sensitivity to A.A. insure a remarkable effectiveness of policy and planning.

Again it is emphasized that none of these five General Service Board Committees are executive in character. They do not manage and conduct the active affairs of the service corporations. They may, however, make any recommendations they wish—to the service corporations themselves or to the Trustees. It will be noted that the General Policy Committee always examines the quarterly reports of the corporate services and such reports of the other General Service Board Committees as may be available at meeting time. The committee can and does comment upon these reports and makes recommendations respecting them.

Next to be considered will be our active service corporations. A.A. World Services, Inc. and The A.A. Grapevine, Inc. Their activities probably represent nine-tenths of our direct Headquarters effort.

The General Service Board owns the stock of these entities.[3] Therefore the Trustees yearly elect all of their directors, seven (at present) in each corporation. This means that so far as the routine direction of our established services is concerned, the Trustees have fully delegated their executive function in these constantly active service areas.

The directorate of A.A. World Services, Inc. (including the A.A. Publishing division) is traditionally composed of two Trustees for custodial oversight, three non-Trustee experts in the work to be done, and two executives, the general manager of the World Office and one of his staff assistants, who are president and vice president respectively. The two Trustee directors usually have seen past service on the Board as non-Trustee experts, and one of them is customarily named Treasurer. A.A. directors thus are those thoroughly experienced with these operations.[4]

The Grapevine situation is similarly structured, with two exceptions. The two Trustee directors of the Grapevine are (1) an ex-editor of the Grapevine, and (2) a finance man who has previously served on the Grapevine Board. The latter Trustee traditionally is made its chairman, and he presides at corporate meetings. This is because neither the editor, who is traditionally the Grapevine president, nor his staff member director, the vice president, ordinarily will have the needed business experience to chair the Grapevine corporate board. This arrangement also places the chairman in a favorable position to mediate differences that may arise between the editorial and business departments of the enterprise. The Grapevine also has an Editorial Board which names its own successors, subject to the approval of the corporate Board.[5]

The Editorial Board assists the editor and his staff in determining the editorial policy, slant and content of the magazine. It relieves the editor (up to now, a volunteer) of some of his work load. It surveys and makes recommendations respecting Grapevine promotional material going to the groups. It gives our makeup men, artists and writers both status and coherence in their joint efforts. And it is a training ground for future editors. Our Editorial Board therefore is the chief guarantor of the magazine's quality and editorial continuity.

Every new generation of workers will raise certain questions about these two corporate questions: "Why can't both of them be consolidated into the General Service Board?" Or, "Why can't the Grapevine be merged into A.A. World Services, Inc., thus placing all active Headquarters operations under a single management?" These questions have already been discussed under previous Concepts. We have concluded that the General Service Board is an unsuitable vehicle for an operating corporation; that because the Grapevine is such a dissimilar operation, and because we ought not concentrate too much money and executive authority in a single entity, there should be no merger of A.A. World Services and The A.A. Grapevine. Upon these points we seem well agreed—at least, as of now.

But this question has some other variations. It will often be asked, "If it is desirable to separately incorporate dissimilar enterprises, why then shouldn't the A.A. Publishing division of A.A. World Services be separately incorporated and managed by a board of directors specially skilled in book and booklet publishing?" Offhand, this looks logical.

Today, however, A.A. Publishing is mostly a business operation. Unlike a commercial publisher, we do not have to ensure the selection, writing and publication of a lot of new books each year. Most of our A.A. books are already written, and it is probable that not many more will be published. Of course we shall issue new pamphlets now and then and revisions of older material occasionally are desirable. But this relatively small amount of creative publishing work can be handled easily by the Literature Committee. Hence the operation of the A.A. Publishing division of A.A. World Services, Inc., is now mostly a matter of printing, distribution, accounting and finance. For management purposes there is therefore no present need for a separate corporation; it is only required that the books of A.A. World Services, Inc. show a separate accounting for its A.A. Publishing division. Only in the highly unlikely event of a large and protracted entry *into the new book business* would we really ever need a separate corporate management.

Another question will be this: "Why don't we merge A.A. Publishing with The A.A. Grapevine, so placing all of our literature under a unified management?" The answer here is based on the complete dissimilarity of the two enterprises. The Grapevine has to produce a brand new quality product every month, on the dot. By contrast, A.A. Publishing success largely depends upon what has already been written.

In the Grapevine the paramount activity is therefore the creative. The Grapevine requires several paid staff members and the constant aid of a large number of specialized volunteers without whose help it could not operate. Why, then, should we load up these people with a lot more straight business activity? Obviously we should not.

Another question often is posed, "Why should A.A. World Services, Inc. not take over *all* the Grapevine's accounting, finances, promotion and distribution. Would not such a consolidation of financing, employees and routine business be more efficient and economical? Would not this relieve the Grapevine of all business headaches?"

This plan, too, looks reasonable at first glance. Nevertheless the chances are it would work poorly. It has serious structural defects. It would violate the basic good-management principle that whoever has the responsibility for a given task must also have the needed authority, funds, personnel and equipment to carry it out. The A.A. Grapevine, Inc. unquestionably holds full responsibility for its own solvency, promotion, policy, and the management of its circulation. It is supposed to have four business directors, expert in these phases of magazine operation. The Conference and the General Service Board will always hold them accountable. If, therefore, any large part of the Grapevine business functions are transferred to a completely different corporate management over which the Grapevine has no authority, what then? This certainly would be double-headed management and a source of continuous conflict. The Grapevine Board would become virtually impotent.

Such a situation also would tend to demoralize the editor, his staff and the Editorial Board, all of them specialized volunteers. This group now has a representation of three directors on the Grapevine Board. In such a corporate body it is now possible to reconcile the editorial desire for excellence in the magazine with the financial realities of the Grapevine situation. But if the business function of the Grapevine was transferred to A.A. World Services, Inc., the status and influence of the GV editorial people would be reduced to almost nothing. World Service directors would be mostly interested in business efficiency and solvency, while the GV editorial representatives would still be looking for quality and magazine improvements. There would be no practical way of reconciling these differences. The business directors of A.A. World Services, Inc., would dominate the editorial workers and therefore the editorial policy. The editorial group would find that they had become a mere committee, taking directions from A.A. World Services. "Who pays the piper calls the tune" would become the actual working arrangement. Having so split the management of the Grapevine in halves and having abandoned the principle of "Participation," it is doubtful if we could make this setup work at all, especially with all those volunteers. We might save some money, but we probably could not save the magazine.

Joint arrangements between The A.A. Grapevine and A.A. World Services for routine operations such as billing, mailing, etc., are not necessarily precluded, though to a lesser degree the same kind of frictions above described can be expected to develop unless there is the clearest possible understanding of "who controls what and when."

We who now work at A.A.'s Headquarters are pretty much in agreement on the foregoing operations. They are recorded in some detail for whatever future benefits they may be. We deeply realize that we should be on guard always against structural tinkering just for money-saving purposes. These departures can often result in so much disharmony and consequent inefficiency that nothing is really saved, and there can often be a real loss.

A detailed description of the active operational side of our General Service Board Committees and active service corporations is too lengthy to set down here. But we should take note, however, of several more principles and problems which are common to both A.A. World Services, Inc. and to The A.A. Grapevine.

1. *The status of executives—executive direction and policy formation distinguished:* No active service can function well unless it has sustained and competent executive direction. This must always head up in *one person*, supported by such assistants as he needs. A board or a committee can never actively manage anything, in the continuous executive sense. This function has to be delegated to a single person. That person has to have ample freedom and authority to do his job, and he should not be interfered with so long as his work is done well.

Real executive ability cannot be plucked from any bush; it is rare and hard to come by. A special combination of qualities is required. The executive must inspire by energy and example, thereby securing willing cooperation. If that cooperation is not forthcoming, he must know when real firmness is in order. He must act without favor or partiality. He must comprehend and execute large affairs, while not neglecting the smaller. He often must take the initiative in plan making.

The use of such executive abilities implies certain realizations on the part of the executive and those who work with him, otherwise there is apt to be misunderstanding. Because of their natural drive and energy, executives will sometimes fail to distinguish between routine execution of established plans and policies, and the *making* of *new* ones. In this area they may tend to make new plans and put them into operation without sufficiently consulting those whose work is to be affected, or those whose experience and wisdom is actually or officially needed.

A good executive is necessarily a good salesman. But he often wants the fast sell and quick results on those very occasions where patient consultation with many people is in order. However this is far better than timid delay and constant requests to be told by somebody or other what to do. The executive who overdrives can be reasonably restrained by the structural situation, and definitions within which he has to work. But a weak and wobbly executive is of little use at any time.

It is the duty of the good executive therefore *to learn discrimination* of when he should act on his own and when limited or wide consultation is proper, and when he should ask for specific definitions and directions. This discrimination is really up to him. His privilege of making these choices is structurally guaranteed by the "Right of Decision." He can always be censured *after* his acts, but seldom before.

In our world services we still have two more important executive problems. One is the lack of money to hire full-time top executives for A.A. World Services, Inc. and for the A.A. Grapevine. In our World Services Office, we can now afford only a part-time general manager.[6] In the Grapevine we must rely on a volunteer.*[7] Of course each of these executives has paid staff assistants. But the fact that one of our top executives can only give half his time and the other one considerably less, is by no means an ideal situation.

A chief-executive-in-fact should be constantly on the job, and ours cannot be. Someday we may be able to correct this defect. Even then, however, we should not

---

* GV finances being much improved, a part-time paid editor was engaged early in 1962.

make the mistake of hiring full-time executives who, lacking the necessary experience and caliber, are willing to work cheaply. No more expensive blunder than this could possibly be made. Outstanding ability in a volunteer, or a part-timer, is definitely preferable to that.

The second executive difficulty is inherent in our A.A. situation. Our key people at Headquarters are A.A. members; they have to be. Therefore the executives and their staffs are friends in A.A., members of the same club. This sometimes makes it hard for an executive to give firm guidance and equally hard for his A.A. friends to accept it. Our A.A. executives find that they not only have to run a business; they must also keep their friends. In turn, those working under them have to realize seriously that we really *do* have a business to conduct as well as a cooperative spiritual enterprise to foster. Therefore a reasonable amount of discipline and direction is a necessity. Those who cannot or will not see this are not well suited for Headquarters work. Although excessive apartness or roughshod authority is to be rejected in an executive, nobody should complain if he is both friendly and firm. These problems are not insoluble; we do solve them right along, mostly by the application of A.A. principles.

Problems of this sort occasionally crop up, but General Service Headquarters is not constantly beset with them. Because of the exceptional dedication of our people, a degree of harmony and effectiveness prevails that is unusual in the conduct of an outside business.

2. *Paid workers, how compensated:* We believe that each paid executive, staff member or consultant should be recompensed in reasonable relation to the value of his or her similar services or abilities in the commercial world.

This policy is often misunderstood. Many A.A.'s no doubt regard A.A. world services as a sort of necessary charity that has to be paid for. It is forgotten that our particular charity is just as beneficial to us as it is to the newcomer; that many of those services are designed for the general welfare and protection of us all. We are not like rich benefactors who would aid the sick and the poor. We are helping others in order to help ourselves.

Another mistaken idea is that our paid workers should labor cheaply, just as charity workers often do elsewhere. If adopted, this concept would mark our service workers for unusual financial sacrifices, sacrifices that we would ask no other A.A.'s to make. We A.A.'s would be saying to each worker, "We send Headquarters $3.00 apiece every year. But it would be just great if you would work for A.A. at $2,000 a year less than you would be worth elsewhere." Seen in this light, the low-pay theory appears as absurd as it really is, especially when we remember that A.A.'s world service overhead is about the smallest per capita of any large society on earth. The difference between fair and poor pay at World Headquarters is a matter only of a few cents a year to each of us.

We should also consider the well-known fact that cheap help is apt to feel insecure and be inefficient. It is very costly in the long run. This is neither good spirituality nor good business. Assuming that service money is readily available, we should therefore compensate our workers well.

3. *Rotation among paid staff workers:*[8] At A.A.'s World Office, most staff members' assignments are changed yearly. When engaged, each staff member is expected to possess the general ability to do, or to learn how to do, any job in the place—excepting for office management where, because of the special skills involved, rotation may sometimes be limited to part of the A.A. staff. But the basis of compensating all staff members is identical. Pay increases are based on time served only.

In the business world, such an arrangement would be unworkable. It would practically guarantee indifference and mediocrity, because the usual money and prestige incentives would be lacking. In our entire operating situation, this is the sole major departure from the structure of corporate business. Consequently there should be proved and compelling reasons for such a corporate heresy, and there are.

Our primary reason for the adoption of rotation and equal staff pay was the security and continuity of the office. We once had the conventional system of one highly paid staff member with assistants at much lower pay. Hers had been the principal voice in hiring them. Quite unconsciously, I'm certain, she engaged people who she felt would not be competitive with her. Meanwhile she kept a tight rein on all the important business of the place. A prodigy of wonderful work was done. But suddenly she collapsed, and shortly afterwards one of her assistants did the same. We were left with only one partly trained assistant who knew anything whatever about the total operation.

Luckily a good A.A. friend of mine, a fine organizer, pitched in and helped to put the office in order. We saw that we had to install a paid staff that simply couldn't break down. Next time there might be no one around to give the necessary amount of time for its reorganization. Besides this breakdown had cost us much confidence out in the field—so much so that we must have lost $50,000 in three years of group contributions.

Thereafter we installed the principle of rotation in a considerably larger staff. Since then we have experienced sudden departures and collapses of A.A. staff members, each of which would have demoralized the place under the former conventional system. But since the remaining staff members always knew every assignment there was, no trouble at all was experienced. Under such a condition replacements can be carefully chosen and trained at leisure. And the usual tendency to select less able associates is largely overcome.

By thus putting our staff members on a complete parity, the removal of the usual money and prestige incentives did not really damage us at all. We A.A.'s had what the commercial venture often lacks: a dedicated desire to serve which replaced the usual ego drives. At the same time many of the temptations to destructive competition and office "politicking" were also removed. The spirit of the Headquarters improved immeasurably and found its way out into the Fellowship.

In the future—at those times when the rotation system does not work perfectly— there will be the natural demand to throw it out in the supposed interest of efficiency. Certainly our successors will be at liberty to try, but past experience surely suggests that they may be jumping from the frying pan into the fire.

One more aspect of rotation: the matter of time. We already know that the more responsible the assignment, the longer the term of service must be, if we are to have effectiveness. For example, a group secretary can be changed every six months and an Intergroup committeeman every year. But to be of any use whatever, a Delegate has to serve two years, and a Trustee must serve four.

In the World Service Office we have found it impractical and unfair to set any fixed term of employment. A staff member has to have several years training. Are we then to throw her out, just as she is getting top grade? And if she realized that she could only serve for a fixed period, could we have hired her in the first place? Probably not. These posts are hard to fill because they require just the right ingredients of personality, ability, stability, business and A.A. experience. If we insisted on a fixed term of service we would often be forced to engage A.A.'s really not qualified. This would be both harmful and unfair.

But we need not fear too many staff members' getting "old in the service." The emotional pace of "A.A. around the clock" is too strenuous for most of them to take for a very long period of time. Already they come and go for this and for other personal reasons. Within reason, most of them can and must rotate from assignment to assignment. But we should attempt no more rotation than this.

Because of certain unusual skills required, rotation among Grapevine staff members is more difficult. If the magazine ever gets a part-time editor who can insist on and help in their training, we may someday bring this about. But in the Grapevine there will never be safety in numbers, as in the World Office. The present Grapevine paid staff of two could serve a circulation of many times today's size.

4. *Full "Participation" of paid workers is highly important:* We have already discussed the necessity of giving key paid personnel a voting representation on our committees and corporate boards.[9] We have seen that they should enjoy a status suitable to their responsibility, just as our volunteers do. But full participation for paid workers cannot be established by voting rights only. Other special factors usually affect the extent of their participation. Let's see what these are, and what can be done about them.

The first is the fact of employment for money; the employer-employee relation. In human affairs authority and money are deeply linked. Possession or control of money spells control of people. Unwisely used, as it often is, this control can result in a very unhappy kind of division. This ranges the "haves" on one side of the fence and the "have nots" on the other. There can be no reconciliation or harmony until a part of that fence is taken down. Only then can proper authority join hands with a responsible willingness to get on with the job.

In our A.A. structure of service we therefore must do more than give our paid workers a place at the A.A. council table. We ought to treat them in all respects as we would volunteers, people who are our friends and co-workers. So long as they work well, the fact that they are dependent upon the money they receive should never, consciously or unconsciously, be used as a lever against them. They must be made to feel that they are on the team. If, however, they cannot or will not do their jobs, that is something else again. We can and should let them go.[10]

Such are the realizations which we can all use every day of our working lives. Add to these the further thought that no organization structure can fully guarantee our Headquarters against the depredations of clashing personalities, that only the sustained willingness to practice spiritual principles in all our affairs can accomplish this, and we shall never need to have any fear for our future harmony.

Concept XII

General Warranties of the Conference: in all its proceedings, the General Service Conference shall observe the spirit of the A.A. Tradition, taking great care that the conference never becomes the seat of perilous wealth or power; that sufficient operating funds, plus an ample reserve, be its prudent financial principle; that none of the Conference Members shall ever be placed in a position of unqualified authority over any of the others; that all important decisions be reached by discussion, vote, and whenever possible, by substantial unanimity; that no Conference action ever be personally punitive or an incitement to public controversy; that though the Conference may act for the service of Alcoholics Anonymous, it shall never perform any acts of government; and that, like the Society of Alcoholics Anonymous which it serves, the Conference itself will always remain democratic in thought and action.

The Concept here considered consists of Article 12 of the Conference Charter. There are good reasons for placing it in this context.

Taken as a whole, our Conference Charter is the substance of an informal agreement which was made between the A.A. groups and their Trustees in 1955. It is the agreed basis upon which the General Service Conference operates. In part, the Charter is an elastic document; its first eleven Articles can be readily amended by the Conference itself at any time.

But Article 12 of the Charter stands in a class by itself. An amendment or a cancellation of any of its vital Warranties would require the written consent of three-quarters of all the directory-listed A.A. groups who would actually vote on any such proposals, and the considerable time of six months is allowed for careful deliberation. Although changes in the Warranties of Article 12 thus have been made difficult, they have not been made impossible.

It is clear that all of these Warranties have a high and permanent importance to A.A.'s general welfare. This is why we believe we should permit change in them only upon positive evidence of their defectiveness and then only by common consent of the A.A. groups themselves. We have ranked them therefore with A.A.'s Twelve Traditions, feeling that they are quite as important to A.A.'s world services as the Traditions are to A.A. as a whole.

The Warranties of Article 12 are a series of solemn undertakings which guarantee that the Conference itself will conform to A.A.'s Twelve Traditions; that the Conference can never become the seat of great wealth or government; that its fiscal policy shall ever be prudent; that it will never create any absolute authority; that the principle of substantial unanimity will be observed; that it will never take any punitive action; that it never will incite public controversy; that it can serve A.A. only; and that it shall always remain democratic in spirit. These Warranties indicate the qualities of prudence and spirituality which our General Service Conference should always possess. Barring any unforeseen defects, these are the permanent bonds that hold the Conference fast to the movement it serves.

There are significant aspects of these Warranties which should be considered. Notice, for example, that all of them are counsels of *prudence*—prudence in personal relatedness, prudence in money matters, and prudence in our relations with the world about us. For us, prudence is a workable middle ground, a channel of clear sailing between the obstacles of fear on the one side and of recklessness on the other. Prudence in practice creates a definite climate, the only climate in which harmony, effectiveness, and consistent spiritual progress can be achieved. The Warranties of Article 12 express the wisdom of taking forethought for the future based on the lessons of the past. They are the sum of our protection against needless errors and against our very natural human temptations to wealth, prestige, power, and the like.

Article 12 opens with this general statement: "In all its proceedings the General Service Conference shall observe the spirit of the A.A. Tradition..." Of all bodies and groups in Alcoholics Anonymous, the Conference should above all feel bound by the A.A. Tradition. Indeed the Conference is named "the guardian of the Traditions of Alcoholics Anonymous." The Traditions themselves outline the general basis on which we may best conduct our services. The Traditions express the principles and attitudes of prudence that make for harmony. Therefore A.A.'s Twelve Traditions set the pattern of unity and of function which our General Service Conference is expected to exemplify at the highest possible degree.

The Warranties of Article 12 are as follows:

Warranty One: "The Conference shall never become the seat of perilous wealth or power." What is meant by "perilous wealth and power"? Does it mean that the Conference should have virtually no money and no authority? Obviously not. Such a condition would be dangerous and absurd. Nothing but an ineffective anarchy could result from it. We must use *some* money, and there must be *some* authority to serve. But how much? How and where should we draw these lines?

The principal protection against the accumulation of too much money and too much authority in Conference hands is to be found in the A.A. Tradition itself. So long as our General Service Board refuses to take outside contributions and holds each individual's gift to A.A.'s world services at a modest figure, we may be sure that we shall not become wealthy in any perilous sense. No great excess of group contributions over legitimate operating expenses is ever likely to be seen. Fortunately the A.A. groups have a healthy reluctance about the creation of unneeded services which might lead to an expensive bureaucracy in our midst. Indeed, it seems that the chief difficulty will continue to be that of effectively informing the A.A. groups as to what the financial needs of their world services actually are. Since it is certain therefore that we shall never become too wealthy through group contributions, we need only to avoid the temptation of taking money from the outside world.

In the matter of giving Delegates, Trustees and staffs enough authority, there can be little risk, either. Long experience, now codified in these Twelve Concepts, suggests that we are unlikely to encounter problems of too much service authority. On the contrary, it appears that our difficulty will be how to maintain enough of it. We must recall that we are protected from the calamities of too much authority by rotation, by voting participation, and by careful chartering. Nevertheless, we do hear warnings about the future rise of a dictator in the Conference or at the Headquarters. To my mind this is an unnecessary worry. Our setup being what it is, such an aspirant couldn't last a year. And in the brief time he did last, what would he use for money? Our Delegates, directly representing the groups, control the ultimate supply of our service funds. Therefore they constitute a direct check upon the rise of too much personal authority. Taken all together, these factors seem to be reliable safeguards against too much money and too much authority.

We have seen why the Conference can never have any dangerous degree of human power, but we must not overlook the fact that there is another sort of authority and power which it cannot be *without*: the spiritual power which flows from the activities and attitudes of truly humble, unselfish, and dedicated A.A. servants. This is the real power that causes our Conference to function. It has been well said of our servants, "They do not drive us by mandate; they lead us by example." While we have made abundantly sure that they will never drive us, I am confident that they will afford us an ever-greater inspiration as they continue to lead by example.

Warranty Two: "Sufficient operating funds, plus an ample Reserve, should be its prudent financial principle."

In this connection we should pause to review our attitudes concerning money and its relation to service effort.

Our attitude toward the giving of time when compared with our attitude toward giving money presents an interesting contrast. Of course we give a lot of our time to A.A. activities for our own protection and growth. But we also engage ourselves in a truly sacrificial giving for the sake of our groups, our areas and for A.A. as a whole.

Above all, we devote ourselves to the newcomer, and this is our principal Twelfth Step work. In this activity we often take large amounts of time from business hours. Considered in terms of money, these collective sacrifices add up to a huge sum. But we do not think that this is anything unusual. We remember that people once gave their time to us as we struggled for sobriety. We know, too, that nearly the whole combined income of A.A. members, now more than a billion dollars a year, has been a direct result of A.A.'s activity. Had nobody recovered, there would have been no income for any of us.

But when it comes to the actual spending of cash, particularly for A.A. service overhead, many of us are apt to turn a bit reluctant. We think of the loss of all that earning power in our drinking years, of those sums we might have laid by for emergencies or for education of the kids. We find, too, that when we drop money in the meeting hat there is no such bang as when we talk for hours to a newcomer. There is not much romance in paying the landlord. Sometimes we hold off when we are asked to meet area or Intergroup service expenses. As to world services, we may remark, "Well, those activities are a long way off, and our group does not really need them. Maybe nobody needs them." These are very natural and understandable reactions, easy to justify. We can say, "Let's not spoil A.A. with money and service organization. Let's separate the material from the spiritual. That will really keep things simple."

But in recent years these attitudes are everywhere on the decline; they quickly disappear when the real need for a given A.A. service becomes clear. To make such a need clear is simply a matter of right information and education. We see this in the continuous job now being done with good effect for our world service by Delegates, Committee Members, and General Service Representatives. They are finding that money-begging by pressure exhortation is unwanted and unneeded in A.A. They simply portray what the giver's service dollar really brings in terms of steering alcoholics to A.A., and in terms of our over-all unity and effectiveness. This much done, the hoped-for contributions are forthcoming. The donors can seldom see what the exact result has been. They well know, however, that countless thousands of other alcoholics and their families are certain to be helped.

When we look at such truly anonymous contributions in this fashion, and as we gain a better understanding of their continuous urgency, I am sure that the voluntary contributions of our A.A. groups, supplemented by many modest gifts from individual A.A.'s, will pay our world service bills over future years, in good times at any rate.

We can take comfort, too, from the fact that we do not have to maintain an expensive corps of paid workers at World Headquarters. In relation to the ever-growing size of A.A. the number of workers has declined. In the beginning our World Service Office engaged one paid worker to each thousand of A.A. members. Ten years later we employed one paid worker to each three thousand A.A.'s. Today we need only one paid helper to every seven thousand recovered alcoholics.[1] The present cost of our world services ($200,000 annually as of 1960) is today seen as a small sum in relationship to the present reach of our Fellowship. Perhaps no other society of our size and activity has such a low general overhead.

These reassurances of course cannot be taken as a basis for the abandonment of the policy of financial prudence.

The fact and the symbol of A.A.'s fiscal common sense can be seen in the Reserve Fund of our General Service Board. As of now this amounts to little more than $200,000—about one year's operating expense of our World Office.[2] This is what we have saved over the last twenty years, largely from the income of our books. This is the fund which has repeatedly prevented the severe crippling, and sometimes the near collapse, of our world services. In about half of the last twenty years, A.A. group contributions have failed to meet our world needs. But the Reserve Fund, constantly renewed by book sales, has been able to meet these deficits—and save money besides. What this has meant in the lives of uncounted alcoholics who might never have reached us had our services been weak or nonexistent, no one can guess. Financial prudence has paid off in lives saved.

These facts about our Reserve Fund need to be better understood. For sheer lack of understanding, it is still often remarked: (1) that the Reserve Fund is no longer needed, (2) that if the Reserve Fund continues to grow, perilous wealth will result, (3) that the presence of such a Reserve Fund discourages group contributions, (4) that because we do not abolish the Reserve Fund, we lack faith, (5) that our A.A. book ought to be published at cost so these volumes could be cheapened for hard-up buyers, (6) that profit-making on our basic literature is counter to a sound spirituality. While these views are by no means general, they are typical. Perhaps, then, there is still a need to analyze them and answer the questions they raise.

Let us therefore try to test them. Do these views represent genuine prudence? Do we lack faith when we prudently insist on solvency?

By means of cheap A.A. books should we engage, as a fellowship, in this sort of financial charity? Should this sort of giving not be the responsibility of individuals? Is the Headquarters' income from A.A. books really a profit after all?

As this is written, 1960, our Headquarters operation is just about breaking even. Group contributions are exceeding our service needs by about 5%. The A.A. Grapevine continues in the red. Compared with earlier days this is wonderful. Nevertheless this is our state in the period of the greatest prosperity that America has ever known. If this is our condition in good times, what would happen in bad times? Suppose that the Headquarters income were decreased 25% by a depression, or that expenses were increased 25% by a steep inflation. What would this mean in hard cash?

The World Service Office would show a deficit of $50,000 a year and the Grapevine would put a $20,000 annual deficit on top of this. We would be faced with a gaping total deficit of $70,000 every twelve months. If in such an emergency we had no reserve and no book income, we would soon have to discharge one-third of our thirty paid workers and A.A. staff members. Much mail would go unanswered, pleas for information and help ignored. The Grapevine would have to be shut down or reduced to a second-rate bulletin. The number of Delegates attending our yearly General Service Conference would have to be drastically reduced. Practically and spiritually, these would be the penalties were we to dissipate our Reserve Fund and its book income.

Happily, however, we do not have to face any such slash as this. Our present reserve and its book income could see us through several years of hard times without the slightest diminution in the strength and quality of our world effort.

It is the fashion nowadays to believe that America can never see another serious business upset. We can certainly hope and pray that it will not. But is it wise for us of A.A. to make a huge bet — by dissipating our own assets — that this could never happen? Would it not be far better, instead, for us to increase our savings in this period when the world about us in all probability has already borrowed more money than can ever be repaid?

Now let us examine the claim that the presence of our Reserve Fund discourages group contributions. It is said that the impression is created that A.A. Headquarters is already well off and that hence there is no need for more money. This is not at all the general attitude, however, and its effect on contributions is probably small.

Next comes the question of whether A.A. as a whole should go in for what amounts to a money charity to individual newcomers and their sponsors — via the selling of our books at cost or less. Up to now we A.A.'s have strongly believed that money charity to the individual should not be a function of the A.A. groups or of A.A. as a whole. To illustrate: when a sponsor takes a new member in hand, he does not in the least expect that his group is going to pay the expenses he incurs while doing a Twelfth Step job. The sponsor may give his prospect a suit of clothes, may get him a job, or present him with an A.A. book. This sort of thing frequently happens, and it is fine that it does. But such charities are the responsibility of the sponsor and not of the A.A. group itself. If a sponsor cannot give or lend an A.A. book, one can be found in the library. Many groups sell books on the installment plan. There is no scarcity of A.A. books; more than a half million are now in circulation. Hence there seems no really good reason why A.A. services should supply everybody with cheap books, including the large majority who can easily pay the going price. It appears to be altogether clear that our world services need those book dollars far more than the buyers do.

Some of us have another concern, and this is related to so-called book "profits." The fact that A.A. Headquarters and most of the groups sell books for more than they cost is thought to be spiritually bad. But is this sort of noncommercial book income really a profit after all? In my view, it is not. This net income to the groups and to A.A.'s General Services is actually the sum of a great many contributions which the book buyers make to the general welfare of Alcoholics Anonymous. The certain and continuous solvency of our world services rests squarely upon these contributions. Looked at in this way, our Reserve Fund is seen to be actually the aggregate of many small financial sacrifices made by the book buyers. This fund is not the property of private investors; it is wholly owned by A.A. itself.

While on the subject of books, perhaps a word should be said concerning my royalties from them. This royalty income from the book buyers has enabled me to do all the rest of my A.A. work on a full-time volunteer basis. These royalties have also given me the assurance that, like other A.A.'s, I have fully earned my own separate livelihood. This independent income also has enabled me to think and act independently of money influences of any kind—a situation which has at times been very advantageous to A.A. as well as to me personally. Therefore I hope and believe that my royalty status will continue to be considered a fair and wise arrangement.

Warranty Three: "None of the Conference members shall ever be placed in a position of unqualified authority over any of the others."

We have learned that this principle is of incalculable value to the harmonious conduct of our Conference affairs. Its application in our structure has already been extensively discussed under the Concept entitled "The Right of Participation," which emphasizes that our world servants, both as individuals and as groups, shall be entitled to voting rights in reasonable proportion to their several responsibilities.

Because this right of participation is so important we have made it the subject of this Warranty, thus providing insurance that Conference action alone can never overturn or amend this right. For any such purpose widespread group consent would be needed, which would probably prove difficult though not necessarily impossible for the Conference to obtain. We believe that our whole service experience fully justifies the taking of this strong stand against the creation of unqualified authority at any point in our Conference structure.

It is to be noted, too, that this Warranty against absolute authority is far more general and sweeping in its nature than a guarantee of voting participation. It really means that we of A.A. will not tolerate absolute human authority in any form. The voting rights urged under our concept of "Participation" are simply the practical means of checking any future tendency to an unqualified authority of any sort. This healthy state of affairs is of course further re-inforced by our concepts of "Appeal and Petition."

Many A.A.'s have already begun to call Article 12 of the Conference Charter "The A.A. Service Bill of Rights." This is because they see in these Warranties, and especially in this one, an expression of deep and loving respect for the spiritual liberties of their fellows. May God grant that we shall never be so unwise as to settle for anything less.

Warranty Four: "That all important decisions be reached by discussion, vote, and, whenever possible, by substantial unanimity."

Here on the one hand we erect a safeguard against any hasty or overbearing authority of a simple majority; and on the other hand we take notice of the rights and the frequent wisdom of minorities, however small. This principle further guarantees that all matters of importance, time permitting, will be extensively debated, and that such debates will continue until a really heavy majority can support every critical decision that we are called upon to make in the Conference.

When we take decisions in this fashion, the Conference voice speaks with an authority and a confidence that a simple majority could never give it. If any remain in opposition, they are far better satisfied because their case has had a full and fair hearing.

And when a decision taken in substantial unanimity does happen to go wrong, there can be no heated recriminations. Everybody will be able to say "Well, we had a careful debate, we took the decision, and it turned out to be a bad one. Better luck next time!"

Like many very high ideals, the principle of substantial unanimity does, however, have certain practical limitations. Occasionally a Conference decision will be of such extreme urgency that something has to be done at once. In such a case we cannot allow a minority, however well-intended, to block a vitally needed action which is evidently in the best interests of A.A. Here we shall need to trust the majority, sometimes a bare majority, to decide whether Conference debate is to be terminated and a final action taken. In certain other cases, the majority will also have to exercise this undoubted right. Suppose, for example, that a small minority obstinately tries to use the principle of substantial unanimity to block a clearly needed action. In such an event it would be the plain duty of the majority to override such a misuse of the principle of substantial unanimity.

Nevertheless our experience shows that majorities will seldom need to take such radical stands as these. Being generally animated by the spirit of "substantial unanimity," we have found that our Conference can nearly always be guided by this valued principle.

In passing it should be noted that the Conference will sometimes have to decide, with respect to a particular question, what the requirements of substantial unanimity are going to be—whether a two-thirds, three-quarters, or even a greater majority, will be required to settle a particular question. Such an advance agreement can, of course, be had on a simple majority vote.

Concluding the discussion on this Warranty, it can be said that without question both the practical and spiritual results of the practice of substantial unanimity already have been proved to be very great indeed.

Warranty Five: "That no Conference action ever be personally punitive or an incitement to public controversy."

Practically all societies and governments feel it necessary to inflict personal punishments upon individual members for violations of their beliefs, principles, or laws. Because of its special situation, Alcoholics Anonymous finds this practice unnecessary. When we of A.A. fail to follow sound spiritual principles, alcohol cuts us down. Therefore no humanly administered system of penalties is needed. This unique condition is an enormous advantage to us all, one on which we can fully rely and one which we should never abandon by a resort to the methods of personal attack and punishment. Of all societies ours can least afford to risk the resentments and conflicts which would result were we ever to yield to the temptation to punish in anger.

For much the same reason we cannot and should not enter into public controversy, even in self-defense. Our experience has shown that, providentially it would seem, A.A. has been made exempt from the need to quarrel with anyone, no matter what the provocation. Nothing could be more damaging to our unity and to the world-wide good will which A.A. enjoys, than public contention, no matter how promising the immediate dividends might appear.

Therefore it is evident that the harmony, security, and future effectiveness of A.A. will depend largely upon our maintenance of a thoroughly nonaggressive and pacific attitude in all our public relations. This is an exacting assignment, because in our drinking days we were prone to anger, hostility, rebellion, and aggression. And even though we are now sober, the old patterns of behavior are to a degree still with us, always threatening to explode on any good excuse. But we *know* this, and therefore I feel confident that in the conduct of our public affairs we shall always find the grace to exert an effective restraint.

We enjoy certain inherent advantages which should make our task of self-restraint relatively easy. There is no really good reason for anyone to object if a great many drunks get sober. Nearly everyone can agree that this is a good thing. If, in the process, we are forced to develop a certain amount of honesty, humility, and tolerance, who is going to kick about that? If we recognize that religion is the province of the clergy and the practice of medicine is for doctors, we can helpfully cooperate with both. Certainly there is little basis for controversy in these areas. It is a fact that A.A. has not the slightest reform or political complexion. We try to pay our own expenses, and we strictly mind our single purpose.

These are some of the reasons why A.A. can easily be at peace with the whole world. These are the natural advantages which we must never throw away by foolishly entering the arena of public controversy or punitive action against anybody.

Because our General Service Conference represents us all, this body is especially charged with the duty of setting the highest possible standard with respect to these attitudes of no punishments and no public controversy. The Conference will have to do more than just represent these principles; it will frequently have to apply them to specific situations. And, at times, the Conference will need to take certain protective actions, especially in the area of Tradition violations. This action, however, never need be punitively or aggressively controversial at the public level.

Let us now consider some typical situations that may often require Conference consideration and sometimes definite action:

Let us suppose that A.A. does fall under sharp public attack or heavy ridicule; and let us take the particular case where such pronouncements happen to have little or no justification in fact.

Almost without exception it can be confidently estimated that our best defense in these situations would be no defense whatever—namely, complete silence at the public level. Unreasonable people are stimulated all the more by opposition. If in good humor we leave them strictly alone, they are apt to subside the more quickly. If their attacks persist and it is plain that they are misinformed, it may be wise to communicate with them in a temperate and informative way; also in such a manner that they cannot use our communication as a springboard for fresh assault. Such communications need seldom be made by the Conference officially. Very often we can use the good offices of friends. Such messages from us should never question the motives of the attackers; they should be purely informative. These communications should also be private. If made public, they will often be seized upon as a fresh excuse for controversy.

If, however, a given criticism of A.A. is partly or wholly justified, it may be well to acknowledge this privately to the critics, together with our thanks—still keeping away, however, from the public level.

But under no conditions should we exhibit anger or any punitive or aggressive intent. Surely this should be our inflexible policy. Within such a framework the Conference and the Headquarters will always need to make a thoughtful estimate of what or what not should be done in these cases.

We may be confronted by public violations of the A.A. Traditions. Individuals, outside organizations, and even our own members sometimes may try to use the A.A. name for their own private purposes. As A.A. grows in size and public recognition, the temptation to misuse our name may increase. This is why we have assigned to our Conference a protective task in respect to such conditions. The Conference, as we know, is the "guardian" of the A.A. Traditions. There has always been some confusion about this term "guardianship," and perhaps we should try to clear it up.

To the minds of some A.A's, "guardianship" of the A.A. Traditions implies the right and the duty on the part of the Conference to publicly punish or sue every wilful violator. But we could not adopt a worse policy; indeed such aggressive public acts would place the Conference in the position of having violated one A.A. Tradition in order to defend another. Therefore aggressive or punitive action, even in this area, must be omitted.

Privately, however, we can inform Tradition-violators that they are out of order. When they persist, we can follow up by using such other resources of persuasion as we may have, and these are often considerable. Manifested in this fashion, a persistent firmness will often bring the desired result.

In the long run, though, we shall have to rely mainly upon the pressures of A.A. opinion and public opinion. And to this end we shall need to maintain a continuous education of public communications channels of all kinds concerning the nature and purpose of our Traditions.

Whenever and however we can, we shall need to inform the general public also; especially upon misuses of the name Alcoholics Anonymous. This combination of counter forces can be very discouraging to violators or would-be violators. Under these conditions they soon find their deviations to be unprofitable and unwise. Our experience has shown that continuous and general education respecting our Traditions will be a reliable preventive and protection in the years to come.

Feeling the weight of all these forces, certain members who run counter to A.A's Traditions sometimes say that they are being censored or punished and that they are therefore being governed. It would appear, however, that A.A's right to object calmly and privately to specific violations is at least equal to the rights of the violators to violate. This cannot accurately be called a governmental action. Some deviators have suffered rather severe personal criticism from individual A.A. members, and this is to be deplored. However this is no reason for us to stop reminding all concerned of the undesirability of breaking A.A's Traditions before the entire public. It can be said in all fairness that the difficulties of those who contravene the Traditions are chiefly troubles of their own making.

Another kind of problem that merits consideration is the occasional severe internal disagreement among us that comes to unwelcome public attention. For example, we once hit the headlines with a pretty hardbitten lawsuit wherein two factions of A.A's were competing for the possession of the A.A. name for Intergroup use, the name having been incorporated by one of them. In another instance in an overseas area there was some rather bad publicity when a considerable section of the groups there became convinced they ought to accept money subsidies from their country's government to promote A.A. work, the A.A. Tradition notwithstanding. This internal difficulty should not have surfaced before the public because there was certainly nothing about it that mutual understanding and good temper could not have readily handled.

Fortunately this sort of episode has been infrequent and relatively harmless. But such difficulties do pose certain questions for the future. What should our General Service Conference do about this sort of thing?

Always remembering group autonomy and the fact that A.A.'s World Headquarters is not a police operation, the most that can be done in most cases is to make an offer of mediation. What the Tradition in this respect means, and what our experience with it has been, can always be offered as a matter of information. We can always urge the avoidance of any breakthrough of such disagreements at the public level. All parties can remember that unfavorable criticism or ridicule which might ensue from such conflicts can so reflect upon A.A. as to keep new prospects from joining up.

Then, too, a great many of these difficulties with the Tradition are of strictly local concern, there being no serious national or international implication. Many of them represent honest differences of opinion as to how the Tradition should be interpreted: whether a lenient or a strict observance would be the better thing. Especially when operating below the public level, our experience with the Traditions reveals gray areas, where neither white or black interpretations seem possible. Here the violations are often so debatable and inconsequential they are hardly worth bothering about. Here we usually refrain from offering suggestions, unless they are insisted upon. We feel that these problems must be solved chiefly by the local people concerned.

There is, too, a grave problem that we have never yet had to face. This would be in the nature of a deep rift running clear across A.A.—a cleavage of opinion so serious that it might involve a withdrawal of some of our membership into a new society of their own, or in their making an alliance with an outside agency in contravention of the A.A. Tradition. This would be the old story of split and schism of which history is so full. It might be powered by religious, political, national or racial forces. It might represent an honest effort to change A.A. for the better. But it would certainly pose the Conference a question of what to do, or not to do.

Such a development is hard to imagine. We A.A.'s usually assume that we have too much at stake and too much in common to succumb to this very ordinary ailment of the world about us. Yet this comforting assurance is no reason for refusing to give this contingency some calm forethought. If it ever came, such a development might be a terrific surprise and shock. Suddenly aroused passions could flare, making any truly constructive solution immensely difficult, perhaps impossible.

Because society everywhere is in such a state of fission today, many of us have given this subject a great deal of consideration. Our considered opinion is this: that the best possible Conference attitude in such a circumstance would be that of almost complete nonresistance—certainly no anger and certainly no attack. We have no doctrine that has to be maintained. We have no membership that has to be enlarged. We have no authority that has to be supported. We have no prestige, power, or pride that has to be satisfied. And we have no property or money that is really worth quarreling about. These are advantages of which we should make the best possible use in the event of a threatened major division; they should make a calm and considered attitude of nonresistance entirely possible and highly practical.

Indeed we have always practiced this principle on a lesser scale. When a drunk shows up among us and says that he doesn't like the A.A. principles, people, or service management; when he declares that he can do better elsewhere—we are not worried. We simply say "Maybe your case *is* different. Why don't you try something else?" If an A.A. member says he doesn't like his own group, we are not disturbed. We simply say "Why don't you try another one? Or start one of your own." When our actors and cops and priests want their own private groups, we say "Fine! Why don't you try that idea out?" When an A.A. group, as such, insists on running a clubhouse, we say "Well, that sometimes works out badly, but maybe you will succeed after all." If individual A.A.'s wish to gather together for retreats, Communion breakfasts, or indeed any undertaking at all, we still say "Fine. Only we hope you won't designate your efforts as an A.A. group or enterprise." These examples illustrate how far we have already gone to encourage freedom of assembly, action, and even schism. To all those who wish to secede from A.A. we extend a cheerful invitation to do just that. If they can do better by other means, we are glad. If after a trial they cannot do better, we know they face a choice: they can go mad or die or they can return to Alcoholics Anonymous. The decision is wholly theirs. (As a matter of fact, most of them do come back.)

In the light of all this experience, it becomes evident that in the event of a really extensive split we would not have to waste time persuading the dissenters to stay with us. In good confidence and cheer, we could actually invite them to secede and we would wish them well if they did so. Should they do better under their new auspices and changed conditions, we would ask ourselves if we could not learn from their fresh experience. But if it turned out they did worse under other circumstances and that there was a steady increase in their discontent and their death rate, the chances are very strong that most of them would eventually return to A.A.

Without anger or coercion we would need only to watch and to wait upon God's will.

Unless we make a problem where there really is none at all, there need be no difficulty. We could still go about our business in good cheer. The supply of drunks in our time will be inexhaustible, and we can continue to be glad that we have evolved at least one formula by which many will come to sobriety and a new life.

We have a saying that "A.A. is prepared to give away all the knowledge and all the experience it has—all excepting the A.A. name itself." We mean by this that our principles can be used in any application whatever. We do not wish to make them a monopoly of our own. We simply request that the public use of the A.A. name be avoided by those other agencies who wish to avail themselves of A.A. techniques and ideas. In case the A.A. name should be misapplied in such a connection it would of course be the duty of our General Service Conference to press for the discontinuance of such a practice—always short, however, of public quarreling about the matter.

The protection of the A.A. name is of such importance to us that we once thought of incorporating it everywhere throughout the world, thereby availing ourselves of legal means to stop any misuse. We even thought of asking Congress to grant us the unusual favor of a Congressional incorporation. We felt that the existence of these legal remedies might prove to be a great deterrent.

But after several years of deliberation, our General Service Conference decided against such a course. The dramatic story of this debate and its conclusion may be found in our history book "Alcoholics Anonymous Comes of Age." Those early Conferences believed that the power to sue would be a dangerous thing for us to possess. It was recognized that a public lawsuit is a public controversy, something in which our Tradition says we may not engage. To make our legal position secure, it would have been necessary to incorporate our whole Fellowship, and no one wished to see our spiritual way of life incorporated. It seemed certain that we could confidently trust A.A. opinion, public opinion, and God Himself to take care of Alcoholics Anonymous in this respect.[3]

Warranty Six: "That though the Conference may act for the service of Alcoholics Anonymous, it shall never perform any acts of government; and that, like the Society of Alcoholics Anonymous which it serves, the Conference itself will always remain democratic in action and in spirit."

In preceding Concepts, much attention has been drawn to the extraordinary liberties which the A.A. Traditions accord to the individual member and to his group: no penalties to be inflicted for nonconformity to A.A. principles; no fees or dues to be levied—voluntary contributions only; no member to be expelled from A.A.—membership always to be the choice of the individual; each A.A. group to conduct its internal affairs as it wishes—it being merely requested to abstain from acts that might injure A.A. as a whole; and finally that any group of alcoholics gathered together for sobriety may call themselves an A.A. group provided that, *as a group*, they have no other purpose or affiliation.

It is probable that we A.A.'s possess more and greater freedom than any fellowship in the world today. As we have already seen, we claim this as no virtue. We know that we personally have to choose conformity to A.A.'s Twelve Steps and Twelve Traditions or else face dissolution and death, both as individuals and as groups.

Because we set such a high value on our great liberties, and cannot conceive a time when they will need to be limited, we here specially enjoin our General Service Conference to abstain completely from any and all acts of authoritative government which could in any wise curtail A.A.'s freedom under God. The maintenance of these freedoms in our Conference is a great and practical guarantee that the Conference itself will always remain democratic in action and in spirit.

Therefore we expect that our Conferences will always try to act in the spirit of mutual respect and love—one member for another. In turn, this sign signifies that mutual trust should prevail; that no action ought to be taken in anger, haste, or recklessness; that care will be observed to respect and protect all minorities; that no action should ever be personally punitive; that whenever possible, important actions will be taken in substantial unanimity; and that our Conference will ever be prudently on guard against tyrannies, great or small, whether these be found in the majority or in the minority.

The sum of these several attitudes and practices is, in our view, the very essence of democracy—in action and spirit.

Freedom under God to grow in His likeness and image will ever be the quest of the

Alcoholics Anonymous. May our General Service Conference be always seen as a chief symbol of this cherished liberty.

To a man, we of A.A. believe that our freedom to serve is truly the freedom by which we live—the freedom in which we have our being.

---

[1] 2015—about one to seventeen thousand, U.S. and Canada.

[2] At December 31, 2015, the net assets of the Reserve Fund (excluding the liability for pension benefits) were $14,584,000, and represented 10.2 months of the $17,075,000 of recurring operating expenses of the operating entities. In 2014, the net assets represented a reserve of 9.8 months of operating expenses.

[3] However, the name Alcoholics Anonymous and the abbreviation A.A. were all legally registered in 1972.